WHAT DO OUR 17-YEAR-OLDS KNOW?

WHAT DO OUR 17-YEAR-OLDS KNOW?

A Report on the First National Assessment of History and Literature

Diane Ravitch

and Chester E. Finn, Jr.

Harper & Row, Publishers, New York

Cambridge, Philadelphia, San Francisco, London
Mexico City, São Paulo, Singapore, Sydney

This book is dedicated with respect and admiration to the many teachers of history and literature in our nation's schools who never stopped believing in the importance of their mission.

A hardcover edition of this book is published by Harper & Row, Publishers, Inc.

WHAT DO OUR 17-YEAR-OLDS KNOW? Copyright © 1987 by Diane Ravitch. All rights reserved. Printed in the United States of America. No part of this book may be used or reproduced in any manner whatsoever without written permission except in the case of brief quotations embodied in critical articles and reviews. For information address Harper & Row, Publishers, Inc., 10 East 53rd Street, New York, N.Y. 10022. Published simultaneously in Canada by Fitzhenry & Whiteside Limited, Toronto.

First PERENNIAL LIBRARY edition published 1988

Designed by C. Linda Dingler

Library of Congress Cataloging-in-Publication Data

Ravitch, Diane.
    What do our 17-year-olds know?

    "Perennial Library."
    Includes index.
    1. United States—History—Study and teaching (Secondary)—United States.   2. History—Study and teaching (Secondary)—United States.
3. American literature—Study and teaching (Secondary)—United States.
4. Literature—Study and teaching (Secondary)—United States.   5. High schools—United States—Curricula.   I. Finn, Chester E., 1944–
II. Title.   III. Title: What do our seventeen-year-olds know?
E175.8.R38   1988   973'.0712   87-45432
ISBN 0-06-091520-X (pbk.)

88 89 90 91 92 CC/FG 10 9 8 7 6 5 4 3 2 1

Contents

Preface

In the months following the original, hardcover publication of this book, its findings ignited considerable controversy. In newspapers and magazines and on television, debate raged about the meaning of the data we reported. There were, predictably, educators and commentators who reacted defensively, insisting that all was well, that the assessment was flawed, or that our interpretation was unduly pessimistic. Some critics asserted that the test results didn't matter because adults may not know more than 17-year-olds, or because high school juniors fifty years ago might not have done any better on such a test. Still others claimed that young people nowadays have no need of such knowledge, since history and literature are not immediately useful or job-related.

Happily, such reactions, though noisy, were atypical. The great majority of teachers, parents, curriculum planners, policymakers, and journalists who commented on the assessment were alarmed and troubled by the results. Like us, they believe that young Americans on the threshold of adult life should have a far stronger command of history and literature than is evidenced by this survey. Like us, they believe that the low average scores registered on this assessment *do* matter—to the quality of our culture, our politics, and our civic life.

And like us, they believe that specific actions can and should be taken to improve the situation.

Some of these actions are under way. The state board of education in California unanimously adopted the new curricular framework for history and the social sciences to which we allude in Chapter 4. It incorporates many of the features that we recommend. It hugely expands the amount of time available for the study of history; mandates three years of world history for all children; emphasizes history, geography, and biography in the early elementary grades; integrates the study of history and literature; and presents history in a rich and absorbing context, drawing together political, social, and economic developments with art, architecture, religion, technology, law, and other salient features of the society under study. Moreover, it encourages textbook publishers to stress narrative history—good story-telling—and provide multivolume series for each course, materials that can be easily revised, supplemented, and interchanged, rather than a single massive textbook.

Also in 1987, the Bradley Commission on History in the Schools was formed to consider proposals to strengthen the teaching of history in the schools. This commission includes some of the nation's most distinguished historians (as well as one of the co-authors of this book). Its creation is noteworthy, for it is the first time since the 1930s that a group of historians has addressed the condition of their subject in the schools. Its recommendations will extend public discussion about ways and means to improve the teaching—and, we trust, the learning—of history in the schools.

Our critical comments about the quality of history textbooks were echoed by a number of thoughtful studies, including Paul A. Gagnon's "Democracy's Untold Story: What World History Textbooks Neglect" and Gil Sewall's "American History Textbooks: An Assessment of Quality."

Our belief that the textbooks are in some measure responsible for students' poor showing on the assessment was strongly supported by a pathbreaking new study by a team of experts in cognitive psychology at the University of Pittsburgh's Center for the Study of Learning. Drawing on the latest research in cognitive theory and information processing, Isabel Beck and her colleagues examined textbooks widely used in fourth through seventh grades to teach history and geography. Their report concluded not only "that the content is not presented so that students will care to remember it," but also "that students are likely to be unable to remember and learn from the presentation."

The Beck report demonstrates that today's textbooks present content in ways that are confusing to the reader; overwhelm the reader with too much miscellaneous information and irrelevant detail; fail to provide sufficient explanations; and suffer from "bad writing, poor organization, and muddled thinking." The researchers note that the textbooks consistently violate what is known from research about the reading process and about learning from written materials. The textbooks, Beck and her colleagues conclude, are "significant obstacles to learning."*

We agree. Yet there is nothing inexorable about poorly written or ill-conceived textbooks. As with the other hindrances to good instruction that are identified throughout this book, change is possible. What needs to be done *can* be done. The fault lies not in our stars nor in the children nor in the conditions of modern life, but in specific institutions, practices, and policies over which we have control as educators, policymakers, citizens, and parents.

Diane Ravitch
Chester E. Finn, Jr.
February 1988

*Isabel L. Beck, Margaret G. McKeown, and Erika W. Gromoll, "Issues That May Affect Social Studies Learning: Examples from Four Commercial Programs" (Learning Research and Development Center, University of Pittsburgh, 1988).

1
Origins of This Assessment

This book contains the results of the first national assessment of 17-year-old students' knowledge of history and literature. On the history portion of the assessment, the national average is 54.5 percent correct; on the literature portion, the national average is 51.8 percent correct. Observers looking for the bright side might suggest that the proverbial glass is half full, rather than half empty. Another way to characterize these results, however, is in the terms traditionally used by teachers: a score of less than 60 percent is failing. If there were such a thing as a national report card for those studying American history and literature, then we would have to say that this nationally representative sample of eleventh grade students earns failing marks in both subjects. A few do exceptionally well; the great majority do not. So long as our schools are expected to educate all of our youngsters, not just the best and brightest, then the results of this assessment are cause for serious concern.

ANTECEDENTS

This assessment is the outgrowth of a study we initiated called the Foundations of Literacy. At the time, we were co-directors of the Educational Excellence Network, which we created in

1981 to bring together educators and scholars committed to school improvement. Among its other activities, the Network sponsored a series of conferences in 1983 and 1984 for high school teachers of the humanities. The purposes of these conferences were to exchange ideas among teachers and scholars of history, literature, and foreign languages, and to develop recommendations for improving the teaching of these subjects. Drawing on material presented at these conferences, we published two volumes of essays, *Against Mediocrity: The Humanities in America's High Schools* and *Challenges to the Humanities*,* which addressed not only problems of classroom technique but also the aimlessness and intellectual torpor that seemed to handicap these fields. Based on what we learned at these conferences and through discussions with the hundreds of participants, we became deeply disturbed about the condition of history and literature in the schools. We learned of schools where history was taught topically, without regard to chronology, and others where history had been replaced by unrelated courses in the social sciences; where literature had given way to coaching for basic skills proficiency tests; where the time for these subjects had been continually whittled away by electives, vocational courses, computer study, and other such subjects. Teachers complained about students who couldn't read, about others who came to high school without knowledge of the most fundamental history or literature, and about time pressures that forced them to "cover" more material than students could absorb within a single year.

As we reflected on these conversations, we began to discuss the value of and need for a reliable nationwide appraisal of students' knowledge of history and literature. Despite the American mania for tests of all kinds, there was no precedent for this one. We knew of occasional polls that showed striking

---

*Chester E. Finn, Jr., Diane Ravitch, and Robert T. Fancher, eds., *Against Mediocrity: The Humanities in America's High Schools* (New York: Holmes & Meier, 1984); Chester E. Finn, Jr., Diane Ravitch, and P. Holley Roberts, eds., *Challenges to the Humanities* (New York: Holmes & Meier, 1985).

ignorance of particular elements of American history, such as the meaning of the Bill of Rights, but there had never been a systematic effort to assess basic historical knowledge on a national scale; nor had anyone ever tried to find out what adults or schoolchildren actually know about major authors and works of literature. It would be useful, we concluded, to go beyond polling and speculation and to determine what young people in fact do know.

Realizing that we needed to engage an experienced organization to develop and administer the test, we initiated discussions with the staff of the National Assessment of Educational Progress (NAEP). NAEP is a federally funded project that has been testing American students regularly since 1969 in such fields as reading, literacy, mathematics, science, and citizenship. NAEP's regular biennial testing cycle normally includes 9-year-olds, 13-year-olds, and 17-year-olds. Although we would have liked to include all three levels, the cost of such an assessment was prohibitive. We chose, therefore, to test only the oldest of the three groups, students enrolled in eleventh grade, reasoning that it would be most informative to test those nearest the completion of their schooling.

NAEP consented to participate, and our proposal for a national assessment of history and literature was funded by the National Endowment for the Humanities. The questions were devised in early 1985, tried out on a pilot basis a few months later, and then administered to a full national sample early in 1986. Nearly 8,000 students were included in the sample, which was divided up by region (i.e., northeast, central, west, and southeast) and by size and type of community. The results of the assessment are representative of students within a large number of subgroups of the population, including gender, race, and number attending public and nonpublic schools. The sampling, the test administration, and the wording and selection of individual questions were all ultimately the responsibility of NAEP.

All of the students answered common background questions about themselves, their families, their schooling, their patterns of doing homework and watching television, their part-time jobs, their reading habits, their perceptions of their history and literature classes, and their attitudes toward these subjects. Though all answered the same background questions, no student was asked to answer every knowledge question on the assessment. The 141 questions in history and 121 in literature were divided up among four "books," each of which was given to an independent, nationally representative sample. This technique is known as matrix sampling, wherein each student takes only a portion of a large test and results are averaged for groups. Teachers of the students in the national sample filled out a separate background questionnaire, but the results of the teacher survey have not yet been compiled and analyzed by NAEP and are therefore not reflected in this book.

We hoped to print the entire test in this book, providing readers with all of the questions and answers in the full assessment, but this was precluded by NAEP's need for confidentiality. It is NAEP's policy to allow only limited public disclosure of its test items, in order to be able to reuse the undisclosed questions in future assessments. Questions that are used again and again provide a gauge for comparing student performance over time. NAEP did give us permission to reproduce test questions that it does not plan to use again, and many of these are shown in Chapter 2.

This assessment provides a snapshot in time; it shows whether students do or do not know the answers to the questions that were posed; it contains rich background information about students, their families, and their attitudes; it captures student descriptions of what happens in their classrooms. But this assessment also has certain limitations. It tests a representative sampling of knowledge but does not claim to test everything worth knowing in these two major fields. It does not explain *why* students perform well or poorly in these subjects, although it does identify significant differences between those who do well and those who do poorly. By the time students are seventeen, their performance on a test of this kind is the result of eleven or twelve years of schooling, as well as whatever they have learned from reading, parents, friends, movies, television, travel, and other experiences. We cannot, and do not, infer that any given classroom practice causes them to do well or poorly, although we are able to describe some of the practices that are typical today.

WHY HISTORY AND LITERATURE?

At the time planning began for this assessment, the nation was in the midst of a major education reform movement. One report after another appeared during the early 1980s, criticizing the performance of American schools and deploring the waste of human talent. Most of these reports and studies called on schools and states to strengthen their academic curriculum and to raise graduation requirements. State after state responded by increasing the number of mandated courses in science and mathematics, and occasionally in social studies, English, and foreign languages.

Yet amid all this educational activism, it was rare that anyone spoke out on behalf of history and literature. The advocates of mathematics and science were not so reticent. They made their case with a bulging portfolio of evidence and an evangelical sense of urgency. They pointed to falling enrollments and test scores in these subjects as proof of the need to improve the quality of instruction, the training of teachers, and the time devoted to these subjects throughout the span of elementary and secondary schooling. It was not hard to convince the public of the importance of mathematics and science, in light of their presumptive utilitarian value. These subjects are linked directly to jobs and careers in engineering and other technical fields. The supply of engineers and technicians, as we have known since the time of Sputnik, also affects the capacity of the nation to keep abreast of technological developments and to maintain a strong economy. Ignorance of mathematics and science, it was rightly said, undermines the quality of the workforce and threatens our nation's ability to compete in world markets. Several major reports went beyond the economic arguments to warn that widespread scientific and technological illiteracy would erode the public's competence to understand complex policy issues, thus jeopardizing the democratic ideal of informed discussion.

In the battle for public attention and curricular time, the humanities were scarcely contenders. No prestigious body of citizens called on American schools to reassess the teaching of history from the first to the last year of schooling, as others had for science. No concerned professors of English banded together to decry their students' ignorance of major works of literature. The representatives of business, labor, government, and education who regularly issued edicts on the need for change in the schools had little to say about history and literature. In our books and conferences, we tried to argue the case for history and literature; so, too, did Ernest Boyer in *High School;* Theodore Sizer in *Horace's Compromise;* and Mortimer Adler in *The Paideia Proposal.* But none of the national or state commissions recommended more time and attention for history and literature. Probably their authors supposed that these subjects are so fundamental that they are always taught, no matter what else changes. Perhaps those who cared about these subjects assumed that they would somehow benefit by any gestures made on behalf of social studies and English.

In fact, proponents of the humanities (and history and literature are the fundamental bearers of the humanities in the schools) were strangely silent. They could not argue that knowledge of history and literature is important in the job market, because they were not sure that this is so; nor could they claim that such knowledge strengthens the nation's economy or contributes to its material well-being, because here, too, proof was lacking. At a time when reshaping the curriculum was high on the agenda of almost every state legislature, those who might have been forceful proponents of history and literature in the schools were unable to articulate why it was important for students to learn these subjects, just as they had earlier failed to defend history and literature against distortion into amorphous courses in social studies and language arts. There were powerful arguments to be made about the importance of history and literature in transmitting and enriching our culture, in developing critical intelligence, in cultivating understanding, character, and judgment. But these arguments were seldom made and, when they were made, not often heard by policymakers.

These subjects were neglected by the education reform movement also because of the absence of the kinds of hard documentation that made claims for science and mathematics so compelling. The evidence that was available from tests of reading and vocabulary—in which achievement scores had fallen sharply since the mid-1960s—was not much help for the disciplines of history and literature. Paradoxically, the erosion of verbal test scores may have made things worse for history and literature in the schools. The most widely publicized score decline was that of the Scholastic Aptitude Test, which more than a million students take annually as part of the college entry process. The revelation in 1975 that the national average had fallen precipitously over a ten-year period stirred a public furor. The news of this decline contributed substantially to demands for educational reform; it aroused public concern about the quality of education; it alerted the media to education issues as no other single indicator had done, doubtless because of its very specificity. Yet no one used the decline of SAT scores to argue that students needed to study more history and literature; no one intimated that the deterioration of verbal scores might in some way be related to decay in the quality of what students were reading. Instead, the celebrated test score decline fueled demands for basic skills, critical thinking skills, reading skills, vocabulary-building, and a host of other nonliterary, content-free exercises.

While we had no brief against the teaching of basic skills—who could?—we believed that this was rather too simplistic a remedy for our educational ailments. The skills of reading, writing, speaking, and listening are clearly fundamental, and no learning of value can proceed until the student has firm command of them. But they are only starting points in the process of education.

As the reform movement gained ground, it seemed clear that the demand for basic skills had become an irresistible rallying cry. These skills are universally valued. They are non-controversial precisely because they lack any cultural content. For the very reason that basic skills and critical thinking skills could become popular banners behind which to march, history and literature were shunted aside. Unlike skill training, teaching the humanities requires people to make choices. Deciding what content to teach risks offending some group or individual, those who prefer a different version of history or different works of literature. How much easier, then, to teach social studies as skills rather than as history, offending practically no one; how much easier to teach the skills of language arts, to fill in blanks and circle words, rather than to bear the burden of selecting particular poems, plays, short stories, and novels and to have to figure out how to make them meaningful for adolescents.

We were convinced that history and literature had lost as much ground in the curriculum as had science and mathematics. The only history studied by most high school students was a single year of American history. Few states or communities require more. A year of world history, once obligatory as a high school graduation requirement in most districts, had become an elective or had disappeared altogether. Even as the need for knowledge of other nations and cultures grew more apparent, willingness to require the study of other nations and cultures faltered. The situation in the elementary and intermediate grades was no better: most elementary school children study history only one year, usually in fifth grade, and history instruction in the middle school years has no pattern, no assured place at all.

THE SAGA OF THE LITERATURE CURRICULUM

The condition of literature was more difficult to ascertain than that of history. While it is often possible to distinguish the presence of a history course under the broad umbrella of social studies, either because of its course title or because of the textbooks in use, the same cannot be said for the teaching of literature. In using the term "literature," we mean works that have received some degree of critical recognition for their quality. Literature in American schools is taught in English classes, but not all English classes teach literature. Some English courses are devoted entirely to reading skills, grammar drills, workbook exercises, and other kinds of nonliterary activities. Even when a significant portion of time is set aside for reading stories and poems, much of the material that is assigned or included in mass-market readers would not be considered "literature" by any reasonable definition of the term.

A generation ago, the literature curriculum in most high schools, though already diverse, had a modicum of coherence since it was centered on major works by renowned British and American writers. Students were likely to read, for example, Eliot's *Silas Marner,* Hawthorne's *The Scarlet Letter,* Shakespeare's *Julius Caesar* or *Macbeth,* Dickens's *Great Expectations* or *A Tale of Two Cities,* essays by Emerson and Thoreau, and poetry by Wordsworth, Byron, Keats, Shelley, Tennyson, Coleridge, Poe, Frost, Dickinson, Stevenson, Sandburg, and Whitman. The range of books and plays read in American high school classes could scarcely be called a canon, since it included hundreds of titles, but certain authors were usually studied, in addition to those already mentioned, such as Austen, the Brontës, Conrad, Crane, Hardy, Hemingway, London, Melville, Orwell, Scott, Steinbeck, Thackeray, Twain, Wharton, and Wilder.*

*For a description of the high school literature curriculum in the early 1960s, see Scarvia B. Anderson, "Between the Grimms and 'The Group'" (Princeton: Educational Testing Service, 1964).

But since the mid-1960s, the professional consensus that supported the established literary curriculum has dissolved as a result of criticism from many quarters—from blacks, because black writers were ignored; from feminists, because women writers were neglected; from those who believed that students would prefer literature that was contemporary and relevant to their own lives; and from those who on principle opposed the very idea of a canon, regardless of its contents or its capaciousness. Today, there is assuredly no canon, and no one could venture a confident guess as to what is read by American students at any point in their schooling. Many college professors believe that their students have read very little; or that they have read nothing in common, which is more likely the case.

What the high school literature curriculum needed, in order to correct its limitations, was a thoroughgoing revision, a reconstruction of the mix of classic and contemporary works and authors. But this did not occur. Instead, the scholars and educators judged the very idea of the traditional curriculum to be irrelevant, claiming that it had lost its power to touch the lives of students and their teachers, to speak to them in a universal voice or even the intensely particular voice that good literature must have. In retrospect, however, it is clear that the real problem lay not in the idea of a coherent literature curriculum, but in the failure of those who could not or would not make the effort to show how traditional and modern literature together can speak to our condition, explain us to ourselves and help us better understand ourselves and our society.

Something of value is lost when there is no coherent literature curriculum, no professional consensus about which writers and which works are superior. Such a curriculum, beginning in the early grades, helps young people understand how the culture came to be what it is, how it was shaped, which writers redefined it and thereby changed the way we see ourselves. The curriculum—and the literary traditions it conveys—is a social and cultural construct that is useful so long as it speaks to our search for meaning. The canon of the past no longer provided a sufficient mirror to show us what we had become; but in its stead we did not get the larger, newer, and better mirror that we needed.

Once the traditional curriculum lost its authority, and there was no consensus about which authors and titles were truly outstanding, the only remaining source of authority for the "language arts" field was the research of reading experts, which yielded technical rather than literary standards for what students ought to read. All too often, the new reading material was such that it could not be called literature by *anyone's* standard. At the precollegiate level, the substitutes for works by the likes of George Eliot, Nathaniel Hawthorne, and Ralph Waldo Emerson were a new genre of realistic melodrama known as "young adult fiction," biographies of current sports stars and other celebrities, and stories written to fit readability formulas, thereby restricting the use of long sentences, polysyllabic words, and uncommon terms.

Whatever its faults, at least the old tradition had a point of view about who we were as a people, what battles we had fought, what self-knowledge we had gained—a point of view that could be disputed, attacked, or controverted. What took its place was not a reformulated and modernized literary tradition that embraced the rich variety of our culture, revealing to us how we had changed during a critical period of our history. The old tradition was dead, but in its stead there was merely cafeteria-style literature, including the written equivalent of junk food. All who had fought the old literature curriculum because they felt left out of its definition of "we" and "us" could only feel cheated to discover that the new approach to literature lacked *any* sense of "we" or "us." Instead of admitting new members to the old boys' club, the club was disbanded.

THE INFORMATION VACUUM

As the great wave of education reform picked up momentum in the 1980s, none of the major commission reports called for even a year of world history, let alone for a three- or four-year sequence of history courses in the high school, and none wondered whether the literature curriculum introduced the young to great works of the past and present. Worse, there was little sure information about the condition of either field, no reliable source to which educators and policymakers might turn in order to gauge what was in the curriculum and whether students were learning it.

It seemed to us that a national assessment could provide some of the missing information. It could try to determine whether students now in their junior year of high school have the fundamental background knowledge that seems appropriate for students of their age. It could seek information about the cultural content offered and assimilated in American classrooms today. It could ask students what books they had read for school and whether they read in their spare time. It could ask about the classroom methods used by teachers. It could ask students how much time they spent watching television, working after school, and doing homework, and then try to determine whether this behavior was associated with competency in history and literature.

We wanted to find out, to the extent that it was possible to do so within the limits of testing technology, whether American students have the information and knowledge that they need to read newspaper stories, magazine articles, books, and other written material that assume a knowledgeable reader. In a daily newspaper, for example, one is likely to encounter references to the New Deal or Reconstruction or the Holocaust in which the writer assumes that the reader understands these terms; in effect, the writer is using a form of cultural shorthand. One is equally likely to come across unexplained references to the Depression, Prohibition, McCarthyism, the Scopes trial, and the *Brown* decision. In casual reading, it is not surprising to find references to an "Achilles' heel" or to someone who has the "patience of Job" or a "Midas touch." Writers in the daily press do not stop to wonder whether their readers know who Stalin or Churchill was. In the United States today, the common reader—not just the college-educated reader—is expected to have a copious supply of historical and literary knowledge ready at hand to make sense of everyday reading.

Given the complexity of these fields, it was clear that whatever test was devised would have limitations. It was equally clear that it would be hard to gain consensus about what should be tested. We were aware that many thoughtful people mistrust multiple-choice tests, especially for complex subjects like history and literature; we shared most of those doubts. We still do. Nonetheless, we were and are convinced that in the absence of *any* reliable data, speculation about student achievement in these two subject areas would continue to be based on hearsay, anecdote, impressions, and samples of a single classroom or even a handful of neighborhood kids.

There has for some time been ample reason to wonder whether the younger generation is culturally illiterate. The spread of remedial reading and writing classes on college campuses has contributed to the sense that our society is breeding a new strain of cultural barbarian, one who cannot read or write except at the most rudimentary level and who possesses virtually no knowledge except that conveyed through the television set. As we wrote this report, we read an article about the author Mary McCarthy, who recently served as visiting professor at a small liberal arts college and lamented that modern students seem "almost totally ignorant of the whole period spanned by my life, to say nothing of what happened before."*

No less worrisome is the possibility that American adoles-

*Michiko Kakutani, "Our Woman of Letters," *The New York Times Magazine* (March 29, 1987): 74.

cents are ignorant of American literature, that they have been raised on a meager diet of stories and books about other teenagers, that their tastes have been pressed into a narcissistic mold, and that most of their knowledge of imaginative fiction has been supplied by television and the movies. There was no objective way, so far as we knew, to gauge whether or not these fears were justified. We wondered, though, whether American 17-year-old students know as much about their national literature as a writer in *The New York Times* claims that Soviet citizens know. According to Serge Schmemann, then chief of the Moscow bureau for the *Times*, "Rare is the Russian who was not reared on *The Deerslayer* and *The Adventures of Tom Sawyer*, who is not familiar with *The Catcher in the Rye*, Ernest Hemingway, William Faulkner, and John Steinbeck. Classics and contemporary American literature are a mainstay of the Soviet reading diet. . . . Russian readers are familiar with Theodore Dreiser, Erskine Caldwell, Sinclair Lewis, John Updike, Kurt Vonnegut, Gore Vidal, Isaac Asimov, and Arthur Hailey." One Russian told the writer, "It would not be an exaggeration to say that in childhood we all were reared on American adventure literature—James Fenimore Cooper, Jack London, Edgar Allan Poe, Mark Twain, O. Henry—a whole constellation of names. . . ."*

We know that such estimates are impressionistic, and that no one knows whether "all" Russians were raised on Cooper, London, Poe, Twain, and O. Henry, just as no one in the United States knows which writers our young people have read. However, the same issue of *The New York Times Magazine* included the results of a national poll of Americans, in which respondents were asked "whether they knew that United States troops had intervened in Russia at the time of the Soviet Revolution; whether they could name the current Soviet leader, Mikhail S. Gorbachev, or identify the K.G.B.;

*Serge Schmemann, "The View from Russia," *The New York Times Magazine* (November 10, 1985): 52–54.

which side the Russians fought on in World War II, and whether they knew that the number of Russian casualties in that war exceeded that of American casualties." Only 14 percent answered more than three of these questions correctly; 24 percent answered none of them correctly.*

Polls of this kind on one subject or another appear frequently in the press, fueling concern about our general level of cultural background. Anecdotes abound about students whose knowledge is derived largely from television and the movies. Many professors have a ready supply of jokes that begin, "Did you hear the one about the student who said . . . ?" But anecdotes are inadequate evidence. Samples of one, or ten, or twenty-five are idiosyncratic and unreliable. Thus we concluded that the time had come for a national assessment.

DISPELLING FALSE DICHOTOMIES

As we worked through some of the issues associated with a national appraisal of history and literature knowledge, we found ourselves wrestling with a pair of what turned out to be false dichotomies. These can be termed the "concepts vs. facts tradeoff" and the "skills vs. content fallacy."

Concepts or Facts?

Some in the social studies field believe that concepts matter more than facts. Indeed, when pressed, those who cherish this dichotomy often acknowledge grave misgivings about the validity of any test that elicits knowledge of facts. What is false about this dichotomy is the assumption that a choice must be made between concepts, on the one hand, and facts, on the other. Of what value is it to young people to learn the terminol-

*Adam Clymer, "Polling Americans," *The New York Times Magazine* (November 10, 1985): 37.

ogy of concepts drawn from the social sciences, like social mobility or cultural diffusion or economic depression, without seeing them demonstrated in the lives of real people and the history of real societies? Such learning is often nothing more than the memorization of social science vocabulary, a practice that is neither interesting nor meaningful. Similarly, a knowledge of disconnected facts that are joined, related, or explained by no concepts is obviously without significance; we learn particular facts in order to grasp ideas and develop generalizations. At best, concepts explain the facts of a given situation, while facts provide examples with which to illustrate or test concepts. We believe that a knowledge of concepts must be grounded in particular facts and situations, particularities of time and place. To study concepts without knowing specific situations in which to test the validity of those concepts is barren. It is also deadly boring.

The power of the facts-versus-concepts dichotomy has grown so great within the social studies field that some professionals now harbor an instinctive distrust of facts per se. An assessment such as this one, which emphasizes factual knowledge—approximate dates as well as specific places and names—is likely to provoke a skeptical, even hostile reaction; a few reviewers of the assessment's objectives darkly warned that its inclusion of questions testing factual knowledge threatened to set the social studies field back by a generation. Are we to presume, then, that children should learn about the Civil War but not care very much about when it occurred? that they should learn about racial discrimination but not bother to learn what Jim Crow laws did or what the *Plessy* decision held? that they should learn the concepts of good citizenship but not take the time to study what Magna Carta is or what is contained in the Constitution and Bill of Rights?

While working on this project, we knew that questions that rely on factual understanding might invite scornful criticism as "mere recall" or even "mere knowledge." Sophisticated questions, we recognized, are supposed to test the student's reasoning powers, not the student's fund of background knowledge. Nonetheless, the learning area committees that developed the assessment's objectives, and the staff from NAEP working with them, rejected the conventional wisdom and concentrated on trying to create questions that would plumb whether students do or do not know the basic facts of American history. The working assumption was that any fact worth knowing illumines at least one important concept: knowing what Magna Carta is helps to explain the evolution of the concept of limitations on the power of the sovereign and the origins of political democracy. Knowing the essence of the *Brown* decision is fundamental to understanding the modern history of race relations and constitutional law in the United States. Knowing approximately when different national groups migrated to the United States is essential in under-standing the demographic and cultural forces that have shaped our history. It is fatuous to believe that students can think critically or conceptually when they are ignorant of the most basic facts of American history. In order for history to make sense, concepts and facts must be blended. It is not necessary to choose between them.

Skills or Content?

There is a tendency in the education profession to believe that *what* children learn is unimportant compared to *how* they learn; to believe that skills can be learned without regard to content; to believe that content is in fact irrelevant, so long as the proper skills are developed and exercised. This assump-tion closely resembles a nineteenth-century pedagogical the-ory which held that the mind is composed of a series of "facul-ties," each of which must be exercised, like a muscle; so long as the muscle is exercised, the content is irrelevant. This pedagogy was used to justify the study of Latin and Greek, on the ground that any subject that was hard must be good for mental discipline. This theory of learning was supposedly discredited in the early twentieth century by educational psychologists, but it has reemerged in a new guise in recent years as a rationalization for teaching skills without regard to content. In his book *Cultural Literacy,* E. D. Hirsch, Jr., calls this approach "educational formalism" and demonstrates how it is used—with dire result—to substitute skills for cultural content in the curriculum.*

The preference for formal skills crops up time and again: when educators claim, for example, that it doesn't matter what children read as long as they read *something;* when they promote workbook activities even though these activities are repetitive, boring, and devoid of any cultural value; when reading experts endorse textbooks that contain little or no significant children's literature but only trivial stories whose purpose is to exercise vocabulary and reading skills. The Dick and Jane readers, with their simple language and their vapid, content-free stories, provided the prototype of the skill-based reader. Although Dick and Jane have been shelved, their bland spirit survives in most of today's mass-market school readers.

In truth, it is neither possible nor desirable to teach reading skills without regard to background knowledge. Yet the usual definition of literacy accepts this dichotomy by treating "literacy" as the formal skill of reading, as a mechanism for decoding the meaning of words on a page, a signpost, or a computer screen. From the outset, the Foundations of Literacy project rejected this approach. The kind of literacy this assessment gauged is not a skill that can be displayed by deciphering a job application, the contents of a cereal box, or the directions on an income tax form.

As Hirsch has shown, students who know the mechanics of reading but lack background knowledge are handicapped as readers; they are, in fact, culturally disadvantaged. An American traveling in India, for example, would find that he was

*E. D. Hirsch, Jr., *Cultural Literacy: What Every American Needs to Know* (New York: Houghton Mifflin, 1987).

able to read English-language signs and newspapers, but his understanding of what he was reading would be severely constricted unless he was also knowledgeable about the culture, traditions, literature, religion, and history of the country. Americans who know little of their own nation's history and literature are similarly handicapped when trying to read anything more complex than a daily newspaper. Indeed they will even be handicapped when trying to read the daily newspaper if they are unfamiliar with common names or references drawn from history, geography, literature, politics, science, popular culture, and other sources. The more background knowledge one has at the ready, the more complex are the transactions that one can have in conversation or in reading.

One's level of cultural literacy determines one's ability to understand what is presented in conversation, newspapers, magazines, books, and even on television. The scale of the literate public inevitably affects the publishing media, by setting ceilings on the kind of public they can write for. Tabloid newspapers sold at the checkout counter in supermarkets assume their readers have scant knowledge beyond the world of television and film stars; newspapers and magazines with higher expectations of their readership assume that writers can refer to historical figures like Freud, Marx, and Einstein without explaining who they were.

In order to have a literate press, it is necessary to have literate readers. Saul Bellow recently wrote about this problem from his perspective as a novelist:*

I readily concede that here and there I am probably hard to read, and I am likely to become harder as the illiteracy of the public increases. It is never an easy task to take the mental measure of your readers. There are things that people *should* know if they are to read books

*Saul Bellow, foreword to Allan Bloom, *The Closing of the American Mind: How Higher Education Has Failed Democracy and Impoverished the Souls of Today's Students* (New York: Simon and Schuster, 1987), 15.

at all, and out of respect for them, or to save appearances, one is apt to assume more familiarity on their part with the history of the twentieth century than is objectively justified.

The widely syndicated political cartoonist Pat Oliphant complained in a similar vein about the growing difficulty of communicating to an audience that lacks a common body of visual images. In an interview in the *Washington Post,* he doubted whether he could continue to use references like Michaelangelo's "Creation" in his political cartoons: "The problem is, as education becomes more and more of a mess in this country, and people learn less and less about the arts and history, the possibility of using those sorts of metaphors is disappearing. It will get to a stage where eventually you won't be able to use the classics at all, or allusions to historical events."*

To the extent that we—educators, parents, and citizens— allow cultural literacy to wane and to be reduced only to knowledge of celebrities from *People* magazine and the electronic media, then the audience for genuine literature will shrink, material written or produced for a literate public will dwindle, and the quality of public discourse and debate in our society will suffer. It is a tragic downward spiral that can only erode the culture, trivialize the intellect, and in time pauperize our civic life.

Although there are reading specialists who continue to believe that literacy consists of little more than mastering the mechanics of decoding and word recognition, most reading experts now believe that the ability to read with comprehension requires a fund of background knowledge. This was the view expressed by the Commission on Reading in 1985, in a major report called *Becoming a Nation of Readers,* which was jointly sponsored by the National Institute of Education, the National Academy of Education, and the Center for the Study

*Washington Post (July 14, 1985).

of Reading. The Commission held that "Reading is a process in which information from the text and the knowledge possessed by the reader act together to produce meaning. . . . No text is completely self-explanatory. In interpreting a text, readers draw on their store of knowledge about the topic of the text."

Some background knowledge is necessary to understand and interpret any text. Even a child who reads a simple story about a dog must know what a dog is. The more advanced the text, the more background knowledge is necessary to read it with understanding. The Commission observed that "Some children may completely lack knowledge of a particular topic, others may know something, while still others may know a lot. Research shows that differences in knowledge influence children's understanding." Furthermore, children who bring background knowledge to their reading not only understand it better than those who lack background knowledge but are better able to answer questions that require reasoning. Put another way, readers' abilities to think conceptually, to make judgments, to draw conclusions, and otherwise to engage in critical thinking are strengthened if they have prior knowledge of the material they are reading.*

LIMITATIONS OF THIS ASSESSMENT

Critics have complained that the concept of cultural literacy encourages superficiality, since it places emphasis on *knowing about* rather than on knowing. This assessment, readers will find, is occasionally guilty of the same charge. We too would prefer an essay examination that determined the depth of students' understanding of historical issues and literary works. We hope that testing agencies will soon develop additional ways to assess knowledge and not rely so exclusively on multiple-choice questions, whose defects we make clear in our

---

*The Report of the Commission on Reading, *Becoming a Nation of Readers* (Washington, D.C.: U.S. Department of Education, 1985), 8–10.

analysis of the test results. We are not content with some of the items in the literature assessment that ask only for simple recognition of authors and titles; we wish that there were more questions about the plots and themes of specific works. At the same time, we are frustrated by the futility of asking such questions of students who have never read—nor, as the results of the literature assessment suggest, even heard of—the very works that we want them to understand deeply. Perhaps in the future this level of questioning will be possible. If so, it will not only have to await the development of testing technology that allows the possibility of gauging understanding and thoughtful analysis, but it will also have to await a time when the shared background knowledge of students goes beyond the childhood stories of Robin Hood, Cinderella, and Noah's Ark. Similarly in history, we do not question the importance of testing students' powers of judgment and reasoning, but neither do we doubt the importance of establishing whether students have a strong grasp of basic chronology, events, trends, and geography.

A problem inherent in any national assessment of literature is the difficulty of knowing which novels, short stories, poems, plays, and nonfiction students have read; clearly, this is less troublesome at the state and local level, where one can more easily determine what is taught in school. To ask students to analyze a literary work that they have never read makes little sense. Where it was expected that the work was known by students, they were asked about its theme or characters. For less well known works and authors, students were asked elementary questions, mainly to establish whether they might understand allusions to these works and authors. This approach may fairly be criticized for superficiality, since it does not guarantee that the student who answers correctly has ever read the work in question or even read anything by the author whose name they recognize. It must be left to future assessments and to classroom teachers to probe whether students have drawn meaning for their own lives from what they have read; the present assessment aimed only to determine which authors and works of literature were familiar to them and, where feasible, whether students could identify a major theme or core issue in what they had read.

GOALS

The goals of this assessment were several. First, it was expected to yield some reliable national information about the present condition of basic knowledge in these areas. What do students know about significant events, individuals, and trends in American history? Do they know the meaning of important terms in the Constitution? Are they familiar with major novels, plays, poems, mythical allusions, biblical references, and writers?

The second goal was to provide baseline data for future tests. The knowledge that it generates should help to improve the way information is gathered about the curriculum of these two important subject fields.

The third goal was to fill in some gaps in current knowledge about the teaching of history and literature in the high schools. Relatively little is known about these fields other than course enrollment data: every high school student takes courses called social studies or language arts, American history or English. Yet no one has reliable information as to how these courses are taught. For lack of any other way to inquire about classroom practice, some researchers scrutinize high school history textbooks; this is an important part of the picture, but it is a limited part. This assessment is the first national survey that asks students about what happens in their history and literature classes.

CONSTRUCTING THE ASSESSMENT

With these goals established, the Foundations of Literacy project was officially launched in January 1985. Two "learning area committees"—one for each field—met for three days in Princeton, New Jersey, where NAEP has its offices. Whenever NAEP prepares a new assessment, it convenes such a group of professionals, coming from different parts of the country and different parts of the field; this committee has the key task of shaping the objectives of the assessment.

The members of the history committee, which included high school social studies teachers and supervisors, as well as historians, were: Diane Brooks, California State Department of Education; Henry N. Drewry, Princeton University; Dana Kurfman, Prince George's County public schools, Landover, Maryland; Donald V. Rogan, New Trier High School, Evanston, Illinois; and Stephan Thernstrom, Harvard University. As project leaders, we (Finn and Ravitch) participated as members of both committees.

The literature committee included high school English teachers, English professors, and writers; its members were: E. D. Hirsch, Jr., University of Virginia; Anna K. Johnston, Colchester High School, Colchester, Vermont; Helen Lojek, Boise State University, Boise, Idaho; Richard Rodriguez, author, San Francisco, California; and Patrick Welsh, T. C. Williams High School, Alexandria, Virginia.

The committees had wide latitude to select content and devise questions for the test in their field so long as they met these two criteria:

First, the questions should cover fundamental material that students of this age might reasonably be expected to know. The aim was not to differentiate among the bright, the average, and the slow, as standardized tests customarily do, but to ask questions that most students *ought* to be able to answer correctly.

Second, the answers should be unambiguous, even at the risk of appearing too simple; the wrong answers (what the testing agencies call "foils" or "distractors") should be completely wrong. The questions were supposed to have a right answer and several wrong answers, not a series of reasonable choices that might mislead students who are imaginative or thoughtful or well read.

Not every question met both criteria, even after NAEP's item developers and field testers were finished. It was virtually impossible to specify which writers or works of literature most students should be expected to know; a few history questions had "distractors" that were not completely wrong. There is a craft to writing good test questions and answers, and those of us who had never done it before discovered that it is not as easy as it appears. While the committees specified the objectives and tried their hand at writing sample questions, the NAEP staff had final responsibility for the wording of the questions and for selecting which questions to use.

The problems of test-making turned out to be quite different for each of these fields. The history committee wrestled for a time with the question of whether there really is a common body of historical knowledge that almost all students should be expected to know. But several hours of animated discussion eventually led to a consensus that there *are* fundamental elements in American history and a few key points in world history that most young people should know.

The literature committee found its task more difficult. Members of the committee were familiar with the literature curriculum in some districts and states, but it was obvious to all that there is no national pattern, no national reading list for tenth and eleventh grades. The committee went through the laborious but fascinating exercise of making voluminous lists of authors and works and then trying to decide which were the most significant. The committee constantly struggled with the problem of whether to test what is actually taught, which includes much that is transient and of dubious literary quality, or whether to test what students should know.

The differences in these two fields will be seen in the dual character of the assessment. In history, the test consistently aims to find out what students know; the history content reflects what is commonly in state curricula and textbooks.

In literature, it was not possible to assume that all students had read or even heard of all of the writers and works included in the assessment. Hence the literature test assesses both the curriculum (what students are exposed to) and the students' knowledge of specific content (what they retain). Some of the literature questions ask about authors like Milton, Chaucer, and Dante, who are probably included in few high school literature courses. Questions of this kind test our society's success in transmitting the inherited culture to the next generation more than they test how well the students have learned what their school teachers have taught them.

Some of the information included on the literature assessment is not commonly covered in the public school classroom. Some—like knowledge of biblical references—is learned at home or in religious school, but is nonetheless necessary for understanding much Western literature. Other literary material included on the test is usually learned through the popular culture, not from school or reading; it is not likely, for example, that the many students who recognize the theme of the novel *Frankenstein* have ever read Mary Shelley's work. But they know the reference and understand its meaning.

Is it fair to test students on material that is not learned in school, knowing that some students may be disadvantaged by their home backgrounds or limited experience? The literature committee decided to include such questions, because such material forms an important part of cultural literacy, even if it is not taught in school. The fact that the greatest numbers of students correctly answered such questions (e.g., Frankenstein, Robin Hood, Romeo and Juliet) showed that not only was there no disadvantage to students from less-privileged homes but also suggested the power of nonschool media like movies and television to disseminate cultural images. The greatest disparity in knowledge on the literature test was found not on questions that assessed what students had learned from religious training or television or movies, but on questions that assessed knowledge of material that is learned—if it is learned—almost exclusively in school.

Members of both committees are astute professionals, mindful of the concerns of their peers. No one was a warm admirer of multiple-choice tests, but everyone accepted that this was the state of testing technology available to us; everyone expected that the assessment would produce information about which all of us were curious. Those on the history panel knew that others in the field would view with alarm anything that might revive the practices of the distant, discredited past, when students were expected to memorize vast quantities of names, dates, battles, and definitions that had no meaning for them. They were also aware of concern that teachers might feel pressured to "teach to the test." Yet the committee judged that the assessment would produce neither result. The questions on the assessment have been used once, and a number of them are opened to public scrutiny in this report; some might be used in altered form on future assessments, but it seems safe to conclude that new questions will also be devised for each succeeding assessment. Of equal or greater importance, this is a *sample* test, and no individual student, school, district, or even state is visible in the results. It renders no judgment on Johnny, Maria, or East Side High, and holds no specific consequences for them.

Members of the literature panel knew that others in their field would criticize any choices that were made and that it was not possible to construct a test that would meet with universal approval. In their effort to decide what should be tested, they settled on genres as a basic organizing concept: poems, plays, novels, epics, myths, Bible stories, and nonfiction. In each genre, which works and authors should students know as a foundation for future literacy? The members of the committee knew that their peers would be concerned about anything that smacked of a monolithic literary canon. They concluded that the questions should not be seen as a mandate about what ought to be read by students in the future. But, perhaps as a result of this assessment, school boards, teachers, and others will engage in thoughtful discussions about the proper content of the literature curriculum. Perhaps they will at least ask what their students *are* currently reading. And then what students should be reading. That would be a worthwhile consequence.

THE LEARNING OBJECTIVES
History

During the course of three intensive days, the two committees arrived at a consensus about what should be tested. The history committee agreed that the assessment would focus on United States history, which all students are supposed to have studied; most students in the assessment were currently enrolled in a junior-year course in American history at the time that the test was given. It was also agreed that chronology would be treated as the fundamental organizing concept in the study of history. The committee recognized that sound historical study encompasses analysis of cause and effect, continuity and change, events and individuals and ideas interacting in a particular context. In its efforts to define the goals of the history assessment, the committee identified a series of issues and facts, set in a chronological context, as central to the study of American history.

The following outline represents the objectives of the history assessment. In accordance with NAEP's customary procedure, the objectives were circulated for field review to fifty-nine professionals in the field of history and social studies, whose comments were used to revise the original draft and to shape the final version, as it appears here:

I. Exploration and Colonization: up to 1763

    A. Exploration
- Factors contributing to exploration (e.g., desire for wealth, technological advances)
- Major countries and explorers involved (e.g., Spain, France, England)

B. Colonization
- Factors contributing to colonization (e.g., religious, economic, and social issues)
- The first colonies (e.g., governments based on English models, leaders of original colonies, and relations with Native American cultures)
- Aspects of colonial life (e.g., diversity of religious and ethnic groups, origins of slavery, types of economy, and immigration)

II. The Revolutionary War and the New Republic: 1763–1815

A. The Revolutionary War
- Factors contributing to the Revolutionary War (e.g., English exploitation of the colonies and emergence of an American society)
- Documents (e.g., Declaration of Independence, the Articles of Confederation, and *Common Sense*)
- Importance of American leadership (e.g., George Washington, Thomas Paine, John Adams, Thomas Jefferson, Benjamin Franklin)
- Events and aspects of the war (e.g., Bunker Hill, Saratoga, foreign alliances)

B. Establishing the new nation
- The Constitution (e.g., major compromises, structure, and steps leading to ratification)
- Forming the new government (e.g., political parties, leaders)
- Expansion (e.g., migration, the Louisiana Purchase, trade with Europe, difficulties maintaining neutrality, and the War of 1812)

III. Nationhood, Sectionalism, and the Civil War: 1815–1877

    A. Economic and social change (e.g., growth of cities, industrialization, transportation)

    B. Jacksonian democracy (e.g., political parties, expanding the franchise, treatment of Native Americans)

    C. Expansion of slavery (e.g., Missouri Compromise, plantation economy, and abolitionists)

    D. The Civil War
- Federal powers versus states' rights (e.g., nullification)
- Factors leading up to the Civil War (e.g., slavery, economic differences between North and South, and secession versus preservation of the Union)
- Abraham Lincoln (e.g., Emancipation Proclamation, Gettysburg Address)
- Effects of the Civil War (e.g., growth of North; destruction of South; Reconstruction; passage of Thirteenth, Fourteenth, and Fifteenth Amendments—abolition of slavery, due process and equal protection, and the right to vote)

IV. Territorial Expansion, the Rise of Modern America, and World War I: 1877–1920

    A. Territorial expansion
- Western expansion (e.g., territories involved, improved transportation, farm protests, Indian Wars, and the reservation system)
- The Spanish-American War (e.g., territorial acquisitions, United States becomes world power)

B. The rise of modern America
- Big business (e.g., leaders, new production techniques, and monopolies)
- Labor unions (e.g., working conditions, American Federation of Labor, problems in organizing unions)
- Progressive Era and reform legislation (e.g., populism, Theodore Roosevelt, muckraking, "trust busting," and conservation)
- Immigration (e.g., shift in patterns, efforts to restrict—National Origins Act)
- Segregation and failure to achieve equality for blacks (e.g., *Plessy* v. *Ferguson*—separate but equal, Jim Crow laws, NAACP)

C. The First World War
- Reasons for United States entry (e.g., rights of neutrality and submarine warfare)
- Characteristics of the war (e.g., countries involved, leaders—Woodrow Wilson)
- Events and effects (e.g., Treaty of Versailles, League of Nations, substantial American contribution, isolationist mood after war)

D. Women's vote—Nineteenth Amendment (e.g., early advocates—Susan B. Anthony, Elizabeth Cady Stanton, Seneca Falls Convention)

V. The Great Depression, the New Deal, and World War II: 1920–1945

A. The 1920s (e.g., temperance movement and prohibition, inventions, Scopes trial)

B. Causes and characteristics of the Great Depression

(e.g., stock market crash, collapse of economy, Dust Bowl)

C. Franklin D. Roosevelt and the New Deal (e.g., changes in role of government, gains for labor, agricultural price supports, Social Security)

D. World War II
  • Factors leading up to United States involvement in the war (e.g., rise of totalitarianism, United States initially neutral, entry after Japanese attack on Pearl Harbor)
  • Characteristics of the war (e.g., global nature with European and Pacific theaters; the Holocaust; leaders—Churchill, Stalin, Hitler, and Roosevelt; effect of war effort on roles of women and minorities; Japanese relocation camps; relationships with Allies—Yalta)
  • End of the Second World War (e.g., Roosevelt dies and is succeeded by Truman; United States uses atomic bomb to end war with Japan)
  • The United Nations (e.g., purpose)

VI. Post–World War II: 1945 to Present

A. The Cold War (e.g., containment of communism, beginnings of arms race, Truman Doctrine, Marshall Plan, NATO, McCarthyism, communist expansion in Europe)

B. Korean conflict (e.g., U.N. forces, MacArthur versus Truman)

C. Postwar prosperity (e.g., demand for consumer goods; the baby boom; the growth of suburbs; inventions and discoveries; Sputnik begins space race)

D. The 1960s
   - President Kennedy and the New Frontier (e.g., space program, Cuban missile crisis, Peace Corps, assassination)
   - President Lyndon Johnson and the Great Society (e.g., increased social legislation and government spending)
   - Civil rights movement (e.g., *Brown* v. *Board of Education* and beyond, Martin Luther King, Jr., civil rights legislation)
   - Vietnam (e.g., growing unpopularity of war, protest movement)

E. The 1970s
   - Opening to China
   - United States withdrawal from Vietnam
   - Watergate, resignation of President Nixon, succession of President Ford
   - Women's Rights Movement (e.g., Betty Friedan, Gloria Steinem, and ERA)
   - Energy crisis
   - Human rights

This outline represents a general overview of the major eras and issues in American history that the committee thought should be included in the assessment. The committee knew that there were many other issues, trends, individuals, and events that might easily have been included; but it reached a consensus that these were the key elements around which the assessment should be built. In order to guide the test-makers at NAEP, the history committee assigned relative weights to the six chronological eras as follows:

I. Exploration and Colonization: 10 percent of the test items would be devoted to this period
II. The Revolutionary War and the New Republic: 17 percent

III. Nationhood, Sectionalism, and the Civil War: 18 percent
IV. Territorial Expansion, the Rise of Modern America, and World War I: 20 percent
 V. The Great Depression, the New Deal, and World War II: 20 percent
VI. Post–World War II to Present: 15 percent

In the assessment that was actually administered to students, these were the weights that determined the distribution of content across the chronological eras. Not every issue that was listed in the outline of historical content ended up on the assessment, but the great majority of issues, individuals, and events did. A few items that appeared on the final assessment were not included in the original outline, such as questions about the Renaissance and the Reformation. In addition to the chronological eras, the assessment included several map questions to check rudimentary knowledge of geography.

The process by which the history committee arrived at the outline above was itself interesting. When committee members first met, they debated whether it was possible to agree on what history virtually all high school students should know. Sensitized by the factionalism within the field of history and social studies during the past two decades, committee members doubted the possibility of finding a common frame of reference. When deliberations began, the questions debated were "*Whose* history will be tested? Which version of American history do we accept? Is there such a thing as 'American history' or are there many different American histories and herstories with little overlap?" Yet after twenty-four hours of intense discussions, the committee had found common ground. Their shared vision of American history contained certain key events, trends, people, and ideas. What emerged from their brainstorming was an American history that reaches beyond the usual boundaries of traditional political history to incorporate elements of black history, women's history, technological developments, social history, immigration history, foreign policy, and the evolution of the American government and laws.

The committee agreed that students must understand basic chronology; that they should know the most important provisions of the Constitution and Bill of Rights; that they should know the major events that shaped the nation and formed its character; that they should know both the achievements and the frailties of the American political system; that all students, not just blacks, should be familiar with the history of civil rights issues and court decisions. The committee sought to construct a bare outline of an American history that belongs to all of us, not just to groups whose ancestors were involved in particular issues or episodes. In a sense, this solution is unremarkable, since it accurately reflects the diversity of the American past. What was remarkable was the discovery among a group of teachers and scholars, none of whom knew each other before, that they could put their heads together and arrive at a reasoned consensus about American history that represented no one's "version" of events. It is possible to define American history, with all its complexity, controversy, and variety, as the story of a people forged from many different pasts but joined together under a common political system. There is, in short, an American people, not just a mosaic of unrelated groups, each with its own story, disconnected from the whole. Perhaps it was the factionalism and the contentiousness of the previous quarter-century that had made such a synthesis possible, but no one questioned the inclusion of questions drawn from women's history, black history, and social history as an integral part of the American story.

Literature

The members of the literature panel had more difficulty reaching a consensus on content than the history panel did, but ultimately they agreed on a set of principles to define the nature of the literature assessment. What they sought to test was the strength among eleventh graders of the core literary culture in this country at this time. They asked not what is it that students are reading in their English classes, but what is the literature that is widely recognized by literate people today. They agreed that it must be literature that has survived the passage of time, that is frequently referred to by other authors, and that therefore serves as a partial basis for communication among literate people. Integral to this notion of a core literary culture was recognition that any such culture changes over time, that some works once considered central have become marginal or arcane, while others have taken their place. The committee recognized that the common literary culture changes as tastes, standards, styles, and the culture itself change. In light of this definition, the committee felt that some new works that are widely read today might be part of the common culture in the future, but had not yet demonstrated the staying power to put them into the same league with the Bible, Aesop, Shakespeare, and Twain.

The committee discussed at length the problems of identifying literature that could fairly be considered fundamental to our culture. In poring over lengthy lists of novels, short stories, poems, plays, etc., the committee found it useful to pose these questions as means of sorting out the consequential from the routine:

- What is basic for understanding and interpreting other literature?
- What helps us define ourselves and our culture?
- What can enlarge our capacity to imagine what is outside our own experiences?
- What helps us to understand both the diversity and similarity of the human experience?
- What can change our lives because of profound insights into the meaning of human experience?
- What is representative of major genres and themes?

To help the committee in its deliberations, the NAEP staff circulated questions from a literature assessment that was given in 1970. The results of that effort were so disparate and discouraging that the subject hadn't received another full-scale assessment until the current project was initiated. Half the 17-year-olds in 1970 did not recognize a thematic illustration from *Gulliver's Travels;* nearly 80 percent did not recognize an illustration of *Don Quixote* as a knight tilting at a windmill; a description of Johnny Appleseed was not recognized by nearly 40 percent; 65 percent failed to identify a character who was like Job; 85 percent could not identify Lewis Carroll's "Jabberwocky"; nearly 90 percent failed to identify a passage that suggested the theme of Faust. What 80 percent or more of the 17-year-old students knew were: Robin Hood, the Tortoise and the Hare, Casey at the Bat, Samson, Noah, and Tom Sawyer. Even more discouraging, though, was that when certain of these exercises were repeated as part of a reading assessment in 1979, the average scores for 17-year-old students dropped five to ten points on most items.

This background information was presented to the literature committee for the Foundations of Literacy project, and it was sobering. It may well have caused some committee members to lower their expectations. After reviewing the objectives from the earlier effort, the committee decided to organize the current assessment by genre. The objectives for the literature assessment, like those for the history assessment, were distributed to field reviewers; thirty-nine teachers, professors, and other specialists in the field proposed revisions. After their review, the following were set forth as the selection criteria:

I. Novels, Short Stories, and Plays
    These works and their authors are significant because of universal characters, plots, and themes. This universality arises when a work portrays an experience or a characteristic common to humanity and so helps us

to understand ourselves and to develop our personal values.

A. Novels
    The emphasis is on American authors and their works (Twain's *The Adventures of Huckleberry Finn*, Cather's *My Ántonia*). Major English and foreign (translated) works are also included *(Robinson Crusoe, 1984, Don Quixote)*. Knowledge and understanding of characters, plots, and themes are essential.

B. Short stories
    Most of the stories are by American authors (Edgar Allan Poe, O. Henry, Shirley Jackson). A knowledge of characters (Walter Mitty) and plots ("Rip Van Winkle") will be assessed.

C. Plays
    The emphasis is equally divided between Shakespearean plays *(Romeo and Juliet, Hamlet)* and classical and modern plays *(Oedipus Rex, Our Town, A Raisin in the Sun)*. Knowledge of characters, plots, and familiar passages will be assessed as well as an understanding of themes.

II. Myths, Epics, and Biblical Characters and Stories
     Knowledge of these is necessary in order to understand other literature in our culture because of the frequency of allusions and references to these texts. This knowledge constitutes a cultural shorthand that enables students to recognize certain universal characters, symbols, and themes. With this knowledge, students may recognize the similarities of human experience, past and present.

A. Myths, heroes, and legends
Classical Greek and Roman mythology (Midas, Venus, Zeus) is the major emphasis in this area. Also included are the Arthurian legend (Merlin), fairy tales (Cinderella), folk heroes (Robin Hood), and fables ("The Tortoise and the Hare").

B. Epics
Included are the earliest epics *(The Odyssey)* and those that came later *(Paradise Lost).*

C. Biblical characters and stories
Major biblical figures (Moses, Judas), events (the Flood), and parables (the Prodigal Son) are the core of this area.

III. Poetry
These poets and works are significant because of themes, allusions, and imagery that enable us to understand the meaning of our human experience, that help alter our sensibilities, and that enlarge our imagination. Some of these works are also frequently quoted and thus have become vehicles for our communication with others.

Included are mostly American poets and their poems (Dickinson, Whitman, Hughes) as well as some English poets (Shelley, Blake). Some familiar passages (from Frost's "Stopping by Woods on a Snowy Evening") are also cited.

IV. Nonfiction
Some of these works and their authors are frequently referred to because they have come to embody the values of our culture. Others are worthy of study because

of their success in the communication of ideas by the use of effective rhetoric.

A variety of American nonfiction has been included: speeches (King's "I have a dream"), historical documents (Declaration of Independence), and autobiographies (Thoreau's *Walden*).

The committee decided to distribute emphasis to the different genres in the following manner:

Novels, Short Stories, and Plays: 50 percent
Myths, Epics, Biblical Characters and Stories: 30 percent
Poetry: 10 percent
Nonfiction: 10 percent

TESTING THE TEST

The two committees completed this part of the project by preparing dozens of test items as examples of what should be tested and how the questions should be framed. When the committees dispersed at the end of three days, the psychometricians, test-makers, and item-writers at NAEP gathered together the objectives, the sample items, and questions that had previously been used in other assessments, and set about constructing the test items. If the objectives set by the learning area committees represent the "ends" of the assessment, the test items are the means of finding out how well these ends have been achieved. Within a few months, a trial run of the history and literature items was administered to a small sample of 17-year-old students in schools across the country. When these results were available, the learning area committees reconvened in Princeton to examine them; some questions were then dropped, others were rewritten, and new ones were added by the NAEP staff.

The results of the field test were little short of appalling. NAEP offered the students five possible answers to most of the questions: a correct answer, three "foils," and "I don't know." On the literature portion of the assessment, a *majority* of the sample answered "I don't know" to a large number of questions about major works and authors. A majority could not correctly answer simple questions about *The Catcher in the Rye,* Joseph Conrad, Ralph Ellison, Richard Wright, Willa Cather, O. Henry, Bret Harte, Henrik Ibsen, John Donne, John Milton, Edna St. Vincent Millay, Byron, Keats, Shelley, Carl Sandburg, Chaucer, Elizabeth Barrett Browning, E. E. Cummings, or Sinclair Lewis.

Because the purpose of the pilot test was to evaluate the questions, not to determine how students would fare on the test, it is possible that students of low-to-average ability were overrepresented in the sample. But given the elementary nature of most of the questions, the returns were nonetheless sobering. In due course, NAEP's item-writers made some of the literature questions easier.

While the preliminary trial of the history assessment also revealed some major problem areas, especially relating to students' grasp of chronology, there was *not a single question* to which a majority of the students responded "I don't know." It became clear that there were many authors and works of literature that most students had simply never encountered. By contrast, there were no questions on the history assessment that were wholly outside the usual curriculum. Here a wrong answer suggested that the students hadn't "got it," didn't understand it when it was presented in the class or the textbook, didn't incorporate it into their repertoire of background knowledge, or had not yet studied it in the American history course.

The actual assessment was administered to the full national sample of 17-year-old students in the spring of 1986. In accordance with its usual procedure, NAEP did not include "I don't know" as a potential answer. It is the test-makers' judgment that this response is somehow inappropriate, that it confuses the analysis of the test results, and that it is more equitable to give everyone a fair guess at the possible answers, rather than to allow uncertain students to opt out with an "I don't know" answer.

We are not psychometricians, so we are not in a position to second-guess NAEP's judgment in those terms. It appears to us, however, that the exclusion of "I don't know" has the consequence of driving up students' scores on many items. And of course it has the consequence of encouraging students to guess when they really have no idea what the answer is. We suspect that it would be better to allow students who genuinely don't know the answer to a question to say so. It has the virtue of honesty.

The results of this assessment reveal serious gaps in 17-year-olds' basic knowledge of history and literature. The findings in the pages that follow should concern all who believe that knowledge of history and literature is vital in transmitting our culture; in preparing young people for the duties of citizenship; in giving our population the background knowledge that is needed to read challenging materials and to communicate with one another beyond the simplest level; and in improving the broad intelligence of our people.

2
What They Know

The assessment consisted of 262 cognitive or "knowledge" questions, 141 of them in history, 121 in literature, and an extensive background questionnaire. The questions were not difficult. Students did not have to analyze or interpret a passage, perform a calculation, intuit a relationship, construct an analogy, or puzzle out a multistage problem. The assessment gauged students' knowledge of basic information in history and literature.

This chapter presents the results of the assessment in rather straightforward fashion. To simplify the reader's task, we deal separately with history and literature. Within each subject area, we array the questions into "clusters" around one or another topic, theme, genre, era, or category. There are sixteen such clusters in the history section, thirteen in literature. Note that most questions fall into *two or more clusters*. A history question typically turns up both within an era and under a topical heading. A literature question will turn up in one of the genre clusters and also as a title-author relationship or literary theme, etc. So there is a great deal of intentional repetition and double-counting built into our cluster results.

Within each cluster, we give at least one sample question, complete with the correct answer, all the wrong answers, and the percentages of students choosing each of these. This is intended to help the reader gain a clearer sense of the nature of the assessment, to showcase some of the more remarkable findings, to display the wild and improbable guesses that students often made (leading us to speculate that a number of youngsters selecting the correct answer are none too sure of it), and to illustrate the range of knowledge that the questions probed.

Though we could not reveal all the questions in their entirety, in many other instances we describe the question and indicate what percent of the students answered it correctly. A close reading of this chapter will therefore yield the vast majority of findings elicited by the 262 questions, without compromising the future utility of individual questions and answers. In the Appendix is a list of all the items tested, with the statistical results for several subgroups of the national sample.

WHO TOOK THE ASSESSMENT?

The assessment was taken by 7,812 students, composed of equal numbers of boys and girls. The results were statistically weighted to produce a sample that is representative of the whole population. For example, the weighted proportion of sample students, by race, was 76.5 percent white, 12.9 percent black, 5.9 percent Hispanic, 2 percent Asian, 1.1 percent Native American, and 1.6 percent "other." In accordance with NAEP's standard procedures, the regions of the country are represented in proportion to their current population estimates: 24 percent of the sample was from the northeast; 21 percent from the southeast; 28.8 percent from the central region; and 26.2 percent from the west. Students were drawn from different types of communities, ranging from extreme rural to urban populations. In the sample, 90.5 percent of the students attended public school; 6.2 percent attended Catholic school; 3.3 percent attended other private schools. This, too, approximates the actual distribution of secondary students in the United States today. The sample was also representative of four different levels of parent education: parents who had not graduated from high school, parents who had graduated from high school but gone no further, parents with some post–high school education, and parents who had graduated from college.

CHOOSING A STANDARD

How should one judge the adequacy of students' knowledge in these subjects? Is there a serviceable scale to apply to these findings? Since it was the original intention that virtually everyone should be able to answer a large majority of these questions, we have adopted the scale that is used by many classroom teachers, in which 100 is "perfect" and below 60 is a failing mark. (In many schools, marks below 65 are treated as failing, but we decided to use a more generous standard.) Scores between 80 and 100 percent correct are treated as if they were Bs and As, i.e., traditionally "honors" grades. We generally use the words "commendable" and "commendably" to describe results in this range.

Similarly, we have treated scores between 60 and 80 percent as if they were Ds and Cs, i.e., traditionally undistinguished but "passing" grades. We use such words as "adequate" and "passable" to describe results in this range.

Truth to tell, we don't think scores in the 60s on this kind of assessment are really satisfactory, and we caution you not to let such words lull you into acceptance of results that your own instincts tell you are wholly unacceptable. Remember, most of the information assessed by these 262 questions represents knowledge that most literate people ought to possess. If, on a given question, 62 percent of the youngsters possess it and 38 percent do not, this is not really sufficient.

Even with this lenient standard of adequacy, it should be noted, the students' overall performance is unsatisfactory. The average student was in the 50s on both parts of the assessment. The average score for all *top quartile* students (those whose performance placed them in the top 25 percent of the distribution) was in the 70s, i.e., in the C range, on both history and literature—certainly not an impressive performance by our best students.

HISTORY

Nearly all of the questions on the history assessment were drawn from American history. The average student correctly answered 54.5 percent of the questions that he/she attempted. Put another way, of all answers given to all history questions, 54.5 percent were correct.

As we explained in Chapter 1, students did not have the option of saying "I don't know"; a lot of guessing ensued and this tended to inflate the results. Moreover, although every question was skipped by at least a few students, and some by more than a few, all our percentage calculations are based on the number of answers actually furnished. When students skipped a question, these unanswered questions are not counted as wrong answers. This, too, probably inflated the results.

Even so, just fifteen of the 141 history questions were answered correctly by at least 80 percent of the students, so the amount of "commendable" performance on this assessment is exceedingly sparse. Barely a tenth of the questions reveal A or B level knowledge on the part of American eleventh grade students. Forty-five other questions were answered correctly by 60 to 80 percent, placing these in the range we have deemed passable. This means sixty of 141 questions were passed while eighty-one were failed, i.e., they were answered correctly by fewer than three-fifths of the students.

The students' overall performance is extremely weak, the more so considering that 78.4 percent of them were enrolled in U.S. history at the time they took the assessment. (Remember, the junior year of high school is the traditional time for the required course in American history.) Virtually all of the remainder had taken U.S. history in ninth or tenth grade. Just 2.4 percent of them said they had not studied the subject in high school; some of these may have been recent immigrants or newcomers to American schools.

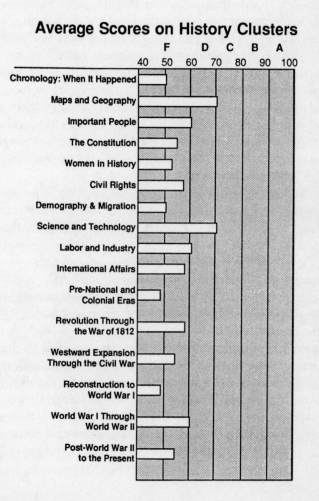

Average Scores on History Clusters

On just five of the sixteen clusters is the students' average performance in the "passing" range and, as the chart suggests, on several of these it is barely that.

Chronology: When It Happened
Average score: 51 percent correct

On twenty-six questions, students were asked to place key events and individuals into the correct year, period or sequence. Chronology is one of the most basic concepts of historical study. Events occur in a particular time and within a particular context. Students who do not have a reasonably accurate sense of "which came first" and "what happened when" are severely handicapped in their capacity to understand relationships between causes and effects. To those without a secure sense of chronology, history seems like a mysterious jumble of unrelated facts. Students cannot even begin to think critically about the meaning of events unless they have a firm grasp of chronology.

On average, the questions about chronology are correctly answered by barely half the students. This means that the youngsters fare somewhat worse on these questions than on the history assessment as a whole.

Only one of the twenty-six questions is answered correctly by more than 80 percent of the students; placing George Washington's presidential term into the correct twenty-year period is the sole chronology question to elicit commendable work (87.9 percent).

Seven others make it into the adequate range of 60 percent or better. These involve the correct dating of the Declaration of Independence (67.8 percent), the Great Depression (72.7 percent), the end of World War II (70.7 percent), Columbus's discovery of the New World (68.1 percent), the writing of the Constitution (60.9 percent), the bombing of Pearl Harbor (60 percent) and Watergate (64.5 percent). Yet in several of these instances, we were disappointed to see how many youngsters got the answer wrong. Surely *everyone* should know that Columbus reached the New World before 1750 (31.9 percent do not); that the Constitution was written between 1750 and 1800 (39.1 percent do not); that the attack on Pearl Harbor occurred between 1939 and 1943 (40 percent do not); and that Watergate occurred after 1950 (35.5 percent do not).

The lowest single score in this cluster involves placing Abraham Lincoln's presidential term into the proper twenty-year period. Fewer than one student in four (24.7 percent) locates it between 1860 and 1880. Three of the four previous twenty-year periods (i.e., 1800–1820, 1820–1840, 1840–1860) also receive more than 20 percent of the student "vote."

As with Lincoln, so with the Civil War. Here is the question/answer combination that to us is the most startling of those in the chronology cluster and quite possibly of all the questions in the entire assessment:

When was the Civil War?	
___ Before 1750	3.7
___ 1750–1800	22.6
___ 1800–1850	38.4
✓ 1850–1900	32.2
___ 1900–1950	2.5
___ After 1950	0.6

NOTE: The answers do not always total 100 percent, because of nonresponses.

Neither Lincoln nor the Civil War is well known to this generation of students. Not even the strongest history students have a secure purchase on the chronological setting of the Civil War. Among the youngsters scoring in the *top quarter* on the history assessment, *three of every ten* cannot place the Civil War in the proper half-century. Yet we would contend that it is impossible to understand American history at all if one lacks any idea of when the Civil War occurred. It is not only the single most traumatic and decisive domestic event since the thirteen colonies won their independence from Britain; it is also the anchoring event of the nineteenth century, the climactic conflict to which other major events led and from which many others resulted.

Here are some other findings in the chronology cluster:

- 57.3 percent of the students correctly assign World War I to the half-century 1900–1950
- 38 percent know that Jamestown was founded before 1750
- 40.2 percent place Reconstruction in the half-century 1850–1900
- 25.9 percent know that the United Nations was founded between 1943 and 1947
- 45.6 percent know that Thomas Jefferson's presidential term was between 1800 and 1820
- 36.9 percent know that Theodore Roosevelt's presidential term was between 1895 and 1912
- 52 percent assign Franklin D. Roosevelt's presidential term to the period 1929–46
- 56.4 percent know that Prohibition occurred in the half-century 1900–1950
- 42.9 percent assign Woodrow Wilson's presidential term to the period 1912–1929

In theory, of course, it is possible to orient oneself in American history around dates and events other than major wars, the terms of famous presidents, and such other celebrated happenings as Columbus's discovery of the New World and the signing of the Declaration of Independence. Events signaling the transfer of power in a nation's history are not the only things worth knowing, but they are certainly not unimportant. It is hard to think why anyone would choose to ignore turning points in a nation's history, or to imagine how students can make sense of history without attention to the chronological relationships among key events.

Maps and Geography
Average score: 71.3 percent correct

The students do relatively well on twelve map questions; their performance in this category is tied for first place with their performance on a set of science and technology questions.

Still, first place here means a grade corresponding to C— on a group of map questions that required only the most elementary knowledge of American and European geography. Five questions asked students to match the names of major nations with their locations on an outline map of Europe. The other seven inquired about prominent physical features of the United States (the Rocky Mountains [81.3 percent], the Mississippi River [70.3 percent]) or large and historically significant sections of the country such as the thirteen original states, the Confederacy, the Louisiana Purchase, Texas, and California.

The Confederacy is correctly identified by 63.4 percent (most of the rest suppose the shaded area on the map is either the Louisiana Purchase or the original thirteen states). Fifty-seven percent spot the territory acquired in the Louisiana Purchase. Two out of three (65.8 percent) can find France, which fares the worst of the European countries; 87.7 percent can find Italy and 92.1 percent correctly identify the Soviet Union.

Among some subgroups of the sample, geographic knowledge is very weak. For example, only 63.8 percent of girls, 44.2 percent of black students, and 54.2 percent of Hispanic students can locate Great Britain.

The geographic knowledge probed by these questions is rudimentary. Students were not asked to designate the route that anyone followed; to distinguish "before and after" in rela-

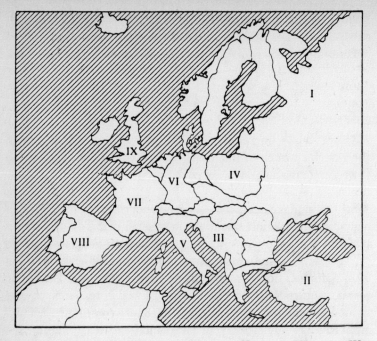

	I	II	VI	IX
Where is Great Britain?	○	○	○	●
	4.2%	11.3%	14.3%	70.2%

	II	III	IV	V
Where is Italy?	○	○	○	●
	1.7	6.2	4.5	87.7

	IV	VII	VIII	IX
Where is France?	○	●	○	○
	9.9	65.8	22.1	2.2

	I	II	VI	IX
Where is West Germany?	○	○	●	○
	3.0	14.5	76.1	6.4

	I	II	V	IX
Where is the Soviet Union?	●	○	○	○
	92.1	3.4	2.2	2.3

tion to geopolitical events; to say *when* anything happened (such as a discovery, an exploration, a conquest); to identify any individual states or cities; or to respond to any questions about five of the seven continents. Had the questions been more demanding, we expect that the number of correct responses would have been much lower. Though the scores on this cluster are higher than on most other parts of the assessment, we do not discern here much evidence that the state of geographic knowledge is strong or secure.

Important People
Average score: 61.6 percent correct

Twenty-five questions asked students to identify famous individuals, all but three of them from American history. The exceptions were Churchill (78.1 percent), Stalin (53.6 percent), and Hitler (87.4 percent).

The youngsters' overall performance here averages out to a D– and it varies widely: from famous inventors (Thomas Edison [95.2 percent], Alexander Graham Bell [91.1 percent]) recognized by nearly everyone, to other celebrated individuals (Jonas Salk [34.3 percent], Betty Friedan and Gloria Steinem [22.8 percent], and Lincoln Steffens [37.1 percent]) known by very few.

On just five questions do students score in the commendable range, i.e., above 80 percent. These pertain to the two just-named inventors, and to the odd trio of Jefferson (87.4 percent), Tubman (83.8 percent), and Hitler.

Seven more are found in the passable range, i.e., with 60 to 80 percent of the students identifying them correctly. These questions involve Hamilton (63.5 percent), Churchill, Washington (79.2 percent), Nixon (77.4 percent), Lincoln (68 percent), Lindbergh (76.1 percent), and Susan B. Anthony (68.9 percent). In each case, at least three students in five knew at least one basic biographical fact about these individuals.

The other thirteen questions, however, elicit wholly unsatisfactory responses. These include such well-known figures in American history as Jane Addams (41 percent), Andrew Carnegie (46.9 percent), Joseph R. McCarthy (42.6 percent), Samuel Gompers (49.8 percent), and Patrick Henry (51.1 percent). (Almost half the students attribute "Give me liberty or give me death" to Samuel Adams, James Madison, or John Hancock.)

In a few instances, such as Gompers's serving as the first president of the American Federation of Labor, we were tempted to express some satisfaction that nearly half the youngsters possess this information. Yet, when five out of ten students guess that the first AFL president was Arthur Goldberg, A. Philip Randolph, or—incredibly—J. P. Morgan, we cannot be content with their grasp of this important chapter in the social and economic history of the United States.

In several other cases, the knowledge gaps are even more astonishing. One student in five (20.8 percent), for example, does not know that George Washington commanded the American army during the Revolution; almost one in three (32 percent) doesn't know that Lincoln wrote the Emancipation Proclamation. Nearly a quarter (22.6 percent) fail to name Richard Nixon as the president whose resignation resulted from Watergate.

The "foils" or "distractors" associated with these questions were not generally designed to be absurd. The idea was that students would have choices—usually four—three of which were entirely incorrect but not completely silly. Hence neither Superman nor Trotsky was among the alternatives to Nixon on the Watergate question. But neither were Jackson, McKinley, and Coolidge. Their choices consisted only of Truman, Eisenhower, and Johnson. Thus it is sometimes difficult to judge how much utterly random guessing is taking place and how much reasonable estimating. Had students' answers been open-ended instead of subject to the constraints of multiple-choice questions, we can only imagine their nominees for various crucial places in history.

As for the three foreign leaders who played key roles in World War II, 87.4 percent correctly identify Hitler; 78.1 percent name Churchill as the British prime minister; but barely half know that Stalin ruled the Soviet Union at this time.

Who was the leader of the Soviet Union when the United States entered the Second World War?

__ Yuri Gagarin	10.2
__ Marshal Tito	5.9
✓ Joseph Stalin	53.6
__ Nikita Khrushchev	30.3

In other instances, biographical knowledge of a factual sort rounds out the story of a well-known historical figure who may otherwise be seen as a two-dimensional image or simply a name without context. The students certainly recognize Martin Luther King, Jr., for example. On the literature assessment, 88.1 percent attributed the "I have a dream" speech to him. Yet we learn from the history assessment that fewer than half (48.9 percent) realize that Dr. King first gained national prominence in the Montgomery bus boycott of 1955. How important is it to know this? Obviously it is not crucial in order to possess a vague sense of King's place in modern American history. But if one really wants to understand what he accomplished and how he became a national leader of the civil rights movement, then it is necessary to know what actually happened.

The Constitution
Average score: 54.4 percent correct

Nineteen questions probed for fundamental knowledge pertaining to the United States Constitution: its antecedents; how and when it came to be written; key provisions, principles and issues; important amendments and Supreme Court decisions. Most of these students are less than a year away from gaining the right to vote; but many lack a clear understanding of the fundamental document that defines the organization and powers of the federal government, as well as the rights and liberties of citizens.

The students' average performance here approximates their overall performance on the entire history assessment, which is to say it is unsatisfactory. Students score commendably on just two of these questions (concerning the Bill of Rights [81.3 percent] and Jefferson's authorship of the Declaration of Independence [87.4 percent]). Adequate answers are furnished to five other questions, leaving twelve in the unsatisfactory range. Four are below 40 percent.

What is Magna Carta?	
__The Great Seal of the monarchs of England	15.9
√ The foundation of the British parliamentary system	30.6
__The French Declaration of the Rights of Man	16.6
__The charter signed by the Pilgrims on the Mayflower	36.8

To be sure, Magna Carta is not an explicit part of American history or of the U.S. Constitution. Yet it is important to know about it to understand the history of Western democracy; the idea of constitutionalism; and the tensions among rights and powers, between government and governed, that created the context for the Revolutionary War and the "miracle at Philadelphia" whose bicentennial we are now observing. The spread of wrong answers given by the students suggests that they were wildly guessing and do not really know anything at all about Magna Carta. Observe that the most popular distractor describes the Mayflower Compact. Some of the 37 percent surely homed in on the simple word association between "carta" and "charter" and proceeded to furnish a wholly inappropriate answer.

Students' knowledge of some key constitutional precepts is also shaky. The system of checks and balances that divides power among the three branches of our government, for example, is a basic concept of our federal government, but only three students in five (59.9 percent) correctly define it.

The idea that each branch of the federal government should keep the other branches from becoming too strong is called

__ strict constructionism	4.4
✓ the system of checks and balances	59.9
__ federalism	18.9
__ implied powers	16.7

Nearly a third of the students (32.4 percent) cannot identify the Declaration of Independence as the document that marked the formal separation of the colonies from Britain. (Half of these guessed at the Articles of Confederation.) The value of knowing that Jefferson wrote the Declaration is diminished by ignorance of its historical significance.

As we noted in the chronology cluster, the sequence of issues and events leading up to and through the Civil War is ill understood. "Nullification" rings the correct bell with just 42.4 percent; only 69.7 percent are clear about the meaning of "secession." One of the key events that preceded the Civil War, the *Dred Scott* decision, is identified accurately by 39.5 percent—fewer than two students in five. Thirty percent of the students instead opt for a plausible but completely opposite foil; they suppose that the Supreme Court held that a slave moving into free territory automatically became free.

As for other celebrated Supreme Court decisions, 61.4 percent recognize the *Plessy* decision (which established the principle of "separate but equal" in law), and 63.7 percent recognize the *Brown* decision (which declared public school segregation unconstitutional)—but nearly four out of ten students know neither. Knowledge of both of these landmark decisions is necessary in order to understand the history of civil rights in the United States.

Only 40.1 percent know that *The Federalist* papers were written to urge ratification of the Constitution.

These questions are gathered into a cluster not only because we happen to be observing the two hundredth anniversary of the U.S. Constitution, but also because they represent perhaps the strongest single reason for studying—and knowing—American history. More is involved than antiquarian interest or intellectual gymnastics. The system by which we govern ourselves today is comprehensible only if its history is understood. Otherwise it is a pastiche of seemingly random rules and capricious practices. Moreover, many of the most profound issues of contemporary society—having to do with civil and individual liberties, equality of opportunity, the tensions between freedom and order, and the relationships between majority rule and minority rights—have their origins and their defining events in the evolving drama of the Constitution. Yet our youngsters do not know enough about that drama, either in general or in specific terms, to reflect on or think critically about its meaning.

Women in History
Average score: 52.6 percent correct

Eight questions probed for knowledge especially pertinent to the history of women in the United States. The results are disappointing. A single question is commendably answered: 83.8 percent know that Harriet Tubman helped slaves escape to the North. Two more queries receive passable answers: Susan B. Anthony is identified by 68.9 percent, and 77.3 percent know that women were heavily involved in production and factory work during World War II.

Who is associated with the founding of settlement houses to help the urban poor?

✔ Jane Addams	41.0
___ Carry Nation	15.6
___ Susan B. Anthony	24.5
___ Mary McLeod Bethune	18.9

The other five questions elicit unsatisfactory answers. A dismal 22.8 percent correctly identify Gloria Steinem and Betty Friedan as leaders of the women's movement in the 1970s, a showing that might result from random guessing. (That a greater number of students choose Elizabeth Cady Stanton and Susan B. Anthony as leaders of the women's movement in the 1970s must cast doubt on their real grasp of Stanton's and Anthony's places in history.)

Just over half (53.7 percent) of the youngsters know when women obtained the vote, while barely a quarter (25.8 percent) correctly identify the Seneca Falls Declaration as an event pertaining to women's rights; 30.5 percent guess that the Homestead Act was concerned with women's rights, and 26.3 percent surmise that the Great Awakening concerned women's rights. The wrong answers apparently were inspired by word associations. On this question (as on a number of others) wholly fictive answers fared well so long as the words in them seemed vaguely plausible.

Would girls do better than boys, we wondered, on history questions that are about women or women's issues? On this small cluster of questions, girls close the gap by which boys otherwise surpass them on the history assessment. Girls do better than boys on four of these eight questions but worse on the other four. But neither boys nor girls do very well on this cluster. Neither gender, we conclude, distinguishes itself for its knowledge of history pertaining to women, which suggests to us that this important aspect of our national history does not receive the attention it deserves, either in the curriculum or in the classroom.

	Percent correct	
Correct answer	Girls	Boys
Harriet Tubman helped slaves escape to the North	84.9	82.8
Women worked in production jobs and factories during World War II	74.2	80.3
Susan B. Anthony was associated with women's suffrage movement	71.9	66.3
Constitutional amendment giving women right to vote was adopted in 1920	57.7	49.7
Constitutional amendments adopted soon after the Civil War omitted women's right to vote	41.0	53.5
Jane Addams founded settlement houses	44.8	37.1
Seneca Falls Declaration was concerned with women's rights	24.4	27.2
Friedan and Steinem were leaders of the women's movement in 1970s	22.2	23.5

Civil Rights
Average score: 58.2 percent correct

Twenty-one questions concerned events and issues in the history of civil rights and civil liberties in the United States. Most pertain to the quest by black Americans for freedom and equality; also included in this cluster are questions about the Bill of Rights, the treatment of Indians after the Civil War, the treatment of Japanese-Americans during World War II, the Holocaust, and the origins of religious toleration in colonial America. Not included here are questions related to women's issues, inasmuch as these occupy a cluster of their own.

The overall performance in this category is not satisfactory. Only four questions are answered correctly by 80 percent or more of the students, and three of these are straightforward identifications of the Ku Klux Klan (83.9 percent), the Underground Railroad (87.5 percent) and Harriet Tubman (83.8 percent). The fourth pertained to the Bill of Rights guarantees of free speech and religion (81.3 percent).

Six more questions are adequately answered, i.e., 60 to 80 percent of the students select the correct alternatives. Included here are Lincoln's authorship of the Emancipation Proclamation (68 percent); the meaning of the term "Holocaust" as a reference to the Nazi's genocide during World War II (75.8 percent); the egalitarian goals of the civil rights movement of the 1960s (71.7 percent); the *Brown* decision (63.7 percent); the *Plessy* decision (61.4 percent); and the fact that it was federal policy to place Indians on reservations in the period after the Civil War (70.5 percent).

Although students score better than average in identifying Lincoln as author of the Emancipation Proclamation, it is nonetheless surprising that nearly one-third of these eleventh graders cannot do so.

President Abraham Lincoln wrote

___ the Bill of Rights	13.6
✓ the Emancipation Proclamation	68.0
___ the Missouri Compromise	9.9
___ *Uncle Tom's Cabin*	8.5

Only 39.5 percent of the students in the sample can identify the essential provision of the *Dred Scott* decision; 38.2 percent can recognize the purpose of the Emancipation Proclamation (though they generally know that Lincoln wrote it they do not know what it did); and 36 percent know the sources of religious toleration in the colonies. This last is of interest both because its correct answer requires a level of understanding deeper than simple recall and because quite a lot of attention has recently been paid to the virtual disappearance of religion from American history textbooks and curricula. A plurality of students (39.4 percent) guess that Puritan assurances of religious freedom in the Massachusetts Bay Colony somehow fostered religious toleration throughout the English colonies, a conclusion that is wholly unjustified.

Though 75.8 percent know about the Holocaust and 83.9 percent about the Klan, only 55.2 percent know about the internment of Japanese-Americans during World War II. Just 30.7 understand the meaning of Jim Crow laws; the other two-thirds choose distractors indicating that these laws in one way or another *improved* the lot of black Americans. Over one-third—more than the number responding correctly—guess that Jim Crow laws were enacted to safeguard the civil rights of the newly emancipated slaves.

Just 63.7 percent of today's 17-year-olds know the significance of the Supreme Court's holding in the 1954 case *Brown* v. *Board of Education*. Fewer than three-quarters (71.7 percent) are aware that the goal of the civil rights movement of the 1960s was political and social equality for minorities.

We naturally wondered whether black youngsters would do better than average on these questions of special significance to them. In several instances, they did. Their average score on questions in this cluster is 54.9 percent correct, which is a substantially narrower gap than on the rest of the history assessment. On six of the twenty-one questions, blacks score higher than the eleventh grade average (twenty-three points higher on the Martin Luther King question). But only 31.8 percent of black students identify Jim Crow laws correctly, and only 55.5 percent accurately describe the *Brown* decision. Moreover, on questions dealing with civil rights issues not specifically pertinent to blacks, their scores are below average. For example, only two in five (40.8 percent) know about the internment of Japanese-Americans; not even three in five (57.5 percent) correctly define the Holocaust.

Black students also do worse than the full sample on a question that asks them to describe the "three-fifths" compromise as the provision concerning the status of slaves that was approved by the Constitutional Convention of 1787. Only 37.7 percent of all students in the sample—a dreadful showing—get this one right. Just 27.3 percent of black youngsters do.

We do not contend that historical knowledge should relate only to one's special interests. To the contrary, the information spanned by this assessment is the kind that we believe all students should possess, since the history of civil rights in America is of real and immediate importance to all of us, not just to members of groups that have been mistreated.

Demography and Migration
Average score: 51.0 percent correct

Eight of the history questions asked students about various aspects of immigration and migration, topics about which they know little. In fact, this is the second worst of the sixteen history clusters in terms of average student performance.

Students appear to be uninformed about basic patterns of migration in American history. Not a single question enters the commendable range and just one makes it into the adequate band between 60 and 80 percent. This was a query about causes of population movement toward the West Coast in the pre–Civil War period; 71.3 percent of the students correctly select the discovery of gold in California. (Almost one in five guesses that the incentive was the completion of the transcontinental railroad—which was a major event of the *post*–Civil War era.)

Two other questions about the reasons that Americans moved westward—the sale of inexpensive public lands in the early nineteenth century (54.7 percent) and the Dust Bowl droughts of the 1930s (53.8 percent)—are understood by barely half.

There is scant understanding among these 17-year-olds about the patterns of immigration to the United States from other parts of the world. If students are vague about or unaware of the great human drama of immigration, then it is not likely that they can have any real understanding of social history or that terms like pluralism and diversity have much meaning for them. For example, the students do not recognize that the principal source of immigration to the United States shifted in the late nineteenth century from northern and western Europe to southern and eastern Europe.

From 1890 through 1910, there was a large increase in the number of immigrants coming to the United States from

___ western and northern Europe	40.9
✓ eastern and southern Europe	37.6
___ west Africa and north Africa	11.1
___ the Near East	10.4

Another question asked which immigrant groups to the U.S. were especially affected by the restrictive legislation of 1921 and 1924. Only 37.3 percent of the students correctly identify those from southern and eastern Europe. The rest guess at other parts of Europe, Mexico and Canada, and even, in a few cases, New Zealand and Australia.

These are not trivial questions. If one has no inkling of the ebb and flow of immigration and the domestic tensions that were associated with them, one cannot easily fathom the relationship between demographic change and ethnic conflict, nor can one understand the process of urbanization, the spread of slums, the progressive movement, the course of anti-Semitism and nativism, the attitudes of many Americans toward the world across the oceans, indeed the isolationist tendencies that so affected Wilson's presidency and our nation's foreign policies. Knowledge of immigration history is essential in order to understand the peopling of our continent, as well as the reactions that different groups had—and have— to one another. Since immigration policy is also one of the great issues of our own time, it is by no means an antiquarian concern. These youngsters have not gained the historical background they need to think critically about one of the major quandaries of their generation.

These questions also require relatively greater understanding of trends, patterns, relationships, and causation than do the questions in many other clusters. Perhaps that is why the students fare less well with them. But that also makes them a better illustration of eleventh graders' inadequate mastery of somewhat less mundane and "factual" history. Moreover, these questions involve knowledge of what is generally termed "social history"—as opposed to wars, dates, presidential elections and biographical information about famous individuals; if anything, the students' grasp of this aspect of social history is even flimsier than their command of traditional history.

Current immigration is no better understood. Only three

students in five (59.5 percent) are aware that significant numbers of immigrants during the past two decades have come from Latin America and Southeast Asia. Not even the children of this wave of immigration recognize its historic scale: just 61.2 percent of Hispanic youngsters got this right, as did 72.3 percent of the "other" (i.e., not black, white, or Hispanic) students in the sample, a group we surmise consists largely of Asian-Americans.

Science and Technology
Average score: 71.3 percent correct

Ten questions pertain to scientific discoveries, technological developments and—in the Scopes trial—issues associated with teaching science. Most of these questions involve simple factual identifications.

This cluster is tied for first place with the map questions. On average, more than seven students in ten select the correct answers to these questions, placing the cluster as a whole well into the passing range.

Two of the ten questions elicit unsatisfactory responses. One of these involves issues of the Scopes trial, which are not well known to students today. Though a plurality (37.2 percent) of the students correctly assert that the trial was concerned with teaching evolution in the schools, more than three youngsters in five (62.8 percent) guess otherwise; more than half surmise that it had to do either with freedom of the press or prayer in schools. This is a pity, especially in view of the durability and contemporary relevance of the Scopes issues. What meaning can a youngster possibly draw from a newspaper headline about "Scopes II" in Tennessee in 1986 if he or she has no sure knowledge of "Scopes I" six decades earlier?

Neither is Jonas Salk's most celebrated achievement known to most of these youngsters. According to almost two-thirds of the students (65.7 percent), the first polio vaccine was the work of Walter Reed, Linus Pauling, or Benjamin Banneker.

More than one-third of these youngsters (37.3 percent) draws a blank on "Sputnik," even though the term is commonly used to symbolize technological breakthrough and was a milestone in space travel.

Sputnik was the name given to the first	
✓ man-made satellite	62.7
___ animal to travel in space	12.7
___ hydrogen bomb	14.2
___ telecommunications system	10.4

We surmised that virtually every student would correctly answer a question about television becoming "a new feature in American homes after 1950." Nearly four-fifths (78.1 percent) do, but more than a fifth of them guess that the radio, the phonograph, even the telephone was a post–1950 innovation.

Finally, it must be noted that one student in five does not know when, where, and by whom the atomic bomb was first dropped. Not even half (48.6 percent) place its detonation in the 1943–47 period. Some believe that the United States dropped it on Germany during World War I, and others suppose that we dropped it on China during the Korean conflict. This question asks a simple historical fact of surpassing importance. For twenty out of a hundred eleventh graders not to know it is remarkable.

Labor and Industry
Average score: 61.1 percent correct

Fourteen questions involve work, workers, industrialization, the economy and the welfare state. In one way or another, each is drawn from important areas of social and economic history.

Overall, the students do better on this cluster than on most others, edging into the passing range. But just barely. Although 75.1 percent of the students can characterize the Great Depression as a period of widespread unemployment, one in four cannot. Furthermore, 28 percent cannot place it in the proper half-century.

Their understanding of the New Deal is even hazier. Barely half (54.7 percent) can date the founding of the Social Security system to that period; two in five assign it to the 1950s or '60s. Only half (52.3 percent) recognize the New Deal as a time of "new welfare measures and increased economic regulation." (One wonders how the guessers would have fared had the word "new" not been contained within the correct answer, allowing them an easy word association.) In the following question, the spread of answers suggests random guessing; the great majority of students do not know what Franklin Roosevelt's New Deal was about:

Which of the following was NOT addressed by New Deal legislation?

___ Agricultural price supports	20.6
___ Labor unions	17.7
___ Social Security	23.9
✓ Restrictions on immigration	37.8

The students frequently seem confused about the relationship between political developments and social and economic policies. Since they know little about what the New Deal did or did not do, it is perhaps not surprising that barely half (52.8 percent) can link the Populist party to government support for farmers, one of that party's central tenets.

Only one of the fourteen questions in this cluster elicits the correct answer from a commendable proportion of the students: 87.2 percent of the sample successfully identify the assembly line as a manufacturing technique pioneered in the early days of the American automobile industry.

Five other questions are answered adequately, while eight fall below 60 percent. Among the information that three-fifths of the students do not possess, besides that already mentioned: the meaning of the term "laissez faire" (51 percent get it right); the link between labor legislation and growth in union membership during the 1930s (38.2 percent); the association of Andrew Carnegie with the steel industry (46.9 percent), and of John D. Rockefeller with the oil trust (57.8 percent).

Why, it may be asked, do students need to know about the history of union membership? Because the free trade union movement is one of the bulwarks of a democratic society and because some of the fundamental economic and social reforms of the past century—such as the banning of sweatshops and child labor—can scarcely be fathomed without knowing something of the saga of the labor movement. The labor movement story is one of men and women, laws and campaigns, ideas and conflict. This is the stuff of history.

In this cluster we again catch a glimpse into students' sparse knowledge of elements of social history. The individual questions do not, in general, deal with broad trends; for the most part, it is necessary to possess specific information in order to furnish the correct answers. But these are the kinds of specifics it is necessary to possess in order to understand how the society we inhabit came to be as it is. Amid contemporary debates about welfare reform, "supply side" economics, budget deficits, Medicare, the sources of poverty, the "underclass" and the proper relationship of government to the family and the economy, a secure knowledge of history creates the foundation for understanding, for forming one's own views, and for becoming an active and informed citizen. Ignorance of social history leaves one without the means to understand what others are debating.

International Affairs
Average score: 58.3 percent correct

The largest cluster of history questions—thirty-eight questions in all—concerns international affairs of diverse sorts: places, people, wars, foreign policies and the like. As befits a subset containing more than a quarter of all the questions in the history assessment, student performance here is close to average—a bit better, actually, but still unsatisfactory overall. It is highly varied, however, ranging from a map question that 92.1 percent get right (find the Soviet Union) to a chronology question (when was the United Nations founded) that barely a quarter (25.9 percent) can answer.

Students do commendably on four questions: two based on the map of Europe (Italy [87.7 percent], the U.S.S.R. [92.1 percent]); one identifying Hitler (87.4 percent); and one associating Pearl Harbor with U.S. entry into World War II (80 percent). Fourteen other questions are passably answered, many of them having to do either with map knowledge or aspects of World War II, a period they seem to know somewhat better than the hundred years preceding it.

But students do very poorly on three questions that evoked European antecedents of American history: identification of the Renaissance (39.3 percent), the Reformation (29.8 percent), and Magna Carta (30.6 percent). All are correctly answered by less than 40 percent, a level that suggests widespread ignorance.

Broad questions about foreign policy also fare badly, as does student understanding of the War of 1812 (47 percent), the Spanish-American War (33 percent) and the First World War (only 57.3 percent know that it occurred between 1900 and 1950, while 64.6 percent correctly identify one of its causes). Though they know somewhat more about World War II, still 29.3 percent cannot correctly name our principal enemies in that conflict and 20 percent do not know about the significance of Pearl Harbor. (Twice that many cannot accurately date the Japanese attack on it.)

Recent history is not well understood, either. Barely half (53.9 percent) are aware of the American role in the Korean conflict. (Two in ten think we were neutral; one in ten thinks we were allied with China.) Asked about Soviet expansionism, only 55.4 percent correctly answer that Israel, alone among the four nations named, has not been invaded by Moscow since World War II.

What nation was NOT invaded by forces of the Soviet Union after the Second World War?

___ Hungary	14.6
___ Czechoslovakia	15.4
___ Afghanistan	14.5
✓ Israel	55.4

Fifty-five percent identify the People's Republic of China as the country that the U.S. established relations with during the Nixon administration. (Almost two in five guess Vietnam or Taiwan.) Half (49.1 percent) do not know the meaning of the Monroe Doctrine, even though the term is frequently invoked by the media in discussing American foreign policy. More than one of every five youngsters thinks it had something to do with the China trade.

A third (32.8 percent) do not know that the United States supplied economic aid to Europe after World War II, and two-thirds (67.7 percent) cannot associate "isolationism" with American foreign policy toward Europe between the world wars. More than half (50.3 percent) guess that the best descriptor is "imperialistic" or "internationalist."

Half (50.3 percent) know that President George Washington warned against entangling foreign alliances, but the other half do not. Fewer than half (47 percent) associate British interference with American shipping with the causes of the War of 1812. (Guessing wildly, 28 percent suppose that conflict had something to do with France's desire to expand her American territories!)

But for being entirely at sea in history, as it were, the prize must go to the 30.1 percent of 17-year-olds who believe that one consequence of the Spanish-American War was the destruction of the Spanish Armada.

Pre-National and Colonial Eras
Average score: 49.0 percent correct

The first of the history clusters to deal with an era or period of time rather than with a set of topics or issues is also the cluster on which students register the lowest average score: less than 50 percent correct on these thirteen questions. Yet 79 percent of the students say they have studied this period while in high school.

This cluster includes that question on which students score lowest in the entire history assessment: what colony did Winthrop and the Puritans found? Nearly half say Plymouth; Providence comes in second; Boston—the right answer—comes in a lowly third, correctly identified by only 19.5 percent of the students. It isn't hard to figure out what went wrong: the students confuse the Puritans with the Pilgrims. Recall that 78.4 percent of all the youngsters in the sample were taking American history during the 1985–86 school year, the year in which they were assessed. Confusions that may be understandable among adults who haven't thought about the seventeenth century for quite some time are less forgivable in young people who presumably began their year where virtually all American history courses have always begun: a quick look at the explorers followed by a close look at the colonial period.

There are paradoxes here, too. Seventy-six percent know that Jamestown was the first permanent English colony—but only 38 percent place its founding in the proper period. (An equal proportion—38.5 percent—place it *after* 1800.) Seventy percent know that most English colonists earned their living by farming, but just 36 percent accurately answer a question about the origins of religious tolerance in those same colonies. Moreover, in one of the assessment's more sophisticated questions, students are asked to pick a feature of life in the United States today that was well established in the colonies. The correct answer, chosen by 58 percent, is representative forms of government. The other 42 percent choose inappropriate distractors, such as compulsory high schooling and the names of today's principal political parties.

Students' grasp of which European nations explored and settled different parts of North America is also manifestly uncertain. Just three in five associate England with the east coast (60.6 percent) and Spain with the southwest (61 percent). A third of them think that England or France explored the southwest. Only half (50.3 percent) select France as the European nation that explored the Mississippi Valley and Canada; more than one in four guesses that it was Spain.

What European nation was primarily responsible for exploring and settling the east coast of the United States?

✓ England	60.6
__ Portugal	11.1
__ France	23.4
__ Italy	4.9

Only 68 percent correctly locate Columbus's discovery of the New World in the period before 1750. We cannot explain the twenty-eight out of a hundred youngsters who suppose that his voyage occurred between 1750 and 1850, let alone the handful who guess still later dates.

Revolution Through the War of 1812
Average score: 58.9 percent correct

Twenty-four questions checked on students' knowledge of that eventful half-century from just before the Revolutionary War until the conclusion of the War of 1812. This is a period that 91 percent say they have studied since ninth grade.

The students' overall performance on the questions in this cluster is far from satisfactory. Only four questions receive answers in the A and B range, while six earn scores in the C and D range.

The three questions that garner the lowest marks involve the shortcomings of the Articles of Confederation (36.8 percent get it right); the Constitution's "three-fifths compromise" regarding the status of slaves (37.7 percent); and the role of Paine's *Common Sense* in presenting arguments for colonial independence (38.3 percent). None of these is something a young person is apt to glean from everyday conversation, nonhistorical writings, or the media; each is the sort of information one acquires only through the study of history. None is correctly answered by as many as two students in five.

The purpose of the authors of *The Federalist* papers was to

__ win foreign approval for the Revolutionary War	15.0
__ establish a strong, free press in the colonies	41.0
✓ gain ratification of the United States Constitution	40.1
__ confirm George Washington's election as the first President	3.9

The three questions on which students score highest involve knowing when Washington was president (87.9 percent)—this is also the question on which students fare best in the chronology cluster; identifying Jefferson as primary author of the Declaration of Independence (87.4 percent); and recognizing the original thirteen states on a map (84.8 percent).

In between, in the satisfactory range, we find that almost two-thirds know of Hamilton's support for a strong national government (63.5 percent); and 67.3 percent understand that the Stamp Act was the first effort by Parliament to impose direct taxes on the colonies.

Yet only 57 percent recognize the area of the Louisiana Purchase on a map. And just 59.4 percent know that the Articles of Confederation were the first constitution drafted by the colonists during the Revolution. (One youngster in four thinks that the Articles of Confederation are the Preamble to the Constitution.)

We are again reminded of the murk through which the Declaration and the Constitution are seen by these eleventh graders. As we have noted, 87.4 percent can correctly attribute authorship of the former to Mr. Jefferson—but one in three cannot place it in the correct fifty-year period and a similar fraction do not know that it signaled the colonists' break from England. As for the Constitution, just 60.9 percent place it in the right half-century, and only 43.8 percent are clear that it established the division of powers between the states and the national government. In the literature assessment, one-third of the students did not recognize the best-known passage from either document.

Territorial Expansion Through the Civil War
Average score: 54.4 percent correct

Students turn in an unsatisfactory performance on these nineteen questions, again showing their lack of understanding of the Civil War and the events giving rise to it. What is more, they display a rather peculiar array of strengths and frailties.

The two questions on which students score best—over 80 percent correct vaulting them, and only them, into the commendable range—involve the Underground Railroad (87.5 percent) and Harriet Tubman (83.8 percent). Eleventh graders generally know what the former did and they understand Tubman's role in relation to it. Perhaps the students remember this story because of its inherent drama and conflict, or perhaps because it was dramatized on television around the time of the test.

Yet they do not understand the political context in which the Underground Railroad and Harriet Tubman operated. Asked, for example, about the main focus of the national debate about slavery in the 1850s, only 51.6 percent choose the correct answer: whether to permit this peculiar institution to expand into new territories. The other half divide almost equally among three plausible but wholly incorrect distractors.

The *Dred Scott* decision (identified correctly by 39.5 percent), the doctrine of nullification (42.4 percent), the Missouri Compromise (43 percent), the central thrust of the Emancipation Proclamation (38.2 percent)—none of these is correctly explained by even half of the students. Here is the question of that group on which students do best:

The Missouri Compromise was the act that

—granted statehood to Missouri but denied the admission of any other new states	11.8
—settled the boundary dispute between Missouri and Kansas	39.9
✓admitted Maine into the Union as a free state and Missouri as a slave state	43.0
—funded the Lewis and Clark expedition on the upper Missouri River	5.4

Only 68 percent know the far simpler and more conventional fact that Lincoln was the author of the Emancipation Proclamation, as discussed before. It is easier to understand the low score (38.2 percent correct) on a question inquiring into the major provision of the Emancipation Proclamation. That is one of the more difficult entries in the history assessment, with at least one seductive (albeit incorrect) distractor. The correct answer was that Lincoln proclaimed the freedom of slaves in the Confederate territories not controlled by the Union. But 41.5 percent of the students opt for the statement that the Emancipation Proclamation ended slavery *within* the Union.

Slavery was not, to be sure, the sole explanation for the Civil War, a bloody conflict that also went a long way toward settling once and for all the domains—and the limits—of state and national authority. Students do not do well in defining the conceptual language associated with the challenge to the Union. Barely two students in five (42.4 percent) correctly associate the doctrine of nullification with the idea of states' rights. (A third suppose it is associated with immigration restriction.) And secession, the ultimate defiance of nation by state, is familiar to just seven in ten.

Faced with a map, only 63.4 percent can identify the region that seceded. A third figure the shaded area is either the Louisiana Purchase or the thirteen colonies.

This era also yields up the students' single worst performance on a map question. Asked which area the United States acquired from Mexico as the result of war, just 36 percent correctly choose the huge region between Texas and the Pacific Ocean. Nearly half opt instead for the sliver of land bordering Mexico today, which was called the Gadsden Purchase. Historians might say *both* were the result of the war with Mexico in the 1840s, but the latter involved a payment, rather than outright conquest of land. We suspect that students based their guess on the proximity of the Gadsden Purchase to Mexico, not on complex reasoning.

Geography is not in such tattered condition as chronology,

however. In none of the other history clusters is it as painfully obvious that the majority of our 17-year-olds simply do not know *when* major events of American history took place. We have already seen that less than one-third associate Lincoln's term of office or the Civil War with the correct period of time, even when these periods are broadly defined. Andrew Jackson's presidency is properly slotted by just 30 percent; more place it between 1840 and 1860 than between 1820 and 1840.

For most of our eleventh graders, the nineteenth century is a vast, hazy blur. Not knowing the sequence of events, or the relationships among them, it is hardly surprising that they are also confused about their significance.

Reconstruction to World War I
Average score: 49.5 percent correct

The two dozen questions in this cluster yield a poor performance. Only three (all discussed in prior sections) make it into the commendable range, and just three more are passable. That means the students fail eighteen of twenty-four questions about this era. Yet 77.8 percent of the boys and girls claim that they have studied this period since ninth grade.

Nine of these twenty-four questions are answered correctly by fewer than 40 percent of the students. These vary greatly in content. Only 21.4 percent know what Reconstruction was, when it occurred (40.2 percent), or—as we have already seen—what Jim Crow laws were (30.7 percent).

An absolute majority (56.3 percent) associate the term "Reconstruction" with physical rebuilding—the obvious guess in terms of literal definitions of words. Twenty-two percent choose other erroneous distractors. Recall, however, that 60 percent place Reconstruction in some half-century *other* than 1850 to 1900. (Most popular among the alternatives is the first half of the nineteenth century, when, it may be recalled, a plurality of the students also believe the Civil War to have occurred.)

Events of the early twentieth century are not in very clear focus in students' minds, either. Sixty-three percent misplace the presidential term of Theodore Roosevelt. Perhaps confusing him with FDR, half (52.3 percent) guess that Teddy Roosevelt was in office at some point between 1912 and 1946.

Most (57.1 percent) get Wilson's term wrong, also. Approximately one-fifth guess at 1895–1912 and an equivalent proportion opt for 1929–1946.

Other famous individuals of the period are not so famous among today's eleventh graders, either. Only 47 percent associate Carnegie with the steel industry (43 percent opt for Ford or Rockefeller). Samuel Gompers, as we have seen, is correctly identified by just 50 percent of the youngsters. And only 57 percent recognize Booker T. Washington as a prominent spokesman for blacks in the period before the First World War. (Malcolm X, Thurgood Marshall, and John Brown all record respectable tallies on this question.)

A majority (63 percent) also misses the boat with muckrakers Ida Tarbell, Upton Sinclair, and Lincoln Steffens; the largest number of students surmise that these people were abolitionists, but significant minorities guess that they might have been trustbusters or carpetbaggers. This, of course, is the kind of question that can be answered correctly if just one of the three names rings the proper bell.

International developments of the period are, if anything, still less well understood. Only one in three knows that the United States became a world power as a result of the Spanish-American War. (Remember, on most questions random guessing would produce an average score of 25 percent.) Thirty-eight percent can identify the shift in immigration patterns that occurred between 1890 and 1910. The foreign policy "motto" of Theodore Roosevelt appears to be familiar to fewer than one-third.

Which of the following characterizes United States foreign policy during the early 1900s?

__ "Fifty-four forty or fight"	11.5
__ The Good Neighbor policy	42.4
__ "The business of America is business"	14.6
✓ "Speak softly, and carry a big stick"	31.6

We initially supposed that the students' confusion about this important era might be explained by the fact that the assessment was administered early in the second half of eleventh grade; perhaps their American history course had not reached the late nineteenth century by that point. But nearly four-fifths of them (77.8 percent) claim that they have studied this period in high school. Moreover, as the next cluster plainly reveals, the youngsters do far *better* on questions pertaining to the two World Wars and the period between them, though these involve still more recent events.

World War I Through World War II
Average score: 60.2 percent correct

The thirty-three questions in this cluster comprise the largest set pertaining to a single era and the set on which students perform best. Three questions are answered commendably and another thirteen adequately. Just six come in below 40 percent.

Still, those six contain some rather basic knowledge about the twenties, the thirties, and World War II. Fewer than two students in five (39.5 percent), for example, put D-Day in the correct four-year period. (A third of them place it between 1939 and 1943 and a quarter guess that it was before 1939.)

Immigration laws, too, are poorly understood. Not even two students in five (37.3 percent) grasp the impact of the restrictive legislation of the twenties or know that these immigration limitations were *not* prominent elements of the New Deal (37.8 percent).

Some of the chronology questions in this era are relatively difficult, involving four-year blocks of time between 1931 and 1947. Perhaps one can be pardoned, at least until the end of the course, for placing Pearl Harbor or D-Day in the adjoining block. But others seek to evoke much more rudimentary knowledge, such as the half-century in which World War I and the Great Depression occurred (known by 57 and 72 percent, respectively) and the decades in which Franklin Delano Roosevelt was president (correctly placed by only 52 percent).

When was the First World War?	
___ Before 1750	3.6
___ 1750–1800	8.5
___ 1800–1850	13.8
___ 1850–1900	16.2
✓ 1900–1950	57.3
___ After 1950	0.6

Nor do dates present the only difficulties. The New Deal is not well understood by these youngsters, nor are certain basic foreign policy issues. Indeed, the lowest score in this cluster (32.3 percent) is to be found on the question about isolationism as the description of U.S. policy toward Europe after World War I.

Students do better in explaining the provocation that propelled the U.S. into the Great War. But observe that more than one in three opts for inappropriate distractors.

The United States was provoked into entering the First World War by

✓ German submarine attacks on American ships	64.6
—— Japanese aggression in the South Pacific	18.3
—— Soviet attempts to blockade Berlin	10.0
—— European grain embargoes	7.1

FDR fares badly. (He doesn't do too well on the literature assessment, either, as some of his most famous statements are misattributed.) As we have seen, only 52 percent place his presidency in the correct decades; just 41 percent choose "Hoover followed by Roosevelt" as the presidents during the Great Depression. The major elements of New Deal legislation are known by only 52 percent. Almost a third (32 percent) guess that the prominent domestic policy changes of the period had to do with declining farm price supports or with decentralization of government.

Only seven students in ten identify Germany and Japan as the major adversaries of the U.S. during World War II. Twenty-nine percent select other answers, involving Cuba, Vietnam, China, Iran, Korea, and the Soviet Union.

Post–World War II to the Present
Average score: 54.7 percent correct

The twenty questions in this cluster pertain to the most recent period of American history, and thus surely contain the most surprises for adults who *lived* through these events and find it difficult to believe that our sons and daughters are not universally familiar with them. Yet not a single question in the group is correctly answered by more than 78 percent of the students. Thus none make it into the commendable range. Seven, however, yield passable scores between 60 and 80 percent.

Recognition of Friedan and Steinem as leaders of the women's rights movement fares worst (22.8 percent), followed by the legislative achievements of Lyndon Johnson's Great Society (23.9 percent) and the founding of the United Nations (25.9 percent). Only 42.6 percent associate Senator Joseph R. McCarthy with anti-Communist investigations; many think he was the Senator McCarthy who led the protest movement against the war in Vietnam. Thus we are raising a generation for whom the term "McCarthyism" has little meaning.

The controversy surrounding Senator Joseph R. McCarthy focused on

✓ investigations of individuals suspected of Communist activities	42.6
___ agitation to secure civil rights for Irish immigrants	15.1
___ leadership of the movement protesting the war in Vietnam	29.4
___ leadership of the movement to improve veterans' benefits	12.9

The same proportion, about two in five, guess that Social Security and the Civilian Conservation Corps were hallmarks of Lyndon Johnson's administration; less than one in four (23.9 percent) opts correctly for Medicare and the protection of voting rights.

Perhaps fittingly, in view of the quantity of it that the youngsters consume, television is recognized by 78 percent of them as a new feature in the American household since 1950; 77.4 percent correctly identify Watergate, and 71.7 percent know that the civil rights movement of the 1960s sought civil and political equality for minorities. Yet it must be recalled that 22 percent of the students associate Watergate with the resignation of a president *other* than Nixon, and 36 percent think it occurred before 1950 (approximately one in five place it before 1900).

We have already called attention to some other surprising knowledge lacunae: that Sputnik is recognized by only 62.7 percent; that only 53.9 percent can correctly depict the American role in Korea; that 45 percent don't know which nations the Soviets have invaded in the years since World War II; that the same fraction select countries other than China as the object of new diplomatic relations during the Nixon administration; and that 36 percent misunderstand the significance of the Supreme Court's 1954 *Brown* decision.

Other noteworthy findings here: 44.4 percent do not know that Eisenhower was president during the 1950s. And only 57.7 percent know that the primary American foreign policy goal of the postwar era was to prevent the spread of communism. (Almost a quarter surmise that we sought to revert to a policy of noninvolvement, while one in ten guess that we sought to resume control over former colonies.)

Overall, students do no better on this most recent era than on the period from the Revolution to the War of 1812. Which obliges us to remember that if they were seventeen in 1986, they were just six years old in 1975. If we think it important that they understand the three decades between the Second World War and their own sixth birthdays, we cannot expect the instructional job to be done for them by the daily newspaper or the nightly news; we have to *teach* this period as the history that it now is.

LITERATURE

The literature assessment comprised 121 cognitive questions, most of them simple recognitions and associations that could be answered correctly on the basis of rather superficial knowledge about major writers and works of Western literature.

Yet on the average question, just 51.8 percent of the students supply correct answers, a lower average score than the 54.5 percent giving the right answer to the average history question.

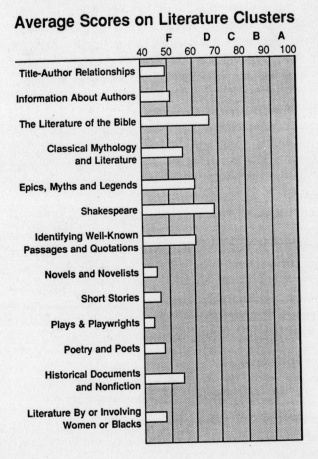

Average Scores on Literature Clusters

The literature assessment also contains more questions that practically nobody answers correctly. A full dozen of these queries elicit the right answers from fewer than 25 percent of the students. In other words, one question in ten is answered correctly by less than one student in four. On the history assessment, by contrast, just six questions of the 141 (roughly one in twenty-four) bring forth such a poor showing.

It seems likely that one reason for this is that the history curriculum has a good deal more coherence across the land than does the literature curriculum. The American history course has an essential similarity regardless of where it is studied. The English curriculum is not comparably constrained. Because of variations in the English curriculum in their state, city, district, school, or classroom, two youngsters can reach the age of seventeen without ever having encountered the same literary titles and authors.

The students' overall performance on the literature assessment is disappointing. Fourteen questions make it into the commendable range, and another thirty-seven into the band we designated adequate, meaning that students perform passably on a total of fifty-one questions and inadequately on seventy.

With just a few exceptions, the students fare far better with the questions they can answer on the basis of "pop culture" knowledge than with those that depend on what is learned in school. (The exceptions include questions about plays by Shakespeare.) If the questions involve something that has turned up in the movies, television, the cartoons, comic books, advertising, or other parts of the popular culture, students are more apt to know it than if it is encountered only in school.

Title-Author Relationships
Average score: 39.5 percent correct

The twenty-nine questions represented here involve perhaps the most rudimentary knowledge about literature: which authors wrote which works?

These questions yield the *lowest* average score of all the clusters in the literature assessment. Overall, only 39.5 percent are able to supply the correct answers.

In the cellar, with less than 20 percent each (a lower score than random guessing would produce), are de Tocqueville (15.5 percent), Joyce (15.6 percent), Dostoevsky (17 percent), Ellison (18.3 percent) and Conrad (19.3 percent), closely followed by Ibsen (20.3 percent), James (22 percent), and Hardy (24.4 percent).

These were not "trick" questions. Students were asked to link these authors to some of their most prominent works and in virtually every instance the students were supplied with the titles of more than one work per author, making it possible to answer the question by correctly associating just one of these with the person who wrote it. Thus, for example, one could get the Dostoevsky question right by linking the great Russian novelist to either *Crime and Punishment* or *The Brothers Karamazov.* Just 17 percent can do so. All three of the distractors (Chekhov, Pasternak, and Solzhenitsyn) are more frequently chosen.

The Ibsen question included the titles of three of his best-known plays: *Hedda Gabler, A Doll's House,* and *An Enemy of the People.* Yet only one student in five gets it right. Nearly half the sample attributes these plays to Samuel Beckett. Ibsen winds up tied for second with Shakespeare, each with the vote of about one student in five.

Three of Thomas Hardy's titles were also supplied, but the scattering of the responses suggests completely random guessing and leads us to believe that Hardy is no longer part of the high school English curriculum:

> **The Return of the Native, Tess of the D'Urbervilles, and The Mayor of Casterbridge** were written by
>
> ___ Sir Walter Scott   34.1
> ✓ Thomas Hardy   24.4
> ___ Oscar Wilde   21.1
> ___ Robert Louis Stevenson   20.4

Among the six authors correctly identified by at least 60 percent—namely Mary Shelley (74 percent), Poe (75 percent), Wilder (65.6 percent), Hemingway (63 percent), London (62.5 percent), and Homer (60.6 percent)—we see at least two whose works are not commonly read by (or during) eleventh grade. This may simply underscore the fact that it isn't necessary to have read a work in order to know who wrote it or to guess correctly on a multiple-choice test, and this we—somewhat glumly—accept. There were enough clues in the *Frankenstein* question (about "a scientist who constructed and gave life to a humanlike creature which he was unable to control") for practically any youngster familiar with Boris Karloff's movie monster to guess the correct answer without ever having heard of Mary Shelley.

On the other hand, Melville was long a staple of the high school curriculum, and even with the help of three references, most students do not recognize him:

> **Billy Budd,** "Benito Cereno," and "Bartleby the Scrivener" were written by
>
> ___ Washington Irving   22.9
> ✓ Herman Melville   35.9
> ___ Jack London   22.7
> ___ James Fenimore Cooper   18.6

Additional examples of the questions in this cluster and the percentages of students who answer them correctly:

- Geoffrey Chaucer wrote *The Canterbury Tales* (36.1 percent)
- F. Scott Fitzgerald wrote *The Great Gatsby* (51.7 percent)
- Henry James wrote books such as *Daisy Miller* and *The Portrait of a Lady,* which compared American and European lifestyles (21.9 percent)
- George Bernard Shaw wrote *Pygmalion, Arms and the Man,* and *Saint Joan* (37.5 percent)
- T. S. Eliot wrote the poems *The Waste Land,* "The Love Song of J. Alfred Prufrock," and "The Hollow Men" (45.4 percent)
- James Joyce wrote *A Portrait of the Artist as a Young Man, Ulysses,* "Araby," and "Eveline" (15.6 percent)

Information About Authors
Average score: 51 percent correct

Rather than asking simply for title-author associations, the ten questions in this small cluster probed for knowledge about characteristics and accomplishments of well-known authors and their works. Students fare somewhat better here, but it should be noted that even though the questions were elementary the overall score is still way below our 60 percent threshold.

Several questions could be answered correctly on the basis of general knowledge: that Shakespeare wrote sonnets, that

Plato and Aristotle were philosophers, that Aesop wrote fables. In these the writer's name and the trade, genre, or product are associated in common discourse, much like Picasso and art or Beethoven and music.

To answer others, it is probably necessary to have encountered the authors at some point in one's English courses. Then one would likely know (as 34.7 percent of those sampled do) that Melville and Conrad wrote novels about the sea; that Byron, Keats, and Wordsworth were poets (though knowing any one of them would permit the correct answer to the question about all three, which 48 percent give); that Langston Hughes was part of the Harlem Renaissance (36.2 percent); or that Faulkner, Welty, and O'Connor situated many of their works in the South (a third of the students know this of Faulkner, while Welty and O'Connor come in at just 14.4 percent).

Most students do know that Plato and Aristotle were philosophers; only 21 percent of the students think they were playwrights, poets, or politicians. Nearly three-quarters (72.7 percent) recognize Charles Dickens, though that question could be correctly answered by recognizing any of four of the author's better-known characters (Oliver, Micawber, Pip, and Gradgrind), one of whom is also the title of a well-known musical.

But just 57 percent know that Shakespeare wrote sonnets as well as plays. And Aesop, once known to every elementary school child, is now familiar to fewer than two-thirds of our sample.

Aesop is best known for having written

✓ fables	65.3
___ dramas	13.2
___ proverbs	10.4
___ epic poetry	11.1

What is the use of such information? It appears superficial precisely because it is so elementary, minor because it is so commonly taken for granted by educated adults and by contemporary writers. It is easy to look down one's nose at the puerile quality of the information that Byron, Keats, and Wordsworth were poets. A generation ago, most high school students would have read at least one of their poems closely and perhaps have known something of the milieu in which they wrote. It would certainly be preferable to determine whether any of today's students have read and enjoyed their poems. But of what use would it be to ask students to analyze one of their poems when 52 percent have never even heard of them?

The Literature of the Bible
Average score: 66.8 percent correct

Fifteen questions pertained to well-known episodes, individuals, or passages from the Old and New Testaments. Obviously not a test of religious belief but a recognition of the profound influence of the Bible on our culture and literature, this cluster of questions elicits a relatively strong performance by the students. One of four literature clusters to make it into the acceptable range, the average score here is second to that achieved on the Shakespeare questions.

Moses (92.3 percent) and Noah (94 percent) are recognized by more than nine out of ten students; 82.4 percent spot "The Lord is my shepherd . . ." as a passage from the Twenty-Third Psalm. No other questions make it over the 80 percent line, though recognizing that the Book of Genesis contains an account of the Creation comes close (79.5 percent), and so does the story of David and Goliath (78 percent).

Four questions fall below 60 percent and thus into the unsatisfactory range: the story of the Prodigal Son (56.5 percent); the significance of Sodom and Gomorrah (33.4 percent); the patience of Job (37.2 percent); and identification of the Bible as the source of the well-known passage (found in Ecclesiastes, though it wasn't necessary to know that to answer the question correctly): "to every thing there is a season. . . . a time to be born and a time to die. . . ." (46.7 percent).

Two-thirds of the students successfully identify Cain and Abel with the biblical story of the young man who kills his brother out of jealousy. But one student in three incorrectly guesses that the unfortunate pair of brothers is David and Goliath, Jacob and Esau, or Isaac and Ishmael.

Three in five know that Jonah was swallowed by a big fish while trying to flee from God. But the other 40 percent guess that he was thrown into a lion's den, that he was shipwrecked for forty days and nights on an island, or that he killed a giant who had terrified everyone else.

That Judas was the betrayer of Jesus is known by 70 percent (though the question included the telltale thirty pieces of silver). Three students in ten settle on John, Pilate, or—incredibly—Mary.

Solomon does not do even that well. Barely three out of five associate him with wisdom.

In the Bible, King Solomon was famous for his	
___ courage	27.9
___ frugality	5.4
___ eccentricity	5.7
✓ wisdom	61.0

So far as we know, the Bible is not routinely taught, even as literature, in most of the nation's public schools. What then accounts for the relatively strong performance of eleventh graders on this cluster? The home, we suppose, as well as the church, and the "general knowledge" resulting from life in a culture strongly influenced by religious traditions.

The Bible is presumably taught in a great many private and parochial schools, however, and this evidently has a salutary effect on students' knowledge of it. On fourteen of the fifteen questions, nonpublic school students earn higher scores than their public school agemates and in most cases by wider margins than their general performance on the literature assessment would predict.

Black youngsters also do relatively well on the questions in this cluster, scoring an average of 64 percent correct. On four of the questions in the Bible cluster, black students' scores are higher than the average for all eleventh graders. Possibly this is a result of schools that pay more attention than usual to the literature of the Bible. We suspect, however, that it is mainly the product of homes that pay close attention to the Bible and of churches that do the same.

Classical Mythology and Literature
Average score: 56.4 percent correct

Although the students' grasp of the information probed by this set of questions is a bit firmer than their overall performance on the literature assessment, it is not satisfactory. On just five of fifteen questions do more than 60 percent of the youngsters supply correct answers. These have to do with simple identifications of Zeus (86.7 percent), Venus (66.5 percent), and Atlas (61.1 percent); recognition of the *Odyssey*'s central theme (73 percent); and knowing that Pandora's box contained a multitude of evils, rather than an enchanted bird, a monster, or glad tidings (64 percent).

In Greek mythology, what happened to Atlas?

___ He was turned into a tree   7.4

_✓_ He had to support the heavens on his   61.1
shoulders

___ He had to map out the heavens   23.4

___ He sat by a pool but was not allowed to drink   8.1

The other ten questions receive unsatisfactory answers, with the reason for Prometheus's punishment eliciting the worst performance (38.5 percent), followed by the defiance of Antigone (39 percent). Almost half the students (48.5 percent) guess that Prometheus was chained to that rock because he had married a beautiful woman (and boasted about her) or killed a sacred animal. And the three students in five (60.8 percent) who do not recognize the story of Antigone as a woman who defies a king in order to honor her dead brother simply distribute their guesses in near-random fashion among Medea, Electra, and Agamemnon.

Slightly more than half the students recognize the Roman war god Mars (56.2 percent), know that Oedipus was the character who unwittingly killed his father and married his mother (51.7 percent), can point to the meaning of "Achilles' heel" (51.5 percent), can identify the tale of Daedalus and Icarus (50.2 percent), and know that Jason pursued a golden fleece (52.5 percent) (although almost two in five guess that he was questing after Troy or the Minotaur).

Speaking of Troy, just 45.4 percent associate the start of the Trojan War with the abduction of Helen by Paris (30 percent hazard the guess that he had kidnapped Penelope). And two in five do not name Midas as the legendary king whose touch turned objects to gold. Instead, they distribute their guesses rather evenly among Agamemnon, David, and Arthur.

Which mythical Greek hero demonstrated his bravery and cunning during his long journey homeward after fighting in the Trojan War?

__ Theseus	22.1	
__ Achilles	23.7	
✓ Odysseus	49.8	
__ Telemachus	4.4	

As with the Bible, the mythology and literature of Greece and Rome undergird much of the art and literature of the West as it has evolved over the past two millennia. Though one can surely get through any given day without such knowledge, it is hard to imagine why our schools should permit the cultural impoverishment implied by the loss of these literary referents.

Other Epics, Myths, and Legends
Average score: 60.7 percent correct

The sixteen questions in this group span some of the best-known and best-loved tales of the Western tradition, several of them in the form of great epic poems.

The students' responses tend to fall into two categories. The majority are reasonably well acquainted with the stories and legends of childhood, which are also the stuff of comic books, movies, and television programs. Thus students are fairly successful—60 percent or more correct—on questions about Cinderella (85 percent), the Tortoise and the Hare (67.7 percent), Rip Van Winkle (76.3 percent), King Arthur (72 percent), Merlin the Magician (80.5 percent), Robin Hood (85.7 percent), Frankenstein (73.8 percent), and Alice in Wonderland (86 percent). Three in five recognize Gulliver, too.

What is the moral of Aesop's fable "The Tortoise and the Hare"?

✓ Slow and steady wins the race	67.7
___ Don't trust flatterers	8.9
___ The race is to the swift and strong	8.0
___ Look before you leap	15.4

They fare markedly less well, however, where the correct answer depends upon having read, or at least knowing a bit about, works of literature that are not routinely encountered in the nursery or on television, but rather in school or as independent reading. Thus fewer than half can handle elementary questions about *Beowulf* (45.8 percent), *The Canterbury Tales* (36 percent), *Paradise Lost* (41 percent), *The Divine Comedy* (32.8 percent), *Pilgrim's Progress* (13.4 percent), or even *Don Quixote* (47.9 percent). Forty-five percent think Bunyan's allegory is about pioneers of the American frontier.

Who is the Spanish knight who attacked windmills, thinking they were giants?

___ Sancho Panza	21.4
✓ Don Quixote	47.9
___ El Cid	15.8
___ Zorro	14.9

Of Hispanic students, 49.2 percent get that one right.

These literary classics are quite challenging and therefore are rarely encountered in high school in anything resembling their full and undiluted texts. Still, stories and episodes extracted from them are commonly found in collections designed for secondary school classes. Moreover, this particular set of questions could be answered correctly on the basis of knowing a bit *about* the works in question. All one has to know about Dante's *Divine Comedy,* for example, is that it is about "a journey through hell, purgatory, and heaven." Yet not quite one-third (32.8 percent) of the youngsters know that, only eight percentage points more than random guessing would produce.

Shakespeare
Average score: 68.4 percent correct

The students achieve greater success with the seven Shakespeare questions than with any other cluster in the literature assessment. The lowest score is 47.3 percent, in response to a question that begins, *"Macbeth* is a play about. . . ."

Yet only four of the seven questions are adequately answered. Save for a single question about Shakespeare the author (he wrote sonnets, too), all the questions pertain to the four plays most commonly encountered in high school: *Romeo and Juliet, Julius Caesar, Macbeth,* and *Hamlet.*

Julius Caesar by Shakespeare is a play about Caesar's

___ discovery of and escape from a plot to kill him	22.1
___ ultimate triumph in the Gallic wars	11.2
✓ death and the fate of his assassins	48.0
___ love affair with Cleopatra	18.8

Three of the questions involve identifying famous passages. Students are asked to recognize the passages that begin with "Friends, Romans, countrymen . . ."; "What's in a name?"; and "To be or not to be. . . ." Approximately three-fourths of them get the first and second of these right, while 87.8 percent correctly attribute Hamlet's best-known soliloquy.

Three other queries pertain to the main story or theme of *Julius Caesar* (48 percent), *Macbeth* (47.3 percent), and *Romeo and Juliet* (89.7 percent). All probe for familiarity and recognition, not for fresh analysis or any but the most rudimentary interpretation. (Is it recognition or interpretation to know that the love affair between Romeo and Juliet was hindered by the feuding of their families? Either way, it is pretty basic. And nine out of ten know it.)

To those who suggest that today's youth are oblivious to Shakespeare, we must reply that it just isn't so. They are acquainted. Unfortunately, an assessment of this sort does not really enable us to determine how well.

Identifying Well-known Passages and Quotations
Average score: 60.5 percent correct

The eighteen "recognition passages" on the literature assessment included at least a couple that not all students would recognize, unless they happened to have read them in school. In this category we might place the "One if by land, two if by sea" line from Longfellow's account of Paul Revere's ride, and Blake's evocative poem, "Tyger! Tyger! burning bright / In the forests of the night. . . ." The Longfellow poem was taught for generations in elementary and junior high schools. Yet it is recognized by just 59 percent of the sample. Only 13.6 percent identify Blake's brightly burning subject, presumably because they have never read the poem. A significantly larger number, revealing better logic than knowledge, guess that the poet was referring to "Fire! Fire! burning bright."

Other passages, however, are harder to dismiss. The assessment included, for example, perhaps the best-known lines from the Declaration of Independence and the Preamble to the Constitution ("We the people of the United States, in order to form a more perfect union . . ."). Each is recognized by two-thirds of the youngsters. That isn't terrible. Yet it is disturbing to discover that 34.3 percent of our 17-year-olds fail to identify key passages—arguably the identifying words—of the two seminal documents of the republic.

"We hold these truths to be self-evident, that all men are created equal, that they are endowed by their Creator with certain unalienable Rights, that among these are Life, Liberty and the pursuit of Happiness."
These words are from

__ *Common Sense*	8.0
√ the Declaration of Independence	65.7
__ Lincoln's Second Inaugural Address	14.2
__ *The Rights of Man*	12.1

Also included were four questions containing famous quotations by American presidents: two from Lincoln, one from Franklin D. Roosevelt, and one from John F. Kennedy. Of these, only the Gettysburg Address makes it into the satisfactory range; 73.9 percent recognize its majestic opening sentence. But fewer than half can associate "With malice toward none, with charity for all" with Abraham Lincoln (45.7 percent), and barely half link the "ask not . . ." line with JFK.

> **Which President said, "And so, my fellow Americans, ask not what your country can do for you; ask what you can do for your country"?**
>
> __ Richard Nixon   11.2
> __ Theodore Roosevelt   29.2
> __ Lyndon Johnson   6.8
> ✓ John F. Kennedy   52.7

FDR fares marginally better; 57.2 percent choose him in response to a very easy question containing *both* "the only thing we have to fear is fear itself" and "a day which will live in infamy." This last quotation included the date of the Japanese assault on Pearl Harbor within the passage itself. But you may recall from the history assessment that few students know when FDR was president, so this fat clue did them little good.

Martin Luther King, Jr.'s "I have a dream" elicits the greatest recognition of all the passages and the fourth highest score of the entire literature assessment. Eighty-eight percent of the youngsters correctly associate the words with Dr. King. But a pair of Churchill's most celebrated lines are properly attributed by just 55.7 percent. One in three supposes that either Hitler or Stalin was offering "blood, toil, tears, and sweat" and calling attention to the descent of an Iron Curtain across Europe.

The students enjoy relatively greater success with three passages from Shakespeare. Hamlet's famous existential dilemma ranks second only to King's dream among all eighteen quotations. Three in four recognize Mark Antony's request for his fellow-countrymen to make him a temporary loan of their auditory appendages, and virtually the same number tap Juliet as the heroine who meditated upon names and roses.

Other poets fare less well. Frost's passages about promises to keep and roads less traveled are attributed to him by just 62.5 percent—though recognizing either one would have yielded the right answer. Frost was once a universal fixture in the high school curriculum; he may not be anymore. That Yeats saw things falling apart elicits the correct association from only 38.9 percent.

Also included, with mixed results, were two passages from the Bible. The Twenty-Third Psalm is spotted by 82.4 percent, but fewer than half (46.7 percent) associate the Bible with the admonition that every thing has its proper season and every purpose its time under heaven.

Though an average score of 60.5 percent edges the students' performance on this cluster into the low end of the passing range, we cannot be sanguine so long as two youngsters in five stare blankly when confronted by a number of the best-known utterances of our culture.

Novels and Novelists
Average score: 44.9 percent correct

The thirty-five questions pertaining to novels and novelists represented a sampling of the core of a high-quality literature curriculum. And the students' responses to them are well below even the average of the literature assessment as a whole.

The problem, of course, is that one tends either to be familiar with a particular book or not, usually depending on whether one has read it. And since the number of novels is vast, while the number that can be squeezed into the high school curriculum is modest, the chances are slim that the assessment-developers successfully matched the questions to what students have actually read in school. We may, therefore, have here a better appraisal of what is and is not included in the curriculum than of what students have learned.

To answer a number of these questions correctly, students

need at least a vague familiarity with a novel's theme, plot, or subject. Such matters are "adequately" familiar to them on only five questions. More than 60 percent know that:

- Robinson Crusoe is the character who, with a few supplies and some ingenuity, was able to survive on an island (83.6 percent)
- *The Adventures of Huckleberry Finn* is about an orphan and a runaway slave rafting down a river (80.5 percent)
- the novel that helped the abolitionist movement was *Uncle Tom's Cabin* (73.4 percent)
- Captain Ahab's obsession in *Moby-Dick* is a desire for revenge (61.8 percent)
- *The Red Badge of Courage* is about a young soldier's struggle to overcome fear while fighting in the Civil War (61.6 percent)

Thirteen questions of the same sort elicited correct answers from fewer than three students in five. Fewer than 60 percent of the students know, for example, that:

- Tom Sawyer is famous for clever ways of getting out of trouble and work (59.8 percent)
- *The Scarlet Letter* is about a woman who committed adultery and the effects of her sin (59.4 percent)
- *To Kill a Mockingbird* is about two children and the conflicts they face when their father defends a black man (59 percent)
- *Don Quixote* is about a Spanish knight who attacked windmills (47.9 percent)
- *The Old Man and the Sea* is a story about a man who battles a great fish and the forces of nature (43 percent)
- *The Grapes of Wrath* is about a family that migrated from the Dust Bowl to California (39.7 percent)
- *Pride and Prejudice* is a story about how the daughters of the Bennet family found husbands (38 percent)
- *Lord of the Flies* is the story of a group of children stranded

on an island who try unsuccessfully to create a civilized
society (35.3 percent)
- Herman Melville and Joseph Conrad wrote novels about the
sea (34.7 percent)
- *Pilgrim's Progress* is an allegory about the temptations that
Christians face in life (13.4 percent)

Where the response drops below 40 percent, we believe that
these novels are not commonly taught in high school. For
example, it was surprising when only 22.5 percent could answer the following question:

**In which novel did a 16-year-old boy who was expelled
from school go to New York City for a weekend to find
himself?**

✓ *A Catcher in the Rye*	22.5
___ *A Tree Grows in Brooklyn*	47.3
___ *The Sun Also Rises*	12.6
___ *A Separate Peace*	17.6

In a demonstration of shrewd but fallacious reasoning, the
students prefer *A Tree Grows in Brooklyn* because of the obvious geographic association between "New York City" in the
question and "Brooklyn" in the answer that the largest number of students choose.

When students are asked to identify a novel by Jane Austen
about how the daughters of the Bennet family found husbands, 38 percent correctly pick *Pride and Prejudice,* and the
remainder divide their votes among *The Heart of Midlothian,
Clarissa,* and *Madame Bovary.*

Often, the students appear to be guessing wildly. For example, when students were offered the solid clue that the book's
theme concerned Heathcliff's "obsessive love of Catherine,"

just 38 percent picked *Wuthering Heights.* In second place, with 28 percent was *Tender is the Night,* followed by *The Hunchback of Notre Dame.*

The novel *1984* received a good deal of attention in the year of its title, yet the majority of the sample do not recognize it.

What is the novel *1984* about?

___ The destruction of the human race by nuclear war	47.9
✓ A dictatorship in which every citizen was watched in order to stamp out all individuality	35.5
___ The invasion and ultimate takeover of the earth by creatures from outer space	8.0
___ A man who went back into time and changed history	8.6

Fourteen different questions asked about title-author relationships. (These are repeaters from the cluster of that designation.) To answer them correctly it was not, of course, necessary to have read the books. Yet only three of these make it into the passing range; the authors involved are:

- Mary Shelley as author of a novel about a monster created by a scientist (73.8 percent). The students could answer this question correctly by connecting the title *Frankenstein* to the description of the novel.
- Ernest Hemingway as author of *For Whom the Bell Tolls* and *The Sun Also Rises* (63.2 percent)
- Jack London as author of *The Call of the Wild* (62.5 percent)
- F. Scott Fitzgerald as author of *The Great Gatsby* (51.7 percent)
- Richard Wright as author of *Native Son* and *Black Boy* (32.3 percent)

- D. H. Lawrence as author of *Sons and Lovers* and "The Rocking Horse Winner" (28.7 percent)
- Willa Cather as author of *My Ántonia, O Pioneers!,* and *Death Comes for the Archbishop* (28.2 percent)
- Thomas Hardy as author of *The Return of the Native, The Mayor of Casterbridge,* and *Tess of the D'Urbervilles* (24.4 percent)
- Henry James as the author who contrasted American and European lifestyles and wrote books such as *Daisy Miller* and *The Portrait of a Lady* (22 percent)
- Joseph Conrad as author of *Heart of Darkness, The Secret Sharer,* and *Lord Jim* (19.3 percent)
- Ralph Ellison as author of *Invisible Man* (18.3 percent)
- Dostoevsky as author of *Crime and Punishment* and *The Brothers Karamazov* (17.1 percent)
- James Joyce as author of *A Portrait of the Artist as a Young Man, Ulysses,* "Eveline," and "Araby" (15.6 percent)

Four questions asked about specific information contained in particular works or works by designated authors, such as a quartet of well-known characters created by Dickens (72.7 percent); Gulliver's adventures in Lilliput (61.7 percent); the war during which *A Tale of Two Cities* is set (59 percent); and the geographic locus of Faulkner's novels (33.3 percent).

The English teachers on the learning area committee thought that Hawthorne's *The Scarlet Letter* was read by almost all students of this age. Nearly six out of ten answer the question about it correctly, while one out of three thinks that the "letter" in the title refers to a "correspondence" between two people:

The novel *The Scarlet Letter* is the story of

___ the correspondence between a woman and her   22.4
fiancé during the Civil War

___ the correspondence between a Revolutionary   10.4
War spy and George Washington

_√_ a woman who was unfaithful and had to   59.4
observe the effects of her sin on others

___ a woman in a New England town who was   7.8
executed for being a witch

How close is the relationship between having read the book and knowing something about it? The background questions for the literature assessment named ten novels and asked students whether they had read them; the same ten novels reappear in the cognitive questions. The following table lists the ten novels, the percentage of students who claim to have read them (whether for school or pleasure) and the percentage who correctly answer the cognitive questions pertaining to those novels:

Novel	Percent who read it	Percent correct on test
A Tale of Two Cities	27.6	59.0
Moby-Dick	33.3	61.8
1984	23.5	35.5
Huckleberry Finn	68.0	80.5
Tom Sawyer	57.3	59.8
The Grapes of Wrath	21.1	39.7
The Old Man and the Sea	28.6	43.0
The Red Badge of Courage	39.9	61.6
The Scarlet Letter	46.8	59.4
To Kill a Mockingbird	52.1	59.1

The most striking point, of course, is that many more of the students seem to know something about each book than have read it. In several cases (e.g., *Tom Sawyer, To Kill a Mockingbird*) the differentials are modest; but in several others they are quite large. More than twice as many youngsters, for example, know which war furnished the setting for *A Tale of Two Cities* than have actually read the book. Big gaps are also conspicuous for *Moby-Dick, The Red Badge of Courage, The Grapes of Wrath,* and *The Old Man and the Sea.*

The overall "have read" average for these ten novels is 39.8 percent, while 56 percent of the youngsters supply correct answers to the pertinent questions about the novels. How can this be? We suspect that we see here some of the effects of random guessing by students in a situation where they are not permitted to confess ignorance, and of canny guessing by test-wise students who adroitly found clues in the questions and distractors, eliminated the less plausible distractors, and improved their chances of success. Of course it is also possible to answer correctly after having seen a movie or television version of the novel or from hearing about it secondhand. Similarly, one may, as we have seen, possess general knowledge of a work without having read it.

Only three of these ten celebrated novels have been read by more than half the students, and only two others by more than a third. And English teachers may be a bit skeptical about even these data. Have a third of the eleventh graders actually read *Moby-Dick?* Or have they read an abridgment, an excerpt, a secondary account, a "classic comic," or even just seen a movie and thought that maybe they had read the book?

Many of the low scores in this cluster surprised us, in several cases because we thought the works and authors were well known. In some instances, lack of familiarity signals a serious omission of the sort that diminishes one's ability to understand our national heritage and history. For example, it is harder to evoke the Great Depression without the help of Steinbeck's imagination. The experiences of black Americans are less well comprehended by those who have not read Richard Wright and Ralph Ellison. And even for youngsters in the 1980s, the menace of totalitarianism is surely better understood with the help of Orwell.

Apparently students won't get such help unless these novels are assigned in school. We note that the two works by Mark Twain are the only books on the list that more than a fifth of the students claim to have read *on their own:* 23.3 percent in the case of Huck Finn (still a far smaller group than those who read it for school) and 29 percent in the case of Tom Sawyer. Six of the ten works yield single-digit figures in answer to the question: have you read it on your own?

Considering this fact together with the relationships shown in the chart, we conclude first that students are far more apt to read novels—at least novels from the realm of "serious literature"—if these are assigned in school; and that—though the correlation is far from perfect—they are more apt to know something about a book if they have read it.

Short Stories
Average score: 46.2 percent correct

Eleven questions were asked about well-known short stories and their authors. Students score in the passing range on four of these. The successes involve recognition of Scrooge as the character who regretted his stingy, selfish ways in "A Christmas Carol" (87.2 percent); "Rip Van Winkle" as the story of a man who slept twenty years and awoke to find the world changed (76.3 percent); Poe as author of three celebrated macabre stories, "The Fall of the House of Usher," "The Tell-tale Heart," and "The Pit and the Pendulum" (75.2 percent); and the great detective Sherlock Holmes as the main character in *The Hound of the Baskervilles*, "The Speckled Band," and "The Red-Headed League" (67.2 percent).

Students may recognize Poe's short stories, but they do not know those of the two other American "power of blackness" writers. Only 43.3 percent identify Hawthorne as author of "Young Goodman Brown," "Rappaccini's Daughter," and "The Minister's Black Veil." A mere 35.9 percent match Melville to three of his best-known short works: "Benito Cereno," *Billy Budd*, and "Bartleby the Scrivener."

One of the most famous daydreamers in all literature, Walter Mitty, is recognized by only 36.6 percent. The short stories of Hemingway ("The Killers" and "In Another Country"), D. H. Lawrence ("The Rocking Horse Winner"), and James Joyce ("Araby") are known by 27.3 percent, 28.7 percent, and 15.6 percent (figures that are no better than random guessing). Only 14.4 percent know Eudora Welty and Flannery O'Connor as authors of tales about the South.

Two authors who are known for their well-crafted stories set in the American South are

√ Eudora Welty and Flannery O'Connor	14.4
___ Louisa May Alcott and Katherine Anne Porter	40.6
___ William Saroyan and Truman Capote	16.1
___ Sherwood Anderson and Sinclair Lewis	28.9

There are, to be sure, innumerable short stories from which the compilers of collections can choose, from which teachers can select, and from which youngsters who read fiction in their spare time can pick. Running into Billy Budd, Walter Mitty, Rappaccini's daughter, or Francis Macomber is to some extent a matter of chance. And short stories are easy to come by. They populate the reading collections that serve as textbooks in many high school English courses. Lots of popular magazines feature new stories in every issue. Because of their brevity, teachers can readily assign them even to youngsters who do not read quickly and fluently. And it is usually possible to distill a story's plot, theme or lesson into reasonably brief and straightforward terms, without the time required for novels, plays, and substantial poems. In short, they lend themselves well to fifty-minute periods, diverse classes, and the instructional needs of harried teachers seeking to present serious literature in relatively brief compass.

Given the size of the short-story universe, it is certainly conceivable that we selected the wrong stars to ask today's eleventh graders about. Maybe they have read a lot of short stories—but not these.

Plays and Playwrights
Average score: 43.6 percent correct

Among the clusters having to do with one or another literary genre, students did least well on this one. Had we included Shakespeare, the average would be higher. But of the eight questions asked, only one makes it into the band of adequacy. It asked students to indicate "which of the following is a play by Thornton Wilder that depicts everyday life in a typical New England village." Almost two-thirds (65.6 percent) correctly answer *Our Town.* But it is hard to know what this signifies. The question itself contained such a robust word-clue (village = town) that a skillful test-taker could readily make a shrewd and successful guess.

As for the other plays and playwrights in this cluster, half of them are correctly identified by fewer than two students in five. And three of these entail simple author-title relationships, leaving us to conclude that the great majority of students are entirely unacquainted with Ibsen as the author of *Hedda Gabler, A Doll's House,* or *An Enemy of the People* (20.3 percent); with Shaw as author of *Pygmalion, Arms and the Man,* and *Saint Joan* (37.5 percent); and Tennessee Williams as author of *A Streetcar Named Desire* and *The Glass Menagerie* (27.6 percent). The fourth abysmal score is earned on the question (already noted in the cluster on classical mythology) about the theme of *Antigone* (39 percent).

Roughly half of the students can identify *Oedipus* as the character who killed his father and married his mother (51.7 percent) and *A Raisin in the Sun* as a drama about a black family planning to move into an all-white suburban neighborhood (53.2 percent). A similar fraction associate Arthur Miller with two of his best-known dramas, *Death of a Salesman* and *The Crucible*.

Which of the following is a play about the experiences of a black family as they made plans to move into an all-white, suburban neighborhood?

___ *The River Niger*	16.2
✓ *A Raisin in the Sun*	53.2
___ *Porgy and Bess*	14.2
___ *Blues for Mister Charlie*	16.4

We do not suppose that many high school students patronize the legitimate theater, although many high schools have active theatrical groups. Nor do many students (or a great many adults of our acquaintance!) read plays in their spare time. During the first half of the 1985–86 school year, 71.8 percent of the youngsters in the sample read *no* plays "for pleasure." Eighteen percent claim to have read one or two on their own; one in ten purports to have read more than two. We note that major plays are seldom presented to prime-time audiences on television, either in their original forms or as adapted for the movies.

We conclude, therefore, that whatever exposure students have to drama is likely to occur in school. And the data suggest that at least some such exposure is indeed taking place; only 35.9 percent of the youngsters in the sample say that they had read no plays in English class during the first half of the year. But 43.6 percent report reading just one or two. If one of these was a work by Shakespeare, there is not much likelihood that Ibsen or Shaw would ever appear.

Poetry and Poets
Average score: 48.6 percent correct

On the seventeen questions pertaining to poetry and those who write it, the students' performance falls below their average score on the literature assessment as a whole. It is not satisfactory. The classic poets of the English language are apparently unfamiliar to most eleventh grade students in our high schools.

As a result of this assessment, we still do not know which poems and poets are actually studied in the nation's high schools. As with most of the literature assessment, one could answer the questions correctly without possessing deep knowledge. Several simply involve forging appropriate links between authors and titles: knowing, for example, that Eliot wrote "The Hollow Men," *The Waste Land,* and "The Love Song of J. Alfred Prufrock" (45.4 percent); that Whitman was the author of *Leaves of Grass* (40.2 percent); Homer, the *Iliad* (60.6 percent); and Chaucer, *The Canterbury Tales* (36.1 percent). Several entail knowledge of the central themes of famous epics and authors. And several others involve the recognition or identification of brief extracts from particular poems. In no case were students asked to engage in an arduous analytic or critical exercise with respect to poetry.

Just five questions elicit passing responses. These involve knowing that the *Odyssey* is about the adventures of a Greek war leader on a long sea voyage home (73 percent) and that Homer was the author of the *Iliad* (60.6 percent); recognizing "Miles to go before I sleep . . ." and "Two roads diverged in a wood . . ." as lines by Robert Frost (62.5 percent); associating Poe with "Annabel Lee" and "The Raven" (67 percent); and knowing that death is a frequent theme in the poems of Emily Dickinson (69.3 percent).

On five other questions, students turn in very poor performances: below the 40 percent mark. These include the Chaucer question noted above; knowing that *The Divine Comedy* is about a journey through hell, purgatory, and heaven (32.8 percent); associating Yeats with "Things fall apart; the center cannot hold . . ." (38.9 percent); linking Langston Hughes to the Harlem Renaissance and to dreams dying (36.2 percent); and choosing the tiger as the brightly burning object in Blake's poem (13.6 percent).

Responses to the remaining seven questions fall between 40 and 60 percent correct. These include literary knowledge that we regard as basic: that Shakespeare wrote sonnets as well as plays (57 percent); that Whitman wrote *Leaves of Grass*; that Byron, Keats, and Wordsworth were poets (48 percent); and that one of the central episodes in *Beowulf* involves the hero's battle with Grendel (45.8 percent). On these questions, the spread of wrong answers suggests random guessing.

Which American poet wrote the volume of poetry *Leaves of Grass*, which includes the line "I celebrate myself, and sing myself"?

___ Robert Lowell	24.5
___ Edna St. Vincent Millay	19.2
___ Archibald MacLeish	16.1
✓ Walt Whitman	40.2

Historical Documents and Nonfiction
Average score: 54.9 percent correct

The dozen nonfiction questions overlap considerably with the cluster dealing with identification of passages and quotations. They include brief excerpts from the Preamble to the Constitution and the Declaration of Independence, quotations from FDR, JFK, Churchill, *Poor Richard's Almanack,* and the two great speeches engraved on the walls of the Lincoln Memorial: the Gettysburg Address and President Lincoln's Second Inaugural Address.

The results are uneven. The opening sentence of the Gettysburg Address ("Fourscore and seven years ago . . .") wins the recognition of 73.9 percent of the students, exceeded only by "I have a dream," which 88.1 percent know to be the words of Martin Luther King, Jr. But as we have seen, only 57.2 percent recognize the quotations from Roosevelt about "a day which will live in infamy" and "the only thing we have to fear is fear itself." Kennedy's statement, "ask not what your country can do for you . . ." is known by 52.7 percent. Just 45.7 percent correctly identify Lincoln with the phrase "With malice toward none, with charity for all" (from his Second Inaugural, though students did not need to know that), and 65.7 percent properly attribute the key passages of the Declaration and the Preamble. Churchill's majestic words are recognized by slightly more than half:

Which twentieth-century European statesman said, "I have nothing to offer but blood, toil, tears, and sweat," and "From Stettin in the Baltic to Trieste in the Adriatic, an iron curtain has descended across the Continent"?

___ Adolf Hitler	15.8
✓ Winston Churchill	55.7
___ William Gladstone	11.0
___ Joseph Stalin	17.5

Benjamin Franklin's common-sense maxims were once standard fare in school readers and literary anthologies, often presented along with excerpts from his autobiography. But less than half of our sample can identify two well-worn maxims.

"A penny saved is a penny earned" and "A small leak will sink a great ship" are two maxims from

___ Solomon's proverbs   22.2
___ Kipling's *Just So Stories*   7.1
___ Aesop's Fables   27.1
 ✓ Franklin's *Poor Richard's Almanack*   43.6

Also included in this cluster are questions about the meaning of the phrase "Achilles' heel" (known by 51.5 percent) and the identity of the European traveler whose perceptive insights were published in the book *Democracy in America* (15.5 percent). De Tocqueville comes in last among the answers to this one, outstripped by Crevecoeur, Lafayette, and even Napoleon.

It is obvious that de Tocqueville's observations on nineteenth-century America are not part of the high school English (or history) curriculum. Nor are those of Henry David Thoreau, who was once a standard fixture in American literature classes. The rugged individualism and love of nature so central to the American psyche find no loftier or more eloquent exposition anywhere than in *Walden*. Yet only 43 percent recognize its fundamental theme: that people should simplify their lives.

But something broader is visible in student responses to some of the background questions: it appears that they have scant exposure in English class to any forms of nonfiction. During the first semester, 60.8 percent had not read any historical documents; 46.2 percent had read no biographies or journals; and 29.2 percent had not read a single essay for English class.

The history classes do not adequately compensate. We learn from background questions on the history assessment that barely half of the students "use documents and other original sources" at any time during the year. The other 44.5 percent never do. About half the students report that the reading of "stories, biographies, or articles about historical people or events" is a regular feature of their history classes. Therefore it is possible that a large proportion of the students have never read the actual words of the Declaration of Independence, much less President Kennedy's, FDR's, or Churchill's speeches. Under the circumstances, it may be remarkable that as many as half the youngsters can link such quotations with their authors.

Literature by or About Women or Blacks
Average score: 48.6 percent correct

Thirteen of the questions involve works by or about women or blacks. The overall student performance on these questions is both unsatisfactory and below average. Only 32.3 percent can identify Richard Wright as the author of *Native Son* and *Black Boy;* just 36.2 percent choose Langston Hughes as the Harlem Renaissance poet who wrote about dreams dying; and not even one in five (18.3 percent) selects *Invisible Man* as the book by Ralph Ellison about growing up in the South and then moving to Harlem. (Students in nonpublic schools are twice as likely to answer the Ellison question correctly as those in public schools.)

Only four questions draw adequate answers: the by-now familiar ones about Frankenstein (73.8 percent), King's "I have a dream" (88 percent), and *Uncle Tom's Cabin* (73.4 percent)—about which one need only know that it helped the abolition movement by depicting the evils of slavery; and a question about the frequent theme of death in Emily Dickinson's poetry (69.3 percent).

Black youngsters, however, do better on these thirteen questions than on the literature assessment as a whole. Here they achieve an average score of 51.7 percent correct, placing them several points ahead of the average score of all youngsters on these thirteen questions (an average, we have already noted, which is not itself satisfactory).

On several questions that have special significance for black youngsters, their performance is well above the average for the entire sample: by almost five points on the Martin Luther King passage (92.7 percent of black students answer correctly, compared with 88 percent of the sample), almost six points for *Invisible Man* (23.9 percent of black students get it, compared with 18.2 percent for all), more than ten for *A Raisin in the Sun* (63.8 percent of black students answer correctly), sixteen points on the Langston Hughes question (52.8 percent of black students answer correctly), and eighteen points on the Richard Wright question (50.2 percent of black students answer correctly).

Who wrote *Native Son*, a novel of black life in Chicago, and *Black Boy*, which is highly autobiographical?

✓ Richard Wright	32.3
___ Eldridge Cleaver	25.2
___ LeRoi Jones	22.3
___ Malcolm X	20.2

Do black students perform better on questions about black writers because these works address their personal situations? Or is it because schools and teachers are more apt to expose black students to works by black authors? Some of each, we surmise. Still, despite their above-average performance on these questions, three-quarters of the black youngsters get the Ellison question wrong and half choose the incorrect answers on the Richard Wright question, nearly as many on Langston Hughes.

As for eleventh grade girls, here as in the rest of the literature assessment they tend to be more successful than the boys, but on the questions of this cluster their margin of superiority is wider than usual. On these questions the boys also fare worse than usual.

On every question about female writers, the girls outscore the boys. But in only a couple of instances does the margin exceed a few points, the widest being 11.3 when, asked to identify the author of *My Ántonia* and two other works, 33.8 percent of the girls choose Cather while just 22.5 percent of the boys do.

Which American poet, who lived mostly in solitude as an adult, wrote frequently about death in such poems as "I heard a Fly buzz—when I died—" and "Because I could not stop for Death—"?

___ Elizabeth Bishop	8.4
___ Gwendolyn Brooks	16.5
✓ Emily Dickinson	69.3
___ Amy Lowell	5.8

Are girls more likely than boys to read Cather or Austen, to know something of Dickinson's subject matter, or to recall that O'Connor and Welty are Southern writers? (Only 14.8 percent of the girls get that one right, but the boys do even worse.) And is it because female writers are involved, or is it because girls generally do a bit better than boys on the literature assessment? We cannot be sure.

Subject of question	Percent correct		
	Whole sample	Girls	Blacks
Martin Luther King, Jr., said "I have a dream . . ."	88.1	89.4	92.7
Mary Shelley wrote *Frankenstein*	73.8	74.1	67.7
Uncle Tom's Cabin contributed to antislavery effort	73.4	75.5	69.3
Emily Dickinson often wrote about death	69.3	71.3	67.1
Theme of *To Kill a Mockingbird*	59.1	62.3	41.6
Theme of *A Raisin in the Sun*	53.2	55.8	63.8
Identify *Don Quixote*	47.9	47.5	34.0
Theme of *Pride and Prejudice*	38.0	42.9	30.5
Identify poet Langston Hughes	36.2	36.8	52.8
Richard Wright wrote *Native Son* and *Black Boy*	32.3	34.2	50.2
Willa Cather wrote *My Ántonia, Death Comes for the Archbishop, O Pioneers!*	28.2	33.8	23.4
Ralph Ellison wrote *Invisible Man*	18.3	17.2	23.9
Flannery O'Connor and Eudora Welty wrote well-crafted stories set in the South	14.4	14.8	19.0
Average	48.6	53.4	51.7

Looking at the overall history and literature assessment, we conclude that the "glass is almost half empty." Though there are topics, eras, genres, and types of questions that elicit passing scores from the eleventh grade sample, and though there are a handful of individual questions on which the students do honors work, the average student fails both halves of the assessment. Put differently, the average question is answered correctly by fewer than 60 percent of the boys and girls in the sample. We cannot tell from a "snapshot" assessment of this kind whether today's students know more or less about history and literature than their predecessors of ten, twenty, or fifty years ago. We do conclude, however, that they do not know enough.

3
Behind the Scores

The assessment included a battery of more than a hundred questions for students about their family backgrounds, schooling, reading, study habits, and out-of-school activities. This chapter describes some of the associations between the students' performance on the assessment and the background information that they provided. Computer analysis makes possible comparisons of many different groups, based on variables such as race, gender, parent education, community size, and so on. In addition, we have extracted comparisons of the top quartile and the bottom quartile of students, based on their performance on the assessment, and have prepared a special analysis of three subsets within the top quartile: black students, students enrolled in nonacademic "tracks" in school, and youngsters whose parents did not attend college. These analyses provide intriguing information about high-scoring students who might not have been expected to do well on the basis of common predictors of school success. In addition, based on the student survey, we are able to outline a sketch of contemporary classroom practices in history and literature.

We caution the reader, and will do so repeatedly in the text, not to assume that an association is a *cause*. An assessment of this kind is a snapshot of a moment in time. We can learn a good deal about the characteristics of high-scoring students, for example, but we cannot infer which (if any) of these characteristics *cause* them to do well on a test of history and literature. Student performance on this assessment is the product of ten to twelve years of schooling and sixteen to eighteen years of living, not just of the history or English courses in which they are presently enrolled. Moreover, this performance is usually enhanced (or undermined) by an array of potent if less purposeful influences, such as family discussions, television, movies, and personal interests. Yet with all these cautionary statements, we believe that the background analysis yields worthwhile insights into the lives and educational experiences of today's adolescents.

FAMILY BACKGROUND

Many previous studies and surveys have demonstrated the importance of family background as a factor in student achievement. The findings of this assessment reiterate the contribution made by families to students' academic performance. Families provide models of behavior, set levels of expectations, choose whether to enroll their children in prekindergarten and kindergarten, express attitudes about the value of education, and determine the extent to which children grow up in a literate environment. In some home settings, children are richly endowed with the attitudes, behaviors, and values that contribute to school success; in others, they are not. Schools are not powerless to reduce the difference between the extremes, nor are individual students incapable of surmounting the disadvantages of poverty, but it would be misleading to ignore the major contribution of family background to students' success in school.

Parent Education

Judging from the results of this assessment, parent education (or the knowledge, values, and priorities for which it is a proxy) is the single most significant element in family background. In our sample, about 39 percent of the students had at least one parent who graduated from college; 22 percent had at least one parent who received some post–high school education; about 27 percent had parents who did not go beyond high school graduation; and about 8.5 percent had parents who did not finish high school (the total is not 100 percent, because some students did not answer this question or did not know how much education their parents had).

There is a close fit between student achievement on this assessment and parent education. Children of college graduates tend to perform better on most items than those whose parents have some post–secondary education, and they in turn perform better than those whose parents are high school graduates; lowest scoring, usually, are the children whose parents did not graduate from high school.

Here and in the tables to follow, we present these differences in performance via a statistical construct that NAEP has developed called "average proficiency." On this assessment, the average proficiency for all students in the sample was 285. The range, for all practical purposes, goes from 225 to 345, i.e., about sixty points on either side of the average.

These average proficiencies are usually shown below the sample information to which they pertain. For example, in the table on the next page, the average proficiency for students whose parents did not graduate from high school is 260.8, while the average proficiency for students who had at least one parent who graduated from college is 297.7. Unfortunately, we were unable to obtain proficiency scores for the black students in the top quartile or for other subgroups within the top quartile.

The reader should bear in mind that the purpose of this kind of analysis is to show characteristics that correlate with significant differences, all of which are relative. Because the base for these comparisons is the average performance actually recorded on this assessment, it would be a mistake to view these numbers in absolute terms of "good" and "bad." As we explained in Chapter 2, the average performance on this assessment seems to us wholly unsatisfactory.

Note, too, that except where we explicitly state that we are using the results of the literature assessment, it should always be assumed that the data being reported come from the history assessment, data that we believe are generally more reliable since almost all students have studied American history, and their courses customarily include the material that was on the test.

In the table and chart correlating parents' education and the average history proficiencies of groups of students, "parent education" refers to the better-educated of a student's parents; if *either* parent had graduated from college, for example, the student would appear under that heading; it was not necessary for both parents to have graduated from college.

PARENT EDUCATION
Percentages of Students Followed by Average History Proficiencies

	No h.s. diploma	H.s. graduate	Some post–h.s.	College graduate
Total	8.5 260.8	27.2 273.8	22.0 289.7	39.1 297.7
White	6.4 267.7	27.0 279.0	23.3 293.8	41.5 301.7
Black	12.2 249.2	30.8 257.7	19.4 266.2	32.3 274.2
Hispanic	24.3 253.5	28.7 256.2	16.9 275.2	21.6 275.9
Others	9.1 250.2	13.6 259.6	14.6 295.3	49.1 301.2

NOTE: Rows in this and other tables do not always add to 100 percent because we omitted data on students who did not know their parents' education or did not reply. The average proficiency score for the entire sample is 285.

As the table shows, black and Hispanic children in our sample are at a significant disadvantage in comparison with whites and other minorities because of their parents' lower level of educational attainment and the close relationship between parents' education and proficiency on this assessment. Note that 41.5 percent of the white youngsters have at least one parent who graduated from college, compared with 32.3 percent of blacks and 21.6 percent of Hispanics. The "others," mainly Asians, included 49.1 percent with a parent who is a college graduate.

Parent Education and Average History Proficiencies

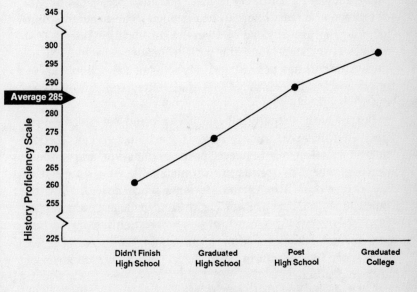

Parents' Highest Level of Education

(Each point on the graph indicates the average history proficiency of the portion of student sample reporting parents' education as shown.)

There is no doubt in our minds that the gap in educational attainment in the parents' generation contributes to the gap in achievement between white youngsters and minority youngsters. Yet having relatively well educated parents is not itself a sufficient condition for high achievement on this assessment. Though black and Hispanic students whose parents are college-educated do significantly better than those whose parents are not, it must also be noted that minority youngsters with parents who are college graduates do not fare as well on the history assessment as white youngsters whose parents are just high school graduates.

Note, too, the sizable number of minority parents who have not finished high school: 24.3 percent of Hispanic parents and 12.2 percent of black parents, compared with 6.4 percent of white parents and 9.1 percent of "others." Students from these families generally turn in the lowest scores on this assessment; they are least likely to have attended preschool or kindergarten and least likely to be enrolled in an academic high school program (instead of a general or vocational track). At almost every step along the path to academic achievement, these students are behind and have less of the school experiences and family resources that contribute to educational success.

But as with virtually all the background variables examined in this assessment, there is no automatic or foreordained relationship between parent education and student performance. The trends are unmistakable. But so are sizable exceptions. Among the students who score in the top quartile, 44 percent are *not* children of college graduates; in fact, 22 percent are from families where neither parent had any formal education after high school. And among those who score in the bottom quartile, 25 percent *are* children of college graduates.

A Literate Home Environment

Students were asked whether their home has a dictionary, an encyclopedia, and more than twenty-five books, and whether their family regularly gets a newspaper and magazines. Together these may be construed as the material com-

ponents of a literate environment, a home where reading and information are valued. It was a pleasant surprise to see how widely distributed these tools of literacy are: 98 percent of the sample report that there is a dictionary in their home; 85.5 percent report having an encyclopedia; 95 percent say that there are more than twenty-five books in their home; 83 percent say that their family regularly receives magazines; and 81 percent report that their family gets a newspaper. Yet even within this high response level, there is variation; parents with the most education provide the most literacy articles in their homes. And children who come from homes that provide all of these items score significantly higher than those whose homes have four, three, or fewer of them. This is true among all demographic groups. To suggest the scale of the difference: three-fourths of the top quartile students report having all five items in their homes; not quite half of the lowest quartile students make that claim.

Another physical resource often provided these days by the family is a home computer with a keyboard and screen. About 30 percent of the students in our sample have them, and their scores are substantially higher than those who do not. Home computers are available to 33 percent of the white students, 21.7 percent of the black students, and 21.5 percent of the Hispanic students. Of the students who score in the top quartile, 43 percent have home computers; of the black students in the top quartile on the history assessment, 40.6 percent do. But of those with scores placing them in the bottom quartile, just 20.6 percent have computers at home. Computer ownership is highest in the northeast and the west; it is highest for children of college graduates (42 percent have them), and lowest for those whose parents did not finish high school (11 percent). Thirty-six percent of the boys have them at home, but only 25 percent of the girls. In every category, those who have them register higher scores than those who do not. There is no reason to believe that the computer contributes directly to this academic advantage (although it might); it may simply serve as a surrogate for preexisting economic and educational advantages. To the extent that it enhances academic ability, it will probably widen the gap between top and bottom students.

Prekindergarten

Students were asked whether they had attended preschool. The sample is almost equally divided between those who have and those who have not; those who have attended score higher on both parts of the assessment. This is true for boys and girls, and for children of all racial groups. Blacks are most likely to have gone to preschool (about 55 percent have, compared with 47 percent of whites), and Hispanics are least likely (about 38 percent). Sixty-five percent of the blacks in the top quartile of history performance attended preschool, a figure higher than that of any other group in the entire sample. Attendance at kindergarten is also associated with higher scores, but almost everyone (92 percent of the sample) reports having attended kindergarten.

A Foreign Language Home

About 11 percent of the sample live in homes where people more than occasionally speak a language other than English. These youngsters do not generally fare as well on either the history or literature assessment as students from English-speaking households. In particular, Hispanic youngsters from non-English-speaking homes (about 56 percent of all the Hispanic students in the sample) have proficiency scores on both history and literature about ten points lower than those whose families never speak a foreign language or who do so only occasionally. There is an exception to the pattern, though, among black youngsters; the 7 percent of them whose families frequently speak languages other than English do *better* on both history and literature than do black students from English-only households.

About 22 percent of the sample say that they themselves

speak a language other than English at home; unfortunately, the questionnaire simply asked for "yes" or "no" answers so we cannot determine how frequently they speak other languages at home. Here, the pattern resembles that seen with the household language. Hispanic youngsters who speak Spanish at home get lower scores than those who do not; but blacks, Asians, and others who speak languages other than English at home do better on the history assessment than those who do not. And black youngsters who speak other languages at home also do somewhat better in literature.

Family Structure

Family structure is associated with a differential in scores on the assessment. Eighty-two percent of the white youngsters live with both parents, compared with 56.7 percent of black students, 71 percent of Hispanic students, and 73 percent of "others." In every instance, students who live with both parents perform somewhat better. Student achievement levels are unaffected, however, by their parents' work patterns; although the highest scoring girls come from families where one parent works full time and the other part time, on the whole it doesn't seem to matter whether both parents work full time, one works part time, or only one works full time. Working mothers can take heart, because student scores do not seem to vary in relation to whether their mothers work or not. In fact, in a comparison between the top and bottom quartile students on the history assessment, an equal proportion of both groups (about 50 percent) have mothers who work at full-time jobs.

Except for the top quartile black students, there is no only-child advantage. For the sample as a whole, scores are roughly similar whether students have no siblings or one or two, although scores are lower for students who live in families with more than three children. Of black students who are high achievers, however, 13 percent are only children. This is a slightly higher proportion than for all students in the top quartile, where only 7 percent have no sibling, and in the whole sample, in which 6 percent have no sibling. Perhaps these academically successful black children have done exceptionally well because their parents concentrate their resources on one child.

More than material resources are involved. In addition to providing books, magazines, computers, and prekindergarten, families influence their children's commitment to words and knowledge in ways that are not measured by instruments like this assessment. Mealtime conversation about the news of the day or television programs or movies can stimulate children's curiosity and verbal skills; tales of the family's history can develop their sense of the past; a family excursion to a play or museum can open up new worlds to the imagination. These are some of the ways that parents can enrich the education received by their children. And while such enrichments may tend to be encountered more frequently in households where the parents are better educated and are employed in white-collar or professional occupations, those households have no monopoly on the provision of additional educational resources for the child.

GIRLS AND BOYS

On the history assessment, boys fare better than girls. The boys' average score is 56.7 percent correct, while the girls' average is 52.2. Differences of approximately this magnitude are found within each racial and ethnic group and in every region. The difference on individual items is occasionally quite substantial. For example, 31 percent of the boys know that Lincoln was president between 1860 and 1880, but only 18 percent of the girls do; 80 percent of the boys know that Germany and Japan were our principal enemies during World War II, but only 60 percent of the girls do; and while 82 percent of the boys can find West Germany on a map of Europe, only 70 percent of the girls can.

The gender gap is not universal, however; for example, girls in the northeast do as well in history as boys in the west and southeast. Similarly, girls in nonpublic schools (whether private or Catholic) get history scores at least as high as public school boys.

On the literature assessment, by contrast, girls score higher than boys, though the margin of difference is narrower than in history. The girls' average literature score is 52.9 percent correct, while the boys' average is 50.8. Gender gaps of this kind are found among whites, Hispanics, and "others," but not among blacks; black boys and girls get about the same scores. The difference is largest when comparing public school girls with public school boys; in nonpublic schools, boys and girls perform at about the same level and both have scores well above average.

These differences can be dramatized by examining the composition of the extremes of student performance: the top quartile of the history group is 62 percent male while the bottom quartile is 57 percent female. In literature, although girls have a higher average score, boys nonetheless comprise 52 percent of the top quartile; however, boys also make up 56 percent of the bottom quartile.

There is good reason for girls to do better in literature than boys: girls read much more than boys in their free time. Two-thirds of the girls have read a novel for their own enjoyment in the previous half year, compared to barely half of the boys; two-thirds of the girls say that they read poems on their own, but just 44 percent of the boys make that claim. Furthermore, girls do more homework than boys; 40 percent of them spend two hours or more each day on homework, compared with 25 percent of the boys.

Why, then, do boys do so much better in history than girls? There is no obvious answer. The same gender gap has been found in other history tests, such as the one regularly given by the California Assessment Program to a representative sampling of that state's students. Even on a simple map question, which asked students to identify in which region of the country the Appalachian mountains are located, the boys in California outscored the girls by 44 percent to 31 percent. The California specialists responded to this by recommending greater emphasis on "the role of women in history-social science."*

On the history assessment, eight questions involve prominent women or issues of women's rights. The girls perform marginally better on simple questions drawn from women's history than the boys do, but still their performance is unimpressive. Seventy-two percent of the girls know that Susan B. Anthony was active in the movement for women's suffrage, compared with 66.3 percent of the boys; but only 57.7 percent of the girls know that the Constitutional amendment granting women the right to vote was adopted in 1920; and only a quarter of them know what the Seneca Falls Declaration was.

We suspect that the Seneca Falls Declaration is not much taught in American history classes, though it should be. But for girls to equalize their knowledge of history with that of boys, and for both groups to absorb more knowledge of history than is the case today, more is required than systematic presentation of the Seneca Falls Declaration. We question the proposition that greater emphasis on women's history will somehow compensate for girls' failure to understand geography or the Constitution. It is one thing to say that there ought to be more women's history in the curriculum, but quite another to expect that girls need not learn about presidents, wars, and technology. Leaving politics and world affairs "to the boys" is not a satisfactory answer to the problem of the gender gap.

RACE AND ETHNICITY

There are large differences in achievement on both assessments among racial and ethnic groups. The scores of white and Asian students are significantly higher, on the whole, than those of black, Hispanic, and American Indian students. Within each group, as we have already seen, student achieve-

*California Assessment Program, Annual Report (Sacramento: California State Department of Education, 1986), 68.

ment is closely associated with parental education; the higher the parents' educational attainment, the higher the average scores of their children.

There are some regional differences that are significantly related to group performance: black students in the southeast are well behind black students in other regions. This may well have something to do with the sizable proportion of southeastern black youngsters living in extreme rural areas, where black achievement levels are lowest. But the lower scores for black students in the southeast also pull down their national average, inasmuch as black students are found in larger numbers in that region than elsewhere (41.3 percent of all black students in the sample live in the southeast, whereas just 19.6 percent of white students live in that region). Hispanic students in the northeast perform well ahead of their counterparts in the other regions of the country, but 72.3 percent of all Hispanic students in the sample live in the west. Asian students in the northeast outscore Asians in other regions on the history assessment, while Asian students in both the southeast and northeast are well above national averages for all groups on the literature assessment.

ASSESSMENT RESULTS BY GENDER AND ETHNICITY

Group	History proficiency	Literature proficiency
All students	285	285
Boys	290.7	282.8
Girls	279.0	287.3
White	290.8	289.9
Black	263.1	267.5
Hispanic	262.5	264.8
Asian	292.3	287.0
Native American	271.0	272.6
Top quartile	334.2	331.5
Top quartile black*	330.2	328.2
Bottom quartile	232.2	234.7

*"Top quartile black" in this and following tables refers to black students in the top quarter of student performance.

Asians

The findings of this assessment should help dispel the stereotypes of Asian students as a group of students gifted in science and math but relatively uninterested or incapable in the study of English language–based fields such as history and literature. This image is not sustained by the evidence in this assessment. On both portions, Asian students perform as well as white students; and Asian youngsters attending nonpublic schools (admittedly a tiny portion of the total sample) surpass the performance of every other group in both history and literature.

The scores are not uniform, however. Among Asian students, as among every other racial and ethnic group, there is a broad range of competence. This range varies, as for other groups, according to such factors as parents' education, size and type of community, and region of the country. Asian students whose parents have a relatively low level of formal education score well below the national average, as do Asian students living in rural or inner-city communities. But Asian students whose parents have some postsecondary education register scores well above the national average.

Hispanics

Among Hispanics, the national average on the assessment is low, but there are wide variations within the group. The Hispanic students who were sampled included youngsters who identify themselves as of Mexican, Puerto Rican, and Cuban origin; among these subgroups there are differences in performance, possibly related to the length of time they have lived in the United States and their relative familiarity with the language and with American schools. This supposition gains strength from the fact that Hispanic youngsters who speak English at home know more history and literature than those who do not. The same pattern is found in relation to the family's language: Hispanic students whose households never or only occasionally speak a language other than English do better than those whose primary family language is not English.

Hispanic performance is strongest in the northeast and weakest in the west, where the vast majority of Hispanic youngsters in the sample reside. Students in nonpublic schools (6 percent of the Hispanic sample) receive the highest scores, with an edge going to the small number in non-Catholic private schools (1.5 percent of the Hispanic sample). Hispanic youngsters attending Catholic schools (4.6 percent of the Hispanic sample) match (and slightly best) the national average for all students in both history and literature. We cannot say whether this academic success is caused by Catholic schooling or whether Catholic schools attract educationally motivated and upwardly mobile Hispanic families. Whatever its cause, the difference is clear.

Blacks

The nearly 13 percent of our sample that is black register a low average score but, like other groups, display wide variation in achievement. As previously noted, scores are lowest among blacks living in rural areas and those whose parents have relatively less education.

We identified three groups of unusually high-scoring black students: those in suburban communities (7.6 percent of the black sample); those attending Catholic schools (4.4 percent of the black sample); and those black students whose very high scores place them in the top quartile in the history assessment. There is undoubtedly a good deal of overlap among these groups, and the top quartile students are probably drawn in significant numbers from the other two. The reader should note that the numbers of students in these groups are small and inevitably the data are not so robust as is the case with larger samples. The results should therefore be read for the impressions that they give, not for statistical precision.

SELECTED SUBGROUPS OF BLACK STUDENTS

Subgroup	History proficiency	Literature proficiency
All black students	263.1	267.5
Rural	246.1	252.9
Suburban	290.7	289.0
Catholic school	288.9	287.3
Parent graduated from college	274.2	274.6
Northeast region	268.3	271.9
Southeast region	257.9	262.5
Top quartile	330.2	328.2

NOTE: The average proficiency score for all students in the national sample is 285.

HIGH-ACHIEVING STUDENTS FROM LOW-ACHIEVING GROUPS

Top Quartile Black Students

Approximately 120 students, or about 10 percent of all black youngsters in the sample, scored in the top quartile of the history assessment. Their average proficiency on the history assessment is 330.2; they correctly answer 76.9 percent of the history cognitive questions; 92 percent of these students attend public schools.

More of these high-achieving black students have mothers who are college graduates than any other subgroup of the sample; more of their fathers are college graduates than any other group except Asians and the top quartile as a whole.

In view of the high educational level of the parents of these successful black students, it is not surprising to discover that they live in a literate home environment. They are as likely as white students to have books, magazines, a dictionary, an

EDUCATIONAL LEVEL OF PARENTS

	No h.s. diploma	H.s. graduate	Some post–h.s.	College graduate
Mother's education (percentage of total)				
Total	13.5	35.9	21.1	24.5
White	10.8	37.8	22.4	25.8
Black	17.4	32.9	19.7	21.7
Hispanic	34.7	28.3	12.0	12.4
Others	16.6	16.3	16.3	31.3
Top quartile	6.4	29.4	25.2	37.1
Top quartile black	4.1	27.3	26.0	37.7
Bottom quartile	22.9	38.9	14.7	14.3
Father's education (percentage of total)				
Total	14.1	26.7	17.8	32.1
White	13.0	26.6	19.4	35.0
Black	14.5	30.9	13.2	21.5
Hispanic	27.9	24.3	12.7	16.0
Others	7.3	18.0	10.2	41.8
Top quartile	7.3	19.4	21.8	47.3
Top quartile black	8.3	21.2	18.9	36.5
Bottom quartile	22.0	32.0	11.7	18.5

encyclopedia, and a newspaper in their homes. Furthermore, they are *more* likely to own computers: 21.7 percent of the entire black sample have home computers; 33 percent of the white sample do; but of these high-achieving black youths, 40 percent have home computers. Whether it contributes to their success or not, the purchase of a home computer represents a significant financial investment in doing well in school. The family commitment to the academic success of these youngsters shows up again in the rate at which they attended preschool: 65 percent of them did, compared with 55 percent of all blacks and 47 percent of all whites.

As would be expected, given their educational level, the parents of these students include a fairly high proportion of professionals and white-collar workers. About 30 percent of their mothers and 20 percent of their fathers are professionals (e.g., doctors, lawyers, social workers, nurses, clergy, and teachers); another 17 percent of their mothers and 14 percent of their fathers are employed in managerial and technical occupations. On the other hand, a substantial proportion of these high-achieving black youngsters do *not* have parents in high-status fields. Twenty percent of their fathers are laborers or operatives (such as welders, bus drivers, or meat cutters) and 36 percent of their mothers are engaged in clerical or service work.

Aside from the advantages that many of their homes provide, these students work hard in school. They attend it more regularly than the sample as a whole; 44 percent say that they missed no days of school in the past month, compared with 36 percent of the whole sample. Furthermore, they do a good deal more homework than others in the national sample. About half say that they do two or more hours of homework each day, which compares very favorably with the 30 percent of white students (and 39 percent of all top quartile students) who study that much at home.

Nearly three-quarters of these high-scoring students are in the college preparatory/academic track in school. The students in this group have also studied more math and science, and taken more advanced courses than whites in the sample. About three-quarters plan to go to a four-year college (as compared to about half the entire sample and half the black sample). It is hard to understand why any of these youngsters is in a nonacademic track. Though it is surely impressive that a quarter of the black students in the top quartile of the history assessment have made it there despite being enrolled in the general or vocational track, it is likely that the school programs in which they find themselves are not making the maximum use of their mental abilities.

Top Quartile Students Whose Parents
Did Not Attend College

Of all students in the top quartile of the history assessment, 62 percent have mothers with at least some postsecondary education and 69 percent have fathers who attended college. As we have seen, parent education is closely associated with student performance, so it is not surprising that the students in the top quartile tend to have well-educated parents.

Yet there are significant exceptions to this pattern. In fact, 22 percent of the students in the top quartile on the history assessment come from families in which neither parent had any formal education beyond high school. Almost two-thirds of these students are boys and more than nine in ten of them attend public schools. Eighty-eight percent are white, 5.6 percent are black, 4.2 percent are Hispanic, 1.5 percent are Asian, and the balance are "others."

These students live in a home environment that is somewhat less likely to have books, newspapers, encyclopedias, and dictionaries than the home of the average student in the sample. They also watch more television than the average student: 38.7 percent watch four or more hours per day (compared with 32.2 percent of the entire sample). They spend about the same amount of time on homework as the sample as a whole: about 37 percent do it for half an hour or less each day, while about 32 percent spend two or more hours per day on homework. These high-scoring students are far less likely to have attended preschool than those in the entire sample: only 36 percent did, compared to 47 percent of all students. When it comes to computer use, they are just as likely as everyone else to have used a computer with a keyboard (89 percent have), and no more likely than the entire sample to have one at home (30 percent do).

The students in this group are more apt to be in the academic track than are those in the full sample, but far less likely to be in the academic track than others in the top quartile:

PERCENTAGE OF STUDENTS IN DIFFERENT SCHOOL "TRACKS"

	Academic	*General*	*Vocational*
Total	52.3	37.8	10.0
Top quartile	73.9	20.9	5.2
*Noncollege group	60.6	27.9	11.3

*Subset of the top quartile of the history assessment, consisting of students whose parents had no formal education beyond high school.

Because two-fifths of this high-achieving group are not in an academic program, they are far less likely than others in the top quartile to have taken advanced courses in math and science. While 64 percent of all top quartile students are taking either advanced placement or college preparatory English, only 50 percent of this group is in such a class. They are also somewhat less likely than their "top quarter" peers—but a good deal more likely than the sample as a whole—to be enrolled in math or science courses during eleventh grade. They are good students; 60 percent of them report a B average or better in school, compared with 48 percent in the sample as a whole. But they are less likely to be A students than their peers in the top quartile; 16 percent of these youngsters report getting "mostly As," compared with 24 percent of the entire top quartile—and 11 percent of the entire sample.

These students have a slightly better than average attendance record. Thirty-eight percent of them missed no school during the previous month, compared with 35 percent of the full sample. They spend about the same amount of time at part-time jobs as the rest of the sample.

Their performance on this assessment places these students in the top quartile among eleventh graders, but they are not much more apt than the average student to be planning to attend a four-year college: 56 percent plan to go to a four-year college, compared with 52.3 percent of the entire sample and 74 percent of the top quartile students.

There is nothing unusual about the family structure of these high-scoring students. Ninety-five percent of them live with their mother; 83 percent of them also live with their father. Eight percent of them are only children; most have one, two, or three siblings. Nearly half their mothers work full time, and those of another 20 percent work part time.

The occupations of the parents of these successful students are predominantly blue-collar—none too surprising when you bear in mind that the parents have no postsecondary education. More than 50 percent of the boys and girls who answered the "parent occupation" questions describe their parents as laborers (e.g., construction, car washer, sanitary worker), craftspersons (e.g., baker, mechanic, painter, plumber), farmers, protective service (e.g., police officer, firefighter), operatives (e.g., meat cutter, assembler, machine operator, welder), or service workers (e.g., barber, beautician, janitor, waiter).

There is nothing in their family background that explains why these students perform so well on the history assessment, and there are not many clues in the data available to us on their school experiences, either. We note that they have taken somewhat more history than most other students: 54.5 percent of them have taken world/Western history, compared to 47 percent of the whole sample. We also note that, when asked whether they have studied the six major eras in American history (from exploration to the present), this group answers "yes" far more often than the sample as a whole. We cannot say with certainty that this additional exposure to American history accounts for the extraordinary record of this group of students, but it is certainly plausible.

From everything that we know about the importance of parental education and a literate home environment, this group would seem to start with one or two strikes against it. Yet they are obviously capable of solid academic achievement, which is sometimes recognized by their schools but not as often as it should be. Their presence in the top quartile demonstrates that the good fortune of parents does not necessarily predetermine the school performance of children and is a stunning reminder that the tracking system may be shunting some talented youngsters into educational and career paths less challenging than they are capable of.

Top Quartile Students Who Are in the General or Vocational Track

In most public high schools, it is common practice to sort students into three "tracks" or programs: academic (which is usually for the college-bound), general (which is less demanding and includes fewer academic courses), and vocational. When students are divided in this fashion, there is a presumption that those in the academic track have greater academic ability or potential than those in the other two tracks. Yet of the students who scored in the top quartile on the history assessment, 25 percent are enrolled in nonacademic tracks. Within this group, 81 percent are in the general track, where students are not likely to encounter much academic challenge, and 19 percent are in the vocational track, where they customarily encounter even less.

While there may be some overlap between these students and the students whose parents did not attend any college, these two groups of "unexpected high achievers" are clearly not identical. This can be seen by examining the educational attainment of the parents of the high-scoring general and vocational students; at least half their parents have had some postsecondary education. Indeed, as is characteristic of top quartile students, their parents have had more education than the average in the sample as a whole.

PARENT EDUCATION OF NONACADEMIC
STUDENTS IN TOP QUARTILE

No h.s. diploma	H.s. graduate	Some post–h.s.	College graduate
Mother's education (percentage of total)			
10.7	34.1	27.4	23.2
Father's education (percentage of total)			
11.7	26.3	25.6	28.2

Of this group of students, 69 percent are boys and 93.4 percent attend public school. Eighty-nine percent are white; 5 percent are black; 3.2 percent are Hispanic; and 2.7 percent are "others." Their families are no more and no less likely than the sample as a whole to possess dictionaries, encyclopedias, newspapers, books, and magazines in their homes. These students watch about the same amount of television as the full sample: 47 percent watch two hours or less each day, but 31 percent watch four hours or more each day. They do less homework than the full sample: 46 percent of them spend half an hour or less each day on homework; only 22 percent spend two or more hours each day. Since all of these students are enrolled in academically undemanding high school programs, it is not surprising that they do little homework.

Like the students whose parents did not attend college, this group includes the children of persons engaged in a wide variety of occupations, primarily blue-collar and technical. Fewer than 15 percent of them report that their fathers hold professional jobs. In the top quartile as a whole, 22 percent of the students have fathers employed in the professions.

This group is more apt to have studied world/Western history (53.7 percent) than is the sample as a whole. And in a pattern very similar to that of the high-scoring students whose parents did not attend college, these young people report somewhat greater exposure to the various chronological eras in American history than does the sample as a whole. In the full sample, for example, 77.8 percent say that they have studied the period from Reconstruction to the First World War, while 82.5 percent of these high-scoring students in nonacademic tracks have. This is a significant difference.

These students do reasonably well in school: 52 percent of them report grades averaging B or better. But 38 percent of them are in the Bs and Cs or mostly Cs range. Nor are they taking a lot of demanding academic courses. Indeed, what is remarkable about these students is that their strong performance in history and, we presume, their better-than-average intellectual abilities are not matched by the program of courses they are taking. Although they have high reading scores, exceptional history scores, and above-average scores on the literature portion of the assessment, their potential is apparently unrecognized by their schools. Of this group, 30 percent are enrolled in advanced placement or college preparatory English classes, and 66 percent are in a general English class. This compares unfavorably with the entire sample, in which 44 percent are enrolled in an academic English course and 50 percent are in general classes. In the remainder of their course of study, these students are even less likely than the previous group of exceptional achievers to be engaged in a solid academic program. They are, for example, less likely than the average student to be enrolled in a math or science course, or to have taken advanced courses in math or science.

One difference between this group and the students whose parents did not attend college is that the nonacademic track students have even lower college aspirations, or less confidence in their academic abilities, than do the youngsters in the other group. Only 48 percent of this group of high-scoring students plan to go to a four-year college, compared with 52.3 percent of the entire sample and 74 percent of the full top quartile. Perhaps they are lazy; perhaps they have been misclassified; perhaps they have misclassified themselves. What-ever the case, it does seem that these capable students have received neither the encouragement nor the academic chal-lenges that they need to develop their abilities to the full.

TOP AND BOTTOM QUARTILES

The quartiles, of course, are statistically derived. There would be a top quartile even if everyone did poorly on the assess-ment, and there would be a bottom quartile even if all had done well. Still, it is worth noting a few distinctive characteris-tics of these groups.

The top quartile students actually do reasonably well in "objective" terms, besides performing better than three-quar-ters of their classmates. On average, top quartile students in history get 78.3 percent of the questions right, putting them in the C+ range on the standard we have been using, an impres-sive twenty-four points ahead of the sample as a whole. The top quartile in literature does not fare quite so well; its average score is 73.2, in the C— to C range. But this, too, is almost twenty-two points above the sample average for literature.

Students who do well on one part of the assessment tend to do reasonably well on the other. Students in the top history quartile have an average score of 65.0 in literature, and stu-dents in the top literature quartile record an average score of 70.9 in history. (Both groups, incidentally, also do quite well on the reading assessment that was given to eleventh graders at the same time.)

Top quartile students are more apt to be white and Asian than the sample as a whole: that is true of 92 percent of the history students and 90.2 percent of the literature students. They are also somewhat more apt to attend private or paro-chial schools: 13.2 percent of the high-scoring history stu-dents and 14.8 percent of the top literature students. Their parents, as we have seen, are generally well educated (though the previous section describes a subset for whom this is not the case). Fifty-six percent of the top quartile students in each assessment have at least one parent who is a college graduate.

Top quartile students are far more likely than average to have taken advanced math and science courses in school and to be enrolled in math and science during eleventh grade. They also tend to get good grades. Almost half on both the history and literature assessments get mostly As or half As and half Bs.

On most of the obvious variables, the bottom quartile students are the obverse of the top. Their assessment scores are very low. The average among those in the bottom history quartile is 30.0 percent correct on the history questions—not much better than random guessing—and 39.3 percent in literature. Those in the bottom quartile of the literature assessment have an average score of 30.5 percent in that subject and 39.9 percent in history. Neither group reads well, either.

In school, the bottom quartile students are more apt to be enrolled in general and vocational tracks. Just 27 percent of the history bottom quartile and 29 percent of the literature bottom quartile are in the academic track. Not surprisingly, they have not taken many advanced academic courses, are not likely to be taking them during eleventh grade, and do not get very good marks in the courses they take. Just 14 percent of the history bottom quartile and 13 percent of the literature bottom quartile characterize their grades as mostly As or half As and half Bs.

Bottom quartile students are more apt to be black or Hispanic. Those two minorities comprise 37.7 percent of the lowest quartile in history and 33.3 percent in literature. Some, but not many of them (4.1 percent in history, 4.3 percent in literature), attend nonpublic schools. Nor are their parents generally very well educated. Fifty-three percent of the bottom quartile in history and 52 percent in literature are young people neither of whose parents went beyond high school.

But here, as elsewhere, there are surprising anomalies and interesting exceptions. One in four of the bottom quartile on the history assessment, for example, has at least one parent who is a college graduate. This suggests that "antideterminism" and social mobility can work in both directions. Just as coming from a relatively disadvantaged background does not preclude high achievement on an assessment of this kind, neither does a reasonably privileged background ensure such achievement.

STUDENT BEHAVIOR

We do not use the term "behavior" in the traditional sense; we are not referring here to the way students cooperate or "act out" in the classroom. By student behavior, we mean the choices that students make in their own lives that may have some bearing on their academic performance. There are four types of student behavior that the assessment asked the students to describe: the amount of time they spend doing homework; the amount of time they spend watching television; the amount of time they spend working at part-time jobs; and the kinds and amounts of reading they do for pleasure.

Homework

Most eleventh graders do not spend much of their day on homework. About 16 percent say either that they don't have any or that they don't do it, and another 18 percent say they give it less than half an hour daily. That is to say, about one high school junior in three does little or no homework. Another third of them spend an hour a day studying at home. The remaining third spend two or more hours each day on homework.

How Much Time Do Top and Bottom Quartile Students Say They Spend Per Day on Homework?

Top Quartile

Bottom Quartile

Those who do no homework at all tend to have lower scores on this assessment than those who spend some time at it. Those who do the most homework (two hours or more) tend to do better.

Who spends two or more hours per day doing homework? Suburban students (44 percent of them); students in the academic track (43 percent); children of college graduates (39 percent); black students (41 percent); students in the northeast (37 percent); "others" (56 percent); and Hispanic students (35 percent). Within each group, those who do more home-

TIME SPENT ON HOMEWORK

Percentages of Students Followed by Average History Proficiencies

	Don't have	Don't do	Less than 1/2 hour	1 hour	2 hours	2+ hours
Total	6.8 265.1	9.6 281.1	18.0 285.5	33.3 284.8	19.8 288.7	12.5 293.7
Male	8.0 270.0	13.6 284.0	20.7 294.2	32.4 292.9	16.7 294.4	8.5 298.6
Female	5.4 257.7	5.4 273.4	15.1 273.0	34.3 276.8	23.0 284.4	16.7 291.1
White	6.8 269.4	10.0 285.6	19.4 290.4	34.2 290.1	19.1 296.0	10.5 304.3
Black	6.2 248.1	6.0 270.0	13.1 259.6	33.2 261.7	23.8 265.8	17.6 268.0
Hispanic	7.4 243.7	12.5 255.0	16.2 262.7	28.8 265.7	18.8 265.6	16.2 266.8
Others	5.9 278.1	6.6 266.2	8.0 274.7	23.5 280.5	21.7 280.3	34.3 297.4
Public schools	7.8 265.0	10.0 280.3	18.3 284.2	33.7 283.9	19.1 286.8	11.5 290.0
Non-public schools	1.5 271.3	5.4 294.4	15.0 299.5	29.7 293.8	26.1 302.0	22.2 312.3
Top quartile	3.3 327.3	8.7 333.4	18.1 334.8	31.0 333.7	22.0 332.4	17.0 337.9
Top quartile black	.5 n/a	8.6 n/a	13.8 n/a	27.0 n/a	25.1 n/a	24.7 n/a
Bottom quartile	11.7 231.3	12.3 231.2	18.7 235.2	31.8 237.0	16.5 236.9	9.0 232.2

NOTE: The average proficiency score for the entire sample is 285.

work tend to get higher scores on this assessment. (One mysterious exception is the 6 percent of black students who say they don't do any homework; their scores are higher than those who do, though still far below the national average. A possible explanation can be found in Signithia Fordham and John U. Ogbu, "Black Students' School Success: Coping with the 'Burden of Acting White,'" *Urban Review* 3 [1986].)

Some comparisons: girls do more homework than boys. The boys still have higher history scores, but the differences are smallest among those who do the most homework. Nonpublic school students do a lot more homework than public school students: 48 percent of the former spend two or more hours a day doing homework, compared with 30.6 percent of the latter.

Thirty-nine percent of the students in the top quartile of the history assessment spend two hours or more on homework, compared with 27 percent of those in the bottom quartile. But the prize for time spent on homework goes to the black students in the top quartile, 49 percent of whom do homework two or more hours daily.

We cannot say that doing homework *causes* students to do better on an assessment of this kind, although we expect that it helps. Subjects like history and literature require more time to learn than the classroom can afford; surely learning these subjects demands extended periods of reading and contemplation, something that is all but impossible during the course of the school day. It is clear that in most instances higher test scores are associated with more time spent on schoolwork. Successful students work harder. Do they work hard because they are already successful and enjoy academic work, or are they successful because they work hard? An assessment of this kind cannot provide a definitive answer to that question.

Television

Seventeen-year-olds probably don't watch as much television as younger children, because many of them work, socialize, and have other commitments. But television viewing takes up a considerable part of their day, far more than homework. Of our total sample, 47 percent watch two hours or less each day; 44 percent watch three to five hours daily; and 9 percent watch six or more hours each day. There is a significant difference in scores on this assessment among these groups and, not surprisingly, scores fall as television viewing increases.

Whatever relationship there is between television and school success is complex. For some groups, like Hispanics and students in rural areas, whose scores generally are lowest of any group, some television watching, about two or three hours a day, is associated with increased scores. This is probably because television in reasonable amounts teaches these children about the larger culture and expands their vocabulary, bringing more information to them than would otherwise be available. Perhaps they even learn things from television about history and literature that they do not learn in school. Children in poor communities who watch *no* television have low scores, while children in affluent suburbs who watch no television have high scores. Even in well-to-do communities, two or three hours a day of television are not associated with declining scores; students who do very well on the assessment watch that much. Beyond three hours daily, however, television watching is associated with lower scores.

The amount of time spent watching television is closely correlated with parental education. Children of college graduates watch the least television, and children whose parents did not finish high school watch the most. Twenty-four percent of the children of college graduates watch four or more hours a day, compared with 42 percent of the children whose parents did not finish high school.

While white and Hispanic students watch about the same amount of television, blacks spend far more time at it than any other group. Nearly four-fifths of black students watch three or more hours a day, compared with about half of white and Hispanic students. Twenty-two percent of blacks watch six or more hours daily, which is about triple the proportion

TELEVISION VIEWING PER DAY

Percentages of Students Followed by Average History Proficiencies

	0–2 hours	*3–5 hours*	*6+ hours*
Total	47.1	43.8	9.1
	291.3	282.1	267.0
Male	45.7	44.4	9.9
	296.5	288.7	274.4
Female	48.6	43.3	8.1
	286.2	475.1	257.6
White	51.6	41.4	6.9
	295.3	288.1	274.8
Black	22.5	55.4	22.1
	267.6	263.6	257.3
Hispanic	45.5	45.8	8.7
	265.2	263.4	243.6
Others	41.1	50.6	8.3
	287.6	284.7	270.4
Parents less than high school graduates	36.7	52.2	11.2
	260.2	263.4	251.0
Parents college graduates	57.4	36.7	5.9
	303.2	292.9	274.9
Academic track	53.4	40.5	6.1
	304.2	294.8	277.7
General track	40.4	48.1	11.5
	274.9	270.4	263.3
Top quartile	56.7	39.0	4.4
	335.3	332.3	334.7
Top quartile black	23.1	60.6	15.9
	n/a	n/a	n/a
Bottom quartile	37.4	47.0	15.5
	233.2	232.9	228.3

NOTE: The average proficiency score for the entire sample is 285.

Television Viewing Per Day
And Average History Proficiencies

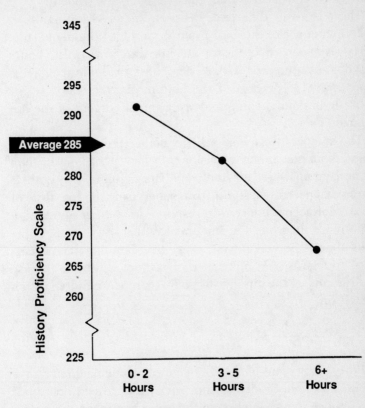

History Proficiency Scale

345

295

290

Average 285

280

275

270

265

260

225

| 0 - 2 Hours | 3 - 5 Hours | 6+ Hours |

Hours of TV Watched

(Each point on the graph indicates the average history proficiency of the portion of student sample reporting daily TV viewing as shown.)

of white or Hispanic students. Even the top quartile black students spend a great deal of time watching television, though somewhat less than the average black student.

There is a vast difference between the television habits of the top quartile of the entire sample and the bottom quartile. Fifty-seven percent of the top quartile watch two or less hours per day, as compared with 37 percent of the bottom quartile. Conversely, 16 percent of the bottom quartile watch six or more hours daily, compared with only 4 percent of the top quartile.

The students were also asked whether their families have rules about how much television may be watched; fewer than 12 percent answered affirmatively. The great majority of their parents apparently abstain from supervising the free time of their adolescent children. In response to another question, a little more than half the students say that someone at home asks about their schoolwork every day. It seems that parents care enough to ask, but that they are not willing to impose restrictions on the number of hours that their children watch television.

Part-time Jobs

Forty-six percent of these 17-year-old students do not have a part-time job. Students who work up to fifteen hours per week score slightly higher on the assessment than those who do not work at all. Perhaps they are more highly motivated. Beyond the fifteen-hour mark, however, students' scores on the assessment begin to decline, and they continue to decline as the number of hours worked each week rises. The 16 percent who work more than twenty hours a week score well below average on the history assessment. The pattern on the literature assessment is virtually identical. Unlike television-watching, work patterns are not related to parents' educational levels: children of college graduates are just as likely to have a part-time job as children whose parents have less education.

School Attendance

It is no surprise that students who attend school with the greatest regularity do well on this assessment. Students were asked how many days of school they had missed in the last month. Those who answered "none" have the highest scores; with each additional day of school missed, the scores slip. Beyond three or four days of absence, scores fall sharply.

Attendance Patterns and Average History Proficiencies

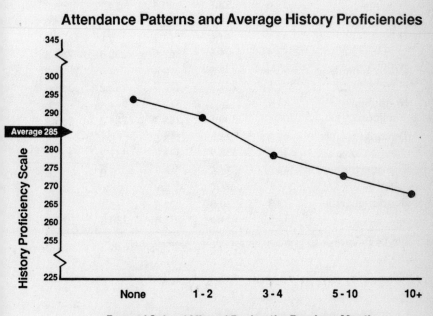

(Each point on the graph indicates the average history proficiency of the portion of student sample reporting monthly school absences as shown.)

ATTENDANCE PATTERNS AND HISTORY PROFICIENCIES
Percentages of Students Followed by Average History Proficiencies

	Days of school missed previous month				
	None	*1–2*	*3–4*	*5–10*	*10+*
Total	34.9 293.6	35.6 289.0	18.1 278.5	8.5 272.8	2.9 268.8
Male	39.4 299.8	33.3 295.4	17.0 284.6	7.3 276.4	2.9 270.6
Female	30.4 285.6	37.9 283.4	19.2 273.0	9.7 270.1	2.9 266.9
White	34.7 298.7	37.2 292.2	17.8 284.5	7.7 279.6	2.6 274.7
Black	37.2 271.7	30.2 267.8	19.4 257.7	10.4 253.6	2.9 251.5
Hispanic	29.6 271.3	28.8 270.7	20.6 256.5	14.7 257.3	6.3 253.6
Others	43.5 293.4	31.6 304.9	15.4 261.6	7.0 258.3	2.6 266.3
Public schools	33.9 291.5	35.5 287.7	18.6 277.7	8.9 272.2	3.0 268.8
Nonpublic schools	44.1 308.1	36.3 300.5	13.3 288.3	4.5 284.2	2.0 268.3
Top quartile	42.3 336.8	37.4 332.9	13.6 331.8	5.1 331.7	1.6 325.3
Top quartile black	43.6 n/a	34.5 n/a	18.1 n/a	3.0 n/a	.6 n/a
Bottom quartile	27.8 233.3	30.0 234.6	23.8 232.6	13.3 230.8	5.1 227.3

NOTE: The average proficiency score for the entire sample is 285.

Again, we have no evidence that missing school *causes* one to know less history and literature, but it seems reasonable to surmise that students who are not in school will not learn whatever is being taught there. Since students do best on this assessment on the kinds of items that can be gleaned from movies or television, and worst on the items that can be learned *only* in school, it appears obvious that absence from school depresses achievement.

Who attends school conscientiously and who does not? Boys go to school more than girls do; 39 percent of the boys missed no school in the last month, compared with 30 percent of the girls. Among racial groups, 37 percent of black students missed no school, compared with 35 percent of whites and 30 percent of Hispanics. Students in the academic track miss less school than those in the general or vocational tracks. Nonpublic school students miss less school than those in public school. In every group, those who attend most often achieve the highest scores on this assessment.

Reading Habits

Students were asked about the amounts and kinds of reading they had done outside school for their own enjoyment during the past half year. Consistently, girls read more on their own than boys. Thirty-seven percent of the girls say that they have read ten or more different works, compared with 26 percent of the boys.

When students were asked whether they ever read on their own at all, about 17 percent of the entire sample say they never do. The nonreaders include more boys (23 percent) than girls (10.6 percent); are more likely to be white and Hispanic than black (only 11 percent of blacks say they read nothing in the previous half year); are more apt to be enrolled in private than public school (20 percent of nonpublic school students read nothing on their own time). Student nonreading is unrelated to the educational level of their parents; children of college graduates are just as likely to be nonreaders as children whose parents did not graduate from high school.

What do students read on their own? About two-thirds say that they have recently read one or more short stories for their own enjoyment. Hispanic and black students are likelier than white students to read short stories. Most of the youngsters who respond affirmatively have read between one and four short stories in the past half year.

About 60 percent of the students report that they have read a novel for pleasure during the past half year; so do nearly three-quarters of the students whose scores vault them into the top quartile on the literature assessment. Reading novels is associated with positive achievement on the literature assessment; those who read no novels for pleasure tend to have scores well below average. The more novels they read, the higher they tend to score. Girls are more likely to read novels than boys: 66 percent of them have read a novel recently, compared with 53 percent of the boys. A third of the girls have read more than three novels in the past half year, compared with 22 percent of the boys. There are no differences among racial groups or regions when it comes to novel-reading, but this activity is positively associated with parental education: the higher the parents' level of education, the likelier the student is to read novels.

When asked whether they read plays for enjoyment, 72 percent of the students responded negatively, even at the top ranges of achievement. Reading plays, oddly enough, seems to be associated with low performance on the literature assessment. Students who say they have read three or more plays on their own tend to have very low scores. We notice, however, that reading plays in the classroom is also associated with declining levels of performance: the students with the lowest scores read the most plays, and this seems to be true for the sample as a whole, as well as for racial and ethnic groups within it. The explanation that seems most plausible to us is that something *like* plays, perhaps dialogues written in simple language, is being widely used for slow readers. We are aware that textbooks for slow readers in the lower grades often contain adaptations of stories in play form, using simplified language. Perhaps the same practice is continued in high school.

Poetry is not in high favor among 17-year-olds. Forty-five percent say that they read no poems on their own in the last half-year. There is no clear-cut association between reading poetry and performance on the assessment. Presumably, poetry appeals to students with different levels of ability and knowledge. Girls read much more poetry than boys: 65 percent of them read poetry on their own, compared with 45 percent of the boys. Among white students, 51 percent say that they have recently read poetry, a far lower level than among minority youngsters. Seventy percent of black students say they have recently read poems for their own enjoyment; the same proportion is found among black students who score in the top quartile of the literature assessment. Sixty percent of Hispanic students also read poetry for pleasure. We wonder what it is about the teaching of poetry in school, where children are likeliest to encounter the genre, that leaves nearly half of them uninterested in reading it on their own time; and what it is about poetry that has touched a chord of interest among minority youngsters. Do the schools take maximum advantage of this evident preference?

Nearly 62 percent of the sample report that they do not read essays for pleasure. This is one of the few categories where the girls read no more than the boys.

When students were asked how often they read for enjoyment in their spare time, an interesting portrait emerged of the association between quantity of spare time reading and literature proficiency.

The following chart reports students' responses when they were asked whether they read for their own enjoyment daily, once or twice a week, less than once a week, or never.

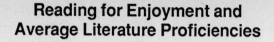

Reading for Enjoyment and Average Literature Proficiencies

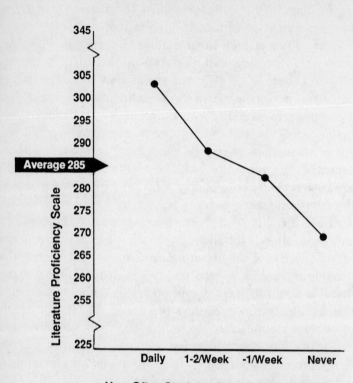

How Often Students Read for Enjoyment

(Each point on the graph indicates the average literature proficiency of the portion of student sample reporting weekly reading as shown.)

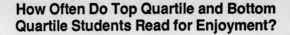

How Often Do Top Quartile and Bottom Quartile Students Read for Enjoyment?

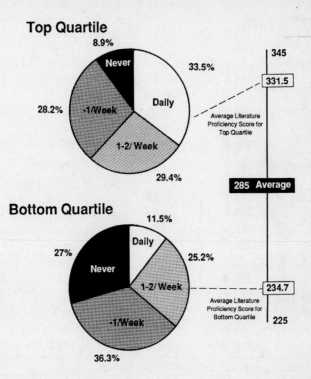

Top Quartile

8.9% Never

33.5% Daily

28.2% -1/Week

29.4% 1-2/Week

345

331.5
Average Literature
Proficiency Score for
Top Quartile

285 Average

Bottom Quartile

11.5% Daily

25.2% 1-2/Week

27% Never

36.3% -1/Week

234.7
Average Literature
Proficiency Score for
Bottom Quartile

225

HOW OFTEN DO YOU READ ON YOUR OWN?

Percentages of Students Followed by Average Literature Proficiencies

	Daily	1–2 times/week	Less than 1 time/week	Never
Total	20.6	25.7	34.8	18.8
	303.5	288.2	282.9	269.8
Male	18.4	24.6	33.0	23.9
	303.4	286.2	282.9	268.3
Female	22.8	26.8	36.6	13.7
	303.5	290.1	282.9	272.4
White	21.5	25.0	34.0	19.5
	307.0	294.1	287.3	273.0
Black	17.3	29.3	40.6	12.7
	285.7	267.6	264.8	257.8
Hispanic	15.5	27.9	34.8	21.8
	276.0	265.7	267.6	252.9
Others	20.4	26.6	33.5	19.5
	308.9	283.1	286.2	257.0
Top quartile	33.5	29.4	28.2	8.9
	337.0	331.4	328.4	323.7
Top quartile black	35.8	26.4	28.8	8.8
	n/a	n/a	n/a	n/a
Bottom quartile	11.5	25.2	36.3	27.0
	234.9	233.9	236.8	232.0

NOTE: The average proficiency score for the entire sample is 285.

In every group, except the bottom quartile, an increase in the amount of reading that students do in their spare time is associated with higher scores on the assessment. The students who read more tend to do better, the students who read less tend to do worse. The students with the highest scores read daily.

Students were also asked whether they prefer to read fiction or nonfiction, neither or both. One of the striking aspects of this response is the demonstration of girls' strong preference for fiction over nonfiction. And once again, nearly 20 percent of the sample report that they don't like to read in their spare time. The rest divide as follows:

DO YOU PREFER TO READ FICTION, NONFICTION, OR BOTH?

	Never	Fiction	Nonfiction	Both
Total	19.4%	34.6%	23.2%	22.8%
Male	25.2	25.5	29.8	19.5
Female	13.6	43.8	16.4	26.2
White	19.9	35.5	21.9	22.7
Black	16.0	29.6	30.8	23.6
Hispanic	20.8	34.8	23.8	20.8
Others	17.5	28.4	25.9	28.3
Top quartile	8.1	45.3	18.9	27.6
Top quartile black	12.0	37.8	26.8	23.2
Bottom quartile	30.2	25.9	26.6	17.4

WHAT DO THEY KNOW ABOUT THE BIBLE AND MYTHOLOGY?

Students were asked how much they know about the Bible. We assume that whatever students know about the Bible is likely to have been learned at home or in Sunday school, unless they attend a denominational school. It is important to know about their exposure to biblical lore because a number of questions on the literature assessment are based on biblical allusions that recur frequently in Western literature. Even though the number of such questions is small relative to the entire literature assessment, students' self-evaluation of their familiarity with biblical lore seems to relate to their performance on the cognitive portion of the literature assessment.

Perhaps students who know a lot about the Bible have had early exposure to the value of the written word and its importance as a source of meaning.

HOW MUCH HAVE YOU HEARD ABOUT OR READ
OF STORIES FROM THE BIBLE?
Percentages of Students Followed by Average Literature Proficiencies

	A lot	*Some*	*Little*	*None*
Total	38.1	32.4	19.2	10.3
	291.7	283.7	280.9	272.9
Male	35.0	32.2	20.9	11.9
	290.6	282.5	278.5	269.7
Female	41.3	32.6	17.4	8.6
	292.7	284.9	283.9	277.6
White	36.4	33.1	20.0	10.5
	298.2	287.9	285.6	276.7
Black	49.6	29.2	14.1	7.1
	272.9	263.4	259.9	258.5
Hispanic	37.5	31.6	19.0	11.9
	268.0	271.5	255.0	250.9
Others	32.0	30.4	20.7	17.0
	290.0	278.6	280.4	274.3
Top quartile	46.2	30.2	17.4	6.2
	332.7	331.2	329.3	329.9
Top quartile black	61.6	21.6	15.2	1.5
	n/a	n/a	n/a	n/a
Bottom quartile	30.0	33.1	22.3	14.5
	236.3	234.6	234.6	232.4

NOTE: The average proficiency score for the entire sample is 285.

The response of the top quartile black students is impressive. It probably says as much about the milieu in which these high-achieving students grew up as it does about their taste in literature.

Greek and Roman mythology used to be taught to all students, beginning in the early grades. It no longer is. Students'

How Much Do Top Quartile and Bottom Quartile Students Say They Know About Greek and Roman Mythology?

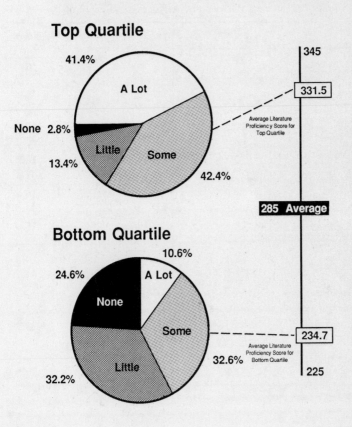

Top Quartile

41.4% A Lot

None 2.8%

Little 13.4%

Some 42.4%

345

331.5

Average Literature Proficiency Score for Top Quartile

285 Average

Bottom Quartile

10.6% A Lot

24.6% None

Some 32.6%

Little 32.2%

234.7

Average Literature Proficiency Score for Bottom Quartile

225

performance on the mythology questions suggests to us that the study of Greek and Roman myths is not a regular feature of the school curriculum. Therefore we are dealing with the response to this question within the context of personal and family reading habits, rather than schooling. Yet knowledge of classical mythology is associated with achievement on the literature assessment; in fact, those who say they know a lot are the highest achievers in *every* group.

HOW MUCH HAVE YOU HEARD ABOUT OR READ OF
STORIES FROM GREEK/ROMAN MYTHOLOGY?
Percentages of Students Followed by Average Literature Proficiencies

	A Lot	*Some*	*Little*	*None*
Total	22.5	41.0	24.5	12.0
	306.2	288.6	273.6	256.6
Male	24.7	41.5	22.0	11.8
	304.2	286.8	267.7	253.0
Female	20.3	40.5	27.0	12.2
	308.8	290.6	278.6	260.2
White	22.2	42.5	24.1	11.2
	312.0	292.8	278.1	261.7
Black	24.2	35.9	25.7	14.2
	286.0	269.8	258.7	244.8
Hispanic	23.3	33.7	28.0	15.0
	284.0	268.0	257.6	239.9
Others	21.1	42.7	21.4	14.8
	306.8	289.3	267.5	244.7
Top quartile	41.4	42.4	13.4	2.8
	336.9	329.3	324.1	321.0
Top quartile black	49.1	35.7	12.8	1.2
	n/a	n/a	n/a	n/a
Bottom quartile	10.6	32.6	32.2	24.6
	236.8	237.2	235.7	229.5

NOTE: The average proficiency score for the entire sample is 285.

There is no difference between students in public and non-public schools in their knowledge of classical mythology; about 22 percent in both types of institutions say they know a lot, and these 22 percent are the top scorers on the assessment.

DO STUDENTS LIKE LITERATURE?

By their own account, the students in the sample engage in certain activities that seem to demonstrate a genuine liking for works they have read. Students were asked, "Have you ever read a poem, story, or article out loud to a friend or member of your family?" This may seem like a strange question to put to teenagers who have grown up surrounded by television, movies, computers, videodisks, and other nonprint media. Stranger still, 73.4 percent respond that they have read something aloud to a friend or family member. Eighty-four percent of the girls and 63 percent of the boys have. In almost every group and every region, about seven out of ten youngsters have. This is the kind of activity that can be construed as meaning, "Hey, I've read something I like: Listen to this." There is no significant difference on this activity between students whose parents had not graduated from high school and those whose parents had graduated from college.

Students were also asked, "Have you ever read more than one book written by an author you like?" The 80.8 percent of the sample who respond "yes" includes 89 percent of the girls and 72.5 percent of the boys. Nearly 70 percent of the Hispanic students, 75 percent of the black students, and 83 percent of the white students say they have read more than one book by a favorite author.

When asked, "Have you ever read a version of a play, movie, or television show that you have seen?," nearly 85 percent say that they have. Perhaps this merely records a fairly common classroom practice, that is, showing a movie or videotape of a performance, and then reading the play or novel. Or it may be that some students have picked up the book "tie-in" to a popular movie. Whatever path brought them to the written word, a large majority of the students have read a version of something they have seen on the screen.

SCHOOLING

Tracking

The students in the sample are juniors in high school. Fifty-two percent of them are in an academic/college preparatory program; 38 percent are in a general (nonacademic) program; and 10 percent are enrolled in a vocational program. In American high schools, these are usually called "tracks," and they are supposed to be based on relative academic prowess. Either the student, the student's parents or, more often, the school decides which track the student "belongs" in. On this assessment, students in the academic track outscore students in both of the other tracks, and the general track youngsters perform somewhat better than the students in the vocational track.

These differences are not surprising, because students in the academic track take more academic courses and are more apt to be college-bound than those in the other tracks. In an assessment of this kind, it is not possible to know whether students in the general and vocational tracks do poorly because they have less academic ability or because they have been less exposed to the subject matter on the test. It is possible that both are true, but from our findings it is certain that the latter is true: students who are not in the academic track take fewer academic courses and study less history and literature than students in the academic track.

Who is in the academic track? About 50 percent of the boys and about 55 percent of the girls; about 55 percent of white students, 47 percent of black students, and 36 percent of Hispanic students. The northeast has the greatest proportion of its students in an academic track (63 percent), compared with 48–50 percent in the other regions. In rural communities and inner-city schools, only about 38 percent are in the academic program, while 71 percent of the eleventh graders in suburban schools are. In public schools, about half the students are in the academic track, compared with about 77 percent of students in nonpublic schools.

PARENT EDUCATION AND SCHOOL TRACK

Percentages of Students Followed by Average History Proficiencies

Parent education	General	Academic	Vocational
No high school diploma	57.3	26.2	16.4
	256.4	277.2	250.4
High school graduate	47.1	38.3	14.6
	264.0	289.3	265.7
Some post–high school	37.3	53.2	9.5
	281.7	298.0	275.3
College graduate	25.6	69.4	5.0
	282.0	305.4	272.7

The higher the parents' level of educational attainment, the likelier it is that the student will be in the academic track. On the other hand, 30 percent of the children of college graduates are *not* in the academic track, and one-fourth of the children whose parents did not finish high school *are* in the academic track. In other words, parent education is important, but not inexorably determinative. This is so, we suspect, because children do not always resemble their parents and because access to higher education is very broad in the United States today. Graduation from college is an accomplishment, to be sure, but it is not hard to get into many colleges, and it is not hard to graduate from some of them. As a social sorting device, higher education today may be thought of as a strainer with very large holes. Thus, having a parent who went to college is surely helpful to students, especially if the parent provides the experiences that create a literate environment, but it does not guarantee school success. Students whose parents did not graduate from high school still find avenues of advancement open to them in school.

Nor is tracking a rigid, immutable process in all schools. Students who persist can often "talk their way" into the track they prefer, as can determined parents. And though not common, it is possible to shift from one track to another during one's high school years. However, when tracking begins in junior high school or even in elementary school, it becomes progressively more difficult for students to make the switch into a more challenging program after years of taking less rigorous or watered-down courses in the basic academic subjects.

Students in all three tracks were almost all currently enrolled in an English course when they took the assessment; 83 percent of the academic and general students and 77 percent of the vocational students were also studying U.S. history. However, there are vast differences among the tracks in their overall school program. By a very wide margin, the academic track student is far more likely to be currently enrolled in a math class and a science class. The academic track student is also far more likely to have taken algebra, geometry, other advanced mathematics courses, biology, chemistry, and physics than students in the other tracks. The general and vocational track students are far more likely to have taken a consumer math course and a general science course than students in the academic track.

Academic students have studied more history and literature than have students in the other tracks. They have studied more U.S. history and more world/Western history (54 percent of the academic students have studied world/Western history, compared with 41 percent of the general students). In the English classes of the academic track, more time is spent on literature. Vocational and general students probably spend more time working on basic skills in their English classes, because two-fifths of these students are in classes where not much time (25 percent or less) is devoted to literature.

Initial differences in ability that may exist between the students in these tracks are heightened by their different educational experiences. Students in the academic track would probably do better on a history and literature assessment anyway, since they are presumably selected for their academic ability, but their advantages on this assessment are increased by the fact that they spend more time in school studying history and literature. The relatively low scores of the general and vocational students suggest that you can't learn what you have not been exposed to and, conversely, the high scores of the academic students suggest that "time on task" increases the chance of learning.

Students in the general and vocational tracks are assigned less literature in school than students in the academic track. However, they say that they like to read on their own time almost as much as the students in the academic track. Eighty-five percent of the students in the academic track report reading a short story or novel or poem or essay on their own in the previous half year, compared with 80 percent of students from the general and vocational tracks. Two-thirds of the students in the lower tracks say that they read one or more short stories for their own enjoyment; half say they read a novel; half say they read poetry. Perhaps the schools have succeeded in developing the interest of these students in reading, even though they do not score well on an assessment that includes classic authors. It appears to us, however, that the schools have failed to use their interest in reading as an avenue to introduce them to major writers and important works of literature.

The tracking system is far from perfect, either as confirmation of a student's ability or as predictor of future academic success. We found that in the top quartile of the history assessment, 20.9 percent of the students come from the general track and 5.2 percent from the vocational track. Since these youngsters are exposed to fairly meager academic fare and take fewer courses in history, their success on this assessment is all the more remarkable. It makes us wonder how many other students are in the "wrong" track, and even to wonder whether tracking as currently practiced makes sense.

Public and Private Schools

Catholic school students do better than public school students on this assessment, and youngsters attending non-Catholic private schools do better still.

This pattern holds true in both history and literature. In the history assessment, public school students earn an average score of 54 percent correct, while students in Catholic schools earn 60 percent and other private school students 63 percent. Corresponding figures in the literature assessment are 51, 58, and 60 percent respectively.

But only in comparative terms is there any cause for satisfaction among patrons and partisans of nonpublic education. For in neither assessment do Catholic or private school attendees earn an average score higher than a low D. Nor is the private school edge very large. Private school students do not, for example, score nearly high enough to place their average performance in the overall top quarter. By way of perspective, Catholic school students fare just a little better than students enrolled in the academic or college preparatory track in public high schools. The difference is slightly greater in literature than in history.

AVERAGE PROFICIENCY SCORES

School	History	Literature
Public (all)	283.4	283.2
Public (academic track)	297.5	297.2
Catholic	298.2	300.4
Other private	304.7	304.8

It is impossible to know from an assessment of this kind to what extent we are dealing with a palpable "school effect" that differs between public and private institutions, and to what extent we are seeing the results of already familiar patterns of family background, race, parent education, and the like.

Nonpublic students in this sample, for example, are 83 percent white, whereas their public school age-mates are 76 percent white. Forty-one percent of nonpublic students' mothers are college graduates, as are 50 percent of their fathers, compared with 23 percent and 30 percent for public school students.

Nonpublic school students are more apt to possess computers; to have attended preschool; to have fathers living at home; and to have parents employed in white-collar and professional jobs. We infer—and data from other surveys tend to corroborate this—that the families of nonpublic school students have higher average incomes than do the families of public school students.

Yet there are also signs of educational and behavioral characteristics associated with higher scores that the school *does* have something, perhaps a lot, to do with. Nonpublic eleventh graders in this sample are much more likely to be enrolled in science courses. Seventy-five percent of them say they are currently taking science, compared with 57 percent of public school students. They are much more apt to be enrolled in the academic track (77 percent vs. 50 percent) and to be planning to attend a four-year college (71 percent vs. 50 percent). They also do a lot more homework; 48 percent of them average at least two hours a night, compared with 31 percent of public school students. And just 7 percent of them admit to doing *no* homework, compared with 17 percent of their public school counterparts.

Nonpublic students watch less television. Thirty-four percent of them claim to watch less than an hour a night, while only 12 percent watch five hours or more. Among public school students, those proportions are much more evenly balanced: 21 and 18 percent, respectively.

Private school students are also more apt to come to school the next day. Just 6 percent of them missed five or more days of school the previous month; twice as large a fraction of public school students are absent that often.

Are we, then, seeing a school effect, a home effect, or both? Both, we suspect, though we cannot prove it. All we can be sure of is that the average private school student knows somewhat more history and literature than the average public school student. But not enough!

Courses in History

Students who took the history assessment were asked about the other courses they had taken in social studies. About a quarter have taken civics or geography or some other social studies course; none of these courses, however, is associated with higher scores on this history assessment. Students who have not taken these courses do as well or better than those who have taken them.

The courses that *are* associated with high achievement on the history assessment are U.S. history and world/Western history. Certainly it is unremarkable that those who have studied U.S. history do better on a test of U.S. history than those who have not. But as the table shows, not all groups are equally likely to have had a full year of American history since ninth grade. Minority youngsters and bottom quartile students are least likely to have studied the subject that much and least likely to achieve high scores on this assessment.

HISTORY COURSES TAKEN

Percentages of Students Followed by Average History Proficiencies

	U.S. history		World/Western history	
	One year	*None*	*One year*	*None*
Total	83.1	3.5	47.3	35.2
	287.8	269.0	293.5	277.2
Male	81.6	3.8	48.1	33.5
	294.4	274.4	300.3	283.0
Female	84.7	3.3	46.4	37.0
	281.3	262.7	286.3	271.8
White	85.3	3.5	48.4	34.1
	293.0	276.0	297.8	284.4
Black	75.5	3.3	44.1	40.3
	264.8	246.4	273.5	253.9
Hispanic	76.6	4.1	41.8	37.5
	264.0	244.5	274.2	252.8
Others	75.7	4.4	44.1	36.3
	291.8	252.8	299.9	272.4
Top quartile	90.0	2.0	59.5	26.6
	334.6	331.2	335.2	332.5
Top quartile black	78.9	0.4	64.9	21.9
	n/a	n/a	n/a	n/a
Bottom quartile	75.3	5.8	33.6	45.8
	233.2	230.2	233.7	232.8

NOTE: The figures do not total 100 percent because figures for students who had taken a course for a half-year or less than a half-year or who answered "I don't know" are not shown.

It is also the case that those who have studied a year of world/Western history perform significantly better than those who have studied it for half a year or less. A generation ago, many school districts required all students to take world history; various surveys reported the elimination of this requirement during the 1960s and '70s. The response to this assessment indicates that it may be making a comeback. Of the sample, 47.3 percent have studied world/Western history. We would guess that it was a required subject for most of those who took it, because there are relatively small disparities among groups, except, of course, between the top and bottom quartile history students.

The black students in the top quartile of the history assessment are more likely to have studied world/Western history than any other group, including the other students in the top quartile. It may sound like a rediscovery of the wheel, but it appears that doing well on a test that assesses basic knowledge of history is associated with studying history.

What Is Covered in Their History Courses?

Have the students in the sample studied the material that was on the assessment? Before they took the history assessment, students were asked to indicate (with a yes or no checkmark) whether they had studied the following six periods of U.S. history since the beginning of Grade 9. These periods, it should be noted, correspond to the eras into which the history assessment questions are "clustered" in Chapter 2.

Exploration
Revolutionary War Through War of 1812
Territorial Expansion Through Civil War
Reconstruction to World War I
World War I Through World War II
Post–World War II to Present

Since the assessment was administered in the early months of 1986, midway through their American history course, it seemed likely that many students would not yet have studied the twentieth century. What is surprising are the divergent answers to the earlier periods.

Exploration: 80 percent of the students say they have studied the exploration period. However, only 74 percent of the black students and 68.7 percent of the Hispanic youngsters have. Students in the central region are least likely to study the exploration period, and students in the academic track are far more likely to study it than are those in either the general or vocational track. However, 90.5 percent of the students in the top quartile have studied this period, as have 92 percent of the black students in the top quartile.

Revolutionary War Through War of 1812: 91 percent of all students have studied this period. In every group except Hispanics, the same proportion holds true. (Only 86.2 percent of Hispanics have studied the Revolutionary War.) Among the top quartile, 94.5 percent have studied this era, as have 97.9 percent of the black students in the top quartile.

Territorial Expansion Through Civil War: 85.4 percent of the total sample say that they have studied this period. Among blacks and Hispanics, only 80 percent have. Of the students in the vocational track, just 78 percent have studied this period. The top quartile students are strikingly different: 92.9 percent have studied this period, as have 94.3 percent of the top black students.

Reconstruction to World War I: 77.8 percent of the total say they have studied this period. But again blacks and Hispanics lag behind, since only about 72 percent of them answer affirmatively. The reason for this may be that students in the general and vocational tracks are somewhat less likely than those in the academic track to have studied this critical era. While 80.7 percent in the academic track have done so, the corresponding figures for the general and vocational tracks are 75.3 and 73 percent. Since there are disproportionate numbers of black and Hispanic youngsters in these two tracks, this may explain their response to this question. Among the top quartile, 86 percent have studied the Reconstruction era, as have 87.1 percent of the black students in the top quartile.

World War I Through World War II: 68.6 percent of the sample have studied this period. On this topic, there is scant variation. Hispanics lag a bit in that 63.5 percent have studied this period, but the difference is barely significant. Almost everyone else registers within the same range as the total. The gap between the top quartile and the other students begins to narrow: 72.6 percent of the top group have studied this era, as have 69.1 percent of the top black students.

Post–World War II to Present: 43.4 percent have studied this period. As was anticipated, this period draws the lowest response, since the eleventh-grade American history course had not yet covered it. There are significant differences among groups: 46.7 percent of the boys have studied it, but only 40 percent of the girls; 45 percent of the white students have studied this period, but only 37 percent of blacks and 36 percent of Hispanics. Students in the northeast are likeliest (50 percent) to have studied the modern era, while those in the southeast are least likely (37.4 percent). Top quartile students are barely ahead of their peers on this topic, since 48.5 percent have studied it, along with 44.3 percent of the black students in the top quartile.

Not surprisingly, those who have studied all six of these topics score highest on the assessment. The downward progression of scores is regular and consistent, depending on the number of topics studied. The highest-scoring students have studied the most history, the lowest-scoring have studied the least. Perhaps the only surprise in this set of data is that there are schools where large numbers of students do *not* study the period of exploration or the period preceding and following the Civil War.

The relationship between the average history proficiency scores and the number of eras studied is shown in the table on the next page.

Number of American History Eras Studied And Average History Proficiencies

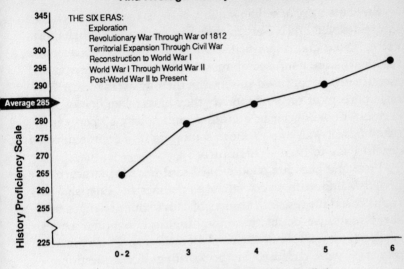

THE SIX ERAS:
Exploration
Revolutionary War Through War of 1812
Territorial Expansion Through Civil War
Reconstruction to World War I
World War I Through World War II
Post-World War II to Present

Number of Eras Students Say They've Studied

(Each point on the graph indicates the average history proficiency of the portion of student sample reporting previous study of number of eras as shown.)

HOW MANY HISTORY ERAS HAVE YOU STUDIED?

Number of Eras	Percentage of students	Average history proficiency
None to two	10.1	263.0
Three	14.4	277.4
Four	21.0	283.0
Five	24.0	288.0
Six	30.5	295.1

Once again, we see evidence of that old educational truism: the more students study, the more they are apt to know.

How Much Literature Have They Studied?

Students were asked how many courses they had taken that were devoted exclusively to either American or English literature. These questions turned out to be useless, because the students were confused about what the questions meant and we are just as confused about what their answers mean. Sixty-five percent of the students say they have taken one or more semesters of American literature, and nearly 60 percent say they have taken one or more semesters of a course devoted exclusively to English literature.

First, the question should have said *British* literature, not *English* literature; everyone takes courses in "English." Second, based on research studies of curriculum changes in recent years, we doubt that many high schools offer courses devoted exclusively to "British" literature, so we surmise that students were confused by the wording of the question.

We are almost as uncertain about the meaning of their response to the question about American literature. The question was intended to survey the number of courses where only American authors are read. We don't know what students had in mind when they answered; perhaps courses in which they read some works by American authors or works written in the English language or works that had something to do with America. The poor results on the literature assessment make us doubt that 65 percent of the students had actually taken courses devoted exclusively to American literature. Our chief conclusion, however, is that the vague wording of these questions makes them invalid.

Of more value, we think, because it is based on the students' direct observation, is the question "Think about your current or most recent English course. What percentage of the time do or did you spend in class studying literature?" This question produced some interesting, albeit predictable, responses. Who spends the most time studying literature in their English classes? Students from the most advantaged backgrounds; stu-

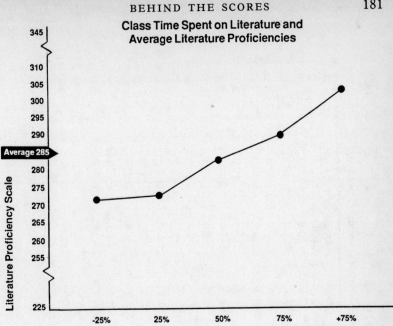

**Class Time Spent on Literature and
Average Literature Proficiencies**

(Each point on the graph indicates the average literature proficiency of
the portion of student sample reporting class time for literature as shown.)

dents in the academic track; students in nonpublic schools; students whose parents are well educated; students in the northeast; students who score in the top quartile. Those who study the most literature in class register the highest scores on the literature assessment. The chart above and table on the following pages demonstrate the amount of class time devoted to literature—ranging from less than 25 percent of class time to more than 75 percent—and the proportion of students in such classes.

PERCENTAGE OF TIME IN ENGLISH CLASS
DEVOTED TO LITERATURE

Percentages of Students Followed by Average Literature Proficiencies

	Less than 25%	25%	50%	75%	More than 75%
Total	12.3	17.6	30.6	19.1	20.4
	271.3	272.3	283.2	289.5	303.2
Male	13.3	18.4	31.7	18.4	18.1
	271.1	269.9	283.2	288.0	299.3
Female	11.2	16.9	29.4	19.8	22.7
	271.7	275	283.2	291.0	306.3
White	12.2	16.7	30.0	19.4	21.7
	275.3	276.5	288.3	294.6	307.0
Black	10.7	22.2	33.2	18.1	15.8
	262.7	261.1	264.6	268.8	282.8
Hispanic	16.9	19.3	30.6	18.9	14.3
	252.8	257.9	265.8	266.6	282.5
Others	11.9	18.2	34.3	15.5	20.1
	262.9	266.0	281.3	292.3	299.9
Public schools	12.4	17.8	31.1	19.0	19.7
	269.5	271.6	282.0	287.9	300.4
Nonpublic schools	10.9	15.9	25.5	20.5	27.2
	290.9	279.8	297.5	303.9	322.0

Parent Education									
No h.s. diploma	16.6	260.0	23.7	261.5	33.4	267.9	14.4	268.1	11.9	275.8
High school graduate	14.9	264.6	22.4	265.9	30.4	273.8	16.8	278.4	15.4	286.1
Some post–high school	12.3	272.8	16.4	280.1	33.3	288.9	17.8	291.4	20.1	300.9
College graduate	9.2	283.7	13.4	281.8	28.4	292.3	22.7	298.6	26.2	315.8
Track									
General	17.0	264.6	21.8	264.3	32.3	273.9	16.0	277.0	12.9	280.6
Vocational	17.5	260.6	25.8	260.9	31.5	268.6	14.5	269.1	10.7	274.3
Academic	7.9	286.5	13.0	286.4	29.0	294.0	22.4	298.7	27.6	313.1
Top quartile	7.3	327.5	10.2	326.7	26.6	329.8	21.0	330.5	34.9	335.7
Top quartile black	7.4	n/a	17.7	n/a	27.8	n/a	19.4	n/a	27.5	n/a
Bottom quartile	18.0	233.2	25.0	232.6	31.4	236.4	15.6	236.6	10.1	235.2

NOTE: The average proficiency score of the entire sample is 285.

Three-fifths of all eleventh graders are in English classes in which the study of literature occupies no more than half the time. Yet as the table shows, youngsters from the most favored circumstances, children of college graduates, those in the academic track, and those in nonpublic schools, are the *most* likely to be enrolled in classes that emphasize literature, and those in classes that spend most of their time on literature fare best on the literature assessment. This is one of the strongest and most consistent relationships in the data.

Conversely, those whose home environment is *least* favorable, blacks, Hispanics, those whose parents do not have a college education, and those in the nonacademic tracks, do not study as much literature in school. This is bound to affect how much they know about literature. Clearly, those students who spend less than 25 percent of their time in English class on literature do not have much time to discuss what they have read. This amount of time translates into about twelve to fifteen minutes for each class period, depending on its length, or a bit more than one class period per week. Given the paucity of time that these youngsters have to study literature, it is not surprising that they have the lowest scores on the assessment, even on some of the easiest questions.

Figures like those displayed above make us wonder whether students do poorly on an assessment of this kind because of their family background or because they have not studied the kinds of literature that are included on this assessment. Schools have no immediate responsibility for, much less influence over, such variables as the educational level of the parents of their students, but they can surely control how much time their students are engaged in various studies and what kind of literature their students study. The persistence of the pattern shown here suggests that in the ways they structure their curriculum and pedagogy the schools may actually be reinforcing rather than mitigating social differences among students.

WHAT DO STUDENTS READ IN SCHOOL?

Students were asked about the kinds of literature they read in English class during the previous school semester. They checked off an estimate of the number of short stories, novels, poems, etc. that they had read for school. In truth, we think that the *number* of works they have read is not terribly important; after all, students may gain more from the careful reading of one novel than from a hurried perusal of three. (The assessment results tend to bear this out; we can find no systematic association between literature proficiency scores and the numbers of works of various genres that students say they read in class during the first semester.) What did strike us as interesting, however, is the proportion of students who state that they have read none of a particular genre. Even though we cannot say precisely what students are reading, they did identify the sorts of things they are *not* reading.

PERCENTAGE OF STUDENTS WHO READ *NONE* OF THE FOLLOWING THE PREVIOUS SEMESTER

	All students	*Top quartile*
Short stories	12.5	13.9
Novels	23.7	19.0
Plays	35.9	35.2
Poems	23.4	21.6
Essays	29.2	29.4
Biographies/journals	46.2	46.7
Historical documents	60.8	56.2

We included in this table the contrast between all students and the top quartile students because the differences between them are so small. This suggests, we think, that the patterns represent not individual preferences or decisions based on what students can reasonably handle, but real and systematic patterns that are presently ingrained in the English curriculum. We were not surprised to see how few students read historical documents, since English teachers don't usually think it is their responsibility to teach the Gettysburg Address or the Declaration of Independence. On the other hand, we are disturbed to note that nearly one out of four of these high school juniors did not read a single novel or poem in the first semester of the school year, and that an even larger number did not read even one essay or play. It is especially vexing that students in the top quartile, who read the most in their free time, are just as likely as students with far less ability or interest to pass a school semester without reading a novel or a poem in class.

Students were asked whether they had read the following ten books in school, on their own or not at all:

PERCENTAGE OF STUDENTS WHO READ
THE FOLLOWING NOVELS: 1986

	In school	On own	No
A Tale of Two Cities	21.1	6.5	72.4
Moby-Dick	16.4	16.8	66.7
1984	11.8	11.8	76.5
The Adventures of Huckleberry Finn	44.7	23.3	32.0
Tom Sawyer	28.3	29.0	42.7
The Grapes of Wrath	15.3	5.9	78.9
The Old Man and the Sea	21.1	7.6	71.4
The Red Badge of Courage	30.4	9.5	60.1
The Scarlet Letter	39.5	7.4	53.2
To Kill a Mockingbird	43.0	9.2	47.9

This list was compiled by the literature committee for the assessment, based mainly on what its members thought are commonly read works in high school. The list could easily have been multiplied many times over without exhausting the novels that are found in high school literature classes. It would be unreasonable to expect that all high school juniors read the same books, in view of the fact that there are scores of excellent novels to choose from. In fact, these figures stand up fairly well when compared with a survey conducted in 1963, in which a large sample of high schools was asked which major works were regularly assigned. This earlier survey tabulated returns by public, Catholic, and independent schools:

PERCENTAGE OF STUDENTS WHO READ
THE FOLLOWING NOVELS: 1963

	Public	*Catholic*	*Independent*
A Tale of Two Cities	33	48	47
Moby-Dick	18	18	24
The Adventures of Huckleberry Finn	27	29	47
Tom Sawyer	10	7	17
The Grapes of Wrath			10
The Old Man and the Sea	12	8	21
The Red Badge of Courage	33	51	37
The Scarlet Letter	32	37	50
To Kill a Mockingbird	8	20	7

SOURCE: Scarvia B. Anderson, "Between the Grimms and 'The Group,'" (Princeton: Educational Testing Service, 1964).

It appears that Dickens's stock is down, Hawthorne has gained ground, and Twain has forged into the lead, at least among these ten books. *1984* was assigned in fewer than 5 percent of the schools in the earlier survey. The two most widely read works in all schools in the 1963 survey were *Macbeth* (read by 90 percent of all students in all kinds of schools) and *Julius Caesar* (read by about 80 percent of all students), neither of which was on our checklist but both of which appear, from the favorable results on the Shakespeare cluster of the literature assessment, to be generally familiar to contemporary eleventh graders.

A STUDENT VIEW OF THE CLASSROOM

When the learning area committees prepared the objectives for each section of the assessment, they also devised questions for students about what happens in their classes. Each committee sought to identify how often students are engaged in certain learning activities in the classroom. We report their answers as "the students' view" and make no claim that this is an accurate description of classroom practices. The portrait the students paint of life in their history and English classes may not be the same as one that would be drawn by an impartial observer, but it nonetheless reflects their perceptions of the classroom experience.

History

Students taking the history assessment were asked how often they engaged in certain activities during their history course. They were offered the following choices: "about once a week"; "about once a month"; "several times a year"; and "hardly ever or never." Their answers provide the students' view of what is typical practice in the classroom.

How often do students work on individual or group projects?

	Once a week	Once a month	Few times a year	Never
Total	16.5%	22.9%	19.7%	40.8%

Boys are more likely than girls to work on history projects, and students in the suburbs are more likely than others to work on projects; otherwise there is little variation across groups. Even among the top quartile of students, about 40 percent never work on history projects.

How often do they write reports over five typed pages long?

	Once a week	Once a month	Few times a year	Never
Total	2.3%	9.2%	20.5%	68.0%

Boys are more likely to write reports than girls (34.8 percent of the boys did at some time during the year, compared with 29.2 percent of the girls); 38 percent of the black and Hispanic students say that they did. Otherwise, there is remarkably little variation among groups. Even 69 percent of the top quartile students answer hardly ever or never. Writing long reports (or "term papers") is not part of the history course for nearly seven out of ten students.

How often do they visit museums and exhibits with the history class?

	Once a week	Once a month	Few times a year	Never
Total	1.2%	1.7%	4.1%	93.0%

Black and Hispanic students and students in the vocational track are somewhat more likely to go on class visits (only 88 percent of them reply never), but again there is remarkably little variation. Hardly anyone goes to museums and exhibits with their history class.

How often do they watch movies or listen to oral history? It is unfortunate that the two activities were merged in a single question, because it seems likely that movie-watching accounts for the strong positive response:

	Once a week	Once a month	Few times a year	Never
Total	33.1%	29.8%	21.3%	15.8%

The only major difference is between public and nonpublic schools; 28.7 percent of the students in nonpublic schools never watch movies (or listen to oral history). However, the patterns for other groups are generally similar to that of the sample as a whole.

How often do students use documents and other original sources (e.g., Declaration of Independence, treaties, etc.)?

	Once a week	Once a month	Few times a year	Never
Total	12.1%	20.6%	22.8%	44.5%

There are a few significant divergences from this pattern. Students in the academic track, nonpublic school students, and children of college graduates are somewhat more likely to use original documents (40 percent of these groups answer never). The highest response comes from suburban students, where 35 percent say never. Even among the top quartile students, 39 percent *never* use original documents.

How often do they take history tests? Unlike some of the other practices, this turns out to be a frequent activity.

	Once a week	Once a month	Few times a year	Never
Total	71.4%	20.6%	5.8%	2.2%

Black students and students in the southeast are most likely to have weekly quizzes (about 80 percent do). Students in the suburbs are least likely to be tested so often, yet 61 percent are. Among the top quartile, 67.4 percent take weekly history tests.

The questions then shifted to inquiries about daily practices. The choices offered students were: "almost every day," "two or three times a week," "about once a week," "less than once a week," and "never."

Students were asked how often they listen to the teacher explain a history lesson. This, not surprisingly, is a very common practice:

	Daily	2–3 times a week	Once a week	Less than once a week	Never
Total	73.4%	16.5%	4.7%	2.5%	2.9%

There is little variation from one group to another except for Hispanics, of whom only 66 percent receive daily explanations. For students who answer never, it is not clear whether this means that the teacher does not explain, or that they don't listen, or that they don't understand when the teacher does explain. The top quartile students are more likely to listen to a teacher's explanation on a daily basis: 78.6 percent do. Among the black students in the top quartile, this figure is 83 percent.

How often do students use a history textbook? According to them:

	Daily	2–3 times a week	Once a week	Less than once a week	Never
Total	59.6%	21.0%	8.5%	6.2%	4.7%

With amazing consistency, the same figures appear for almost every group across the spectrum, with only one major exception: In the advantaged suburbs, just 46.5 percent of the students use the textbook every day. About 30 percent of the suburban students use it once a week or less often.

How often do they read stories, biographies, or articles about historical people and events?

	Daily	2–3 times a week	Once a week	Less than once a week	Never
Total	16.9%	19.1%	20.6%	26.3%	17.1%

There are some curious patterns in the response to this question. The black and Hispanic students with the lowest scores are more likely than other groups to read stories on a daily basis. Even among girls, the lowest-scoring students are most apt to report reading stories on a daily basis. These associations led us to wonder whether simple stories and biographies are used largely with low-ability students. We wondered further whether biographies and historical narratives have been unfairly stigmatized by the uses to which they are put.

How often do students memorize information?

	Daily	2–3 times a week	Once a week	Less than once a week	Never
Total	22.6%	18.9%	22.3%	18.9%	17.3%

Boys are more likely to memorize daily than girls, and blacks more than whites or Hispanics. The top quartile black students memorize more than any other group: 49 percent report memorizing daily. Otherwise the pattern here displayed is consistent across all groups, regardless of region, ethnicity, high school track, or parent education. What is more, youngsters who never memorize tend to have lower scores than others in the sample.

How often do students discuss and analyze historical events in small groups?

	Daily	2–3 times a week	Once a week	Less than once a week	Never
Total	11.7%	10.2%	11.4%	23.7%	43.1%

Most experts on teaching insist that there is too much telling and not enough discussion in the classroom, and the figures bear them out. Nearly half the sample says that they never discuss history in their classes. Among the top quartile, an even smaller proportion attend classes where discussion is frequent. The figures are somewhat higher for some low-scoring students (18 percent of the black students, for example, say that they discuss and analyze daily, as do 15 percent of Hispanic and vocational students); perhaps their teachers are making an extra effort to get the lesson across. On the whole, though, it appears that classroom discussions are not an important feature of the history course as the students see it.

How often do students do history homework at home?

	Daily	2–3 times a week	Once a week	Less than once a week	Never
Total	24.9%	29.3%	19.1%	13.6%	13.0%

Most groups report doing about the same amount of history homework, but black students and students in nonpublic schools are most likely to have daily history homework (about 30 percent of them do). The group that does the most history homework is the top quartile black students: 39 percent do it daily.

How often do history students get comments from their teacher on their work? About half the students report that they receive comments less than once a week or never. The 13 percent who get daily comments are often weaker students; the top quartile students are least likely to get daily attention from the teacher.

In the eyes of the students, the typical history classroom is one in which they listen to the teacher explain the day's lesson, use the textbook, and take tests. Occasionally they watch a movie. Sometimes they memorize information or read stories about events and people. They seldom work with other students, use original documents, write term papers, or discuss the significance of what they are studying.

Literature

The learning area committee for the literature assessment posed a series of "yes-no" questions, rather than the frequency questions put to the history students. Again, the object was to try to determine what classroom practices are typical from the students' perspective.

Students were asked, "Does or did your teacher do the following things in your current or most recent English course?":

- "Talk about the historical period during which an author wrote?" Answering yes are 76.2 percent of the students. This is a practice that is strongly associated with high-performance students. Of those in the top quartile, 90 percent are in classrooms where teachers talk about the historical setting of the author. The students who checked no tend to have scores that are far below the national average. In most groups—boys and girls, whites and blacks, and different regions of the country—three-fourths of the students say that their teacher talks about the historical period. But there are significant variations. Only 65 percent of Hispanic students and inner-city students say their teachers do this, compared with 81 percent of those in suburban schools. Eighty-five percent of students in nonpublic schools checked yes, compared with 75 percent of students in public schools. Students in the academic track are far more likely to be in such classes than students in either the general or the vocational track.

- "Talk about an author's style and use of language?" According to the students, 85.4 percent have teachers who do this. This is a practice that is strongly associated with higher student performance. Moreover, 90 percent of the students in the academic track, in nonpublic schools, and in suburban schools report that their teachers talk about style and use of language; so do the teachers of 95 percent of the top quartile. The figure dips down to about 75–77 percent of Hispanic students, inner-city students, and students in the general and vocational tracks. The students whose teachers do *not* talk about an author's style and use of language are at the low end of the performance scale.

- "Talk about plot and character development?" Eighty-seven percent of the sample say that their teachers do this. This seems to be a nearly universal practice among English teachers, except that it is reported by only 79 percent of Hispanic and inner-city students. The small minority of students whose teachers do not talk about plot and character development tend to have scores at the low end of the performance scale.

- "Talk about themes, meaning, and interpretations of a work of literature?" This too is a nearly universal practice among English teachers: 86.4 percent of the students checked yes. Yet even with a practice so universal, there are significant divergences among student groups. This practice is reported by 95 percent of students in the top quartile, 92 percent of students in the suburbs, the academic track, and nonpublic schools, as compared to 77 percent of the vocational students, 82 percent of inner-city students, 81 percent of Hispanics, and 86 percent of public school students.

- "Talk about how a work of literature relates to students'

experiences?" To this question, 46.7 percent of the students say that their English teachers relate what they are reading to students' lives, and 53.3 percent say that their teachers do not do this. This balance between yes and no responses holds true across all groups, regardless of race, parent education, public or nonpublic, or type of community. The only significant variation from this pattern is among the top quartile black students, where 53 percent report that their teachers try to make literature relevant to their lives; however, in the top quartile as a whole, 53.8 percent say that their teachers do *not* do this. There is no association that we can discern between the students' proficiency scores on this assessment and the teacher's use or nonuse of this practice.

- "Ask students to give their opinions about what they read?" Eighty-one percent of the sample say that their teacher asks for their opinions. There are some variations to this response. Nonpublic school students are likelier to be asked their opinion than public school students, by a ratio of 88 to 80 percent. Students in the academic track are far more likely to be asked their opinion than those in the general or vocational tracks. Eighty-four percent of the students in the northeast contribute their views in class, compared with 78 percent of those in the west. Blacks are more likely to be asked their opinion by their teachers than are white students, by a ratio of 86 to 80 percent. Ninety-three percent of the black students in the top quartile say that they are in such classes. Students in classes where their opinions are invited tend to have somewhat higher scores than those who are not.

- "Ask students to write plot summaries of what they read?" Answering yes are 58.3 percent of the students. This practice seems to be used most with the weakest students; positive answers are given by 70 percent of the black students and 66 percent of the Hispanic students, as well as 65 percent of inner-city students. Nonpublic school students are less likely to write plot summaries than public school students, by a ratio of 49 to 59 percent. Among the top quartile students, 51.5 percent write plot summaries, while 63 percent of the top black students do.

- "Ask students to write analyses of plot, characters, mood, setting, and use of language in what they read?" Sixty percent of the students checked yes. Among boys and girls, students in public and nonpublic schools, and blacks, Hispanics, and whites, there is a nearly identical response. But there are a few significant variations. Students in the northeast, students in the academic track, and students whose parents graduated from college are more likely than others to write analyses. Sixty-four percent of the top quartile report writing analyses. Students who write such analyses in their classes tend to have slightly higher scores on this assessment than those who do not.

- "Show a movie or videotape or play a recording about a work of literature?" Sixty-seven percent answer yes. Seeing a movie or listening to a recording in English class is more frequent among students in the academic track (71 percent), the suburbs (73 percent), the top quartile (75 percent), and whites (69 percent). It is least frequent among the bottom quartile (60 percent), the vocational track (60 percent), black students (59 percent), Hispanics (56 percent), and inner-city students (53 percent). This surprised us, as we supposed that teachers faced with less able or more difficult classes would be more apt to use films and recodings as entertaining diversions. More likely, we now think, is that teachers seriously and successfully engaged in the teaching of literature use a multimedia strategy, enlisting films and recordings to increase student interest and to reinforce understanding of written works.

If the students' view is correct, the typical English teacher talks about plot and character development, about an author's style and use of language, and about themes, meaning, and interpretations of whatever literature is read. The students are frequently asked to give their opinion of what they have read. Often they see a movie or listen to a recording about a piece of literature that they are reading. Sometimes they write analyses of the plot, characters, mood, setting, and use of language in the literature they read. Weaker students are given the assignment of summarizing the plot. About half the students have teachers who try to show them how the literature they are reading has meaning for their own lives.

This snapshot of classroom practice is limited, in that it tells us little about what students are reading. Are they analyzing superb stories, poems, novels, and plays, or are they closely studying popular fiction of dubious literary merit? We cannot answer that question with the material available from this assessment, but we think that it should be asked—regularly.

We emphasize, as we did at the outset, that the reader ought not infer that a particular classroom practice "works" because it is associated with high-scoring students or that some other classroom practice is a failure because it is associated with low-scoring students. An association is not a cause. An assessment of this kind is not a controlled experiment. From the data available, we can identify some of the practices that are found in high-scoring districts in the suburbs or among high-scoring students in the academic track. But it would be foolish to assert that the scores of these students are high *because* of a given practice. Many different elements produce and encourage high academic achievement; we think some of them may have been isolated on the background questionnaire for this assessment. But all of them certainly were not.

Readers of this book will reach different conclusions about the relationship between the practices described here and the achievement of the students. We encourage such speculation, because there are many divergent paths to academic achievement. Debate, discussion, criticism, and renewed dedication to improving the quality of our children's education will move us farther along; neglect and indifference will not.

4

A Generation at Risk

If you believe that the specific information included in this assessment is both valuable in its own right *and* a reasonably representative selection from a far larger menu of important knowledge that ought to belong to all our youngsters by the time they complete high school, it is impossible to avoid the conclusion that something is gravely awry: despite exceptions, notwithstanding variation, and with due deference to the shortcomings of all such assessments, our eleventh graders as a whole are ignorant of much that they should know. We cannot be certain that they were taught it; but the evidence is unmistakable that they do not know enough of it.

We do not assert that American youth know less about the past than their predecessors. This may be true, but one cannot verify it from the data presented in this book. This assessment was administered once, and there are no previous test results with which it can be compared. Based on the findings reported here, we are not able to state that history and literature in the schools are taught (and learned) either better or worse than they used to be. We simply don't know.

Yet the absence of earlier baseline data must not keep us from establishing a standard of present expectations. Ours is based on the premise that there are some things almost all students should know by the time they are juniors in high school. We—and the learning area committees that designed the objectives and approved the test items—expected that students would be able to answer the great majority of the questions on the history portion; with only a few exceptions, they are questions about people, places, events, and trends that are included in the most widely used textbooks in American history. Nor, with few exceptions, are the questions difficult. Judged by these expectations, which we think reasonable and by no means demanding, the national average of 55 percent on the history portion is a shameful level of performance.

Our expectations were not as high for the literature assessment, because we were not sure what students read in their English courses. We recognized that some of the questions pertained to authors and works that had probably not been encountered by many students (e.g., James Joyce, T. S. Eliot, Henrik Ibsen, William Blake). But when we saw the results we were surprised to discover that only a small minority of the students recognized other authors who we thought were firmly established in the high school curriculum, authors such as Ralph Ellison, Joseph Conrad, Willa Cather, and Thomas Hardy. Even more surprising was the poor performance of many students on simple questions of general knowledge, such as those drawn from biblical or mythological literature. It sometimes appeared that the only common threads in students' knowledge may be those provided by movies or television, via their translations of literary themes into the popular culture.

We do not assert that American 17-year-olds are stupid, that they are apathetic, or that they are short on savvy, creativity, and energy. We do not contend that the "younger generation is going to the dogs." We merely conclude that it is ignorant of important things that it should know, and that it and generations to follow are at risk of being gravely handicapped by that ignorance upon entry into adulthood, citizenship, and parenthood.

This assessment is not an exercise in finding fault with the youngsters themselves or in placing blame on them for the gaps in their knowledge. We suspect that the generation whose representatives were sampled in this assessment is an enormously capable group. They have been the beneficiaries of one of the best, most highly developed school systems in the world. Few people their age, whether in this country or abroad, have had equivalent educational opportunities. Not only do they have more years of schooling than most young people in the world today (and most Americans of yesterday), they are also surrounded by the riches of an "information society": television, newspapers, magazines, computers, movies, books, radio, libraries, and countless educating institutions, such as Scouts, unions, museums, universities, political parties, and so on.

Far from being constrained and sheltered, this generation is bombarded by information, far more than its members can understand and assimilate, and by agencies trying to persuade them to do something, to buy something, to try something. These boys and girls are busy: all of them go to school, about half of them have part-time jobs, most of them do some homework, and almost all of them watch television, in many cases vast quantities of it. In addition, they surely set aside some time for their social lives, their hobbies, their sports, and their other personal interests. This is not a parochial generation: through the television sets in their homes, they have seen more of the world than any others before them.

But can they make sense of what they see and hear? Do they have the perspective to separate what is important from what is trivial? What is durable from what is ephemeral? Can they interpret the significance of the day's news? Are they able to discern patterns in trends and events? Are they capable of introspection? Can they relate their experiences to universal themes that have been explored by great writers through the ages? These are only a few of the potential benefits of the study of history and literature.

As we review the findings, we wonder whether this generation knows enough of the past to enjoy these benefits, enough to be able to reflect on what others did and believed long before they were born, enough to compare their own experiences with those of previous generations. We wonder how they will be able to "stand on the shoulders of giants" if they do not know who are the giants and who are the pygmies. Like others in the education profession, we value critical thinking; we earnestly believe that critical thinking requires context, perspective, and breadth, precisely the kinds of vicarious experiences that can be gained through the study of history and literature.

We did not anticipate that this assessment would identify budding historians or would-be literary critics; we expected that it would produce reliable data about whether juniors in high school have learned basic elements of these two subjects, without which higher levels of reasoning are not likely to occur, at least not in any worthwhile manner. This assessment has now generated a goodly quantity of such data, surely more than anyone has ever had with respect to these subjects and this age group. And we are deeply uneasy about what it portends for these boys and girls, for the society they will inhabit, and for the children *they* will rear.

The youngsters are not the causes of their own ignorance. Of course, it would be grand if more of them had innate enthusiasm for history and literature and a high degree of motivation to learn these subjects. But we do not believe that many children naturally gravitate to academic subjects or spontaneously immerse themselves in the lore of their civilization. Children are often not the best judges of what they need to do and know. In general, we believe that children learn pretty much what the important adults in their lives make a point of seeing that they learn: in school, at home, and through myriad other means.

Nor is it fair to pin the blame on teachers, to make them scapegoats for the extent of cultural illiteracy that the assessment found. Teachers customarily do not establish state curricula, do not set graduation requirements, do not control textbook selection, do not determine the content of primetime television. They are constrained by the behavior and attitudes of many other agencies, institutions, and individuals. No single actor or agency among them can set things right. All must work together to achieve the literacy we want for all American children.

By what mechanisms, then, do adults see that children learn things? Five, mainly: (1) by developing a clear sense of what children *ought* to learn, i.e., by setting curricular objectives and standards; (2) by making available the necessary information, whether through books, the media, or other means, i.e., by providing the appropriate instructional materials; (3) by explaining, questioning, coaching, and cajoling until children understand what adults want them to understand, i.e., by teaching them; (4) by illustrating the benefits and virtues of knowing such things, i.e., by setting a good example; and (5) by creating feedback and accountability mechanisms such that children and adults both know how much and how well the former have learned what was taught.

Though we phrased that paragraph in the argot of formal education, in fact those "mechanisms" apply to virtually every instructional relationship of a purposeful sort that exists between adults and children. If you believe, as we do, that children are not likely to learn about the Declaration of Independence or the Great Depresson or the voyage of Odysseus or the uncertainties of Hamlet unless adults see to these things in a purposeful way, and if you conclude, as we do on the basis of this assessment, that today's youngsters have not learned nearly enough of such things, then you must hold the adults ultimately responsible. The grownups who determine what and how well the children learn are not living up to their responsibilities. In the remainder of this chapter we will offer some suggestions as to how we—the adults, the grownups, the members of our generation—might yet do a better job so as to reduce the risk to the generations that follow.

PROPOSALS FOR IMPROVING THE TEACHING
AND LEARNING OF HISTORY

RECOMMENDATION: Teach history in context so that people and events are seen in relation to consequential social and economic trends and political developments. A richly drawn portrait of a given time and place must also include a sense of the life of the times: the ideas that influenced people's behavior; their religious, philosophical, and political traditions; their literature, art and architecture; the state of their knowledge and technology; their myths and folktales; their laws and government.

History is a story about what happened (or did not happen) in a given time and place. Learning history involves the systematic study of time and place, when and where, chronology and geography. Skilled historians write vividly about events and people. They are capable of setting a scene in which political, social, and economic trends establish the background of events; they know that their readers' interest will flag unless they bring the past to life through absorbing stories of extraordinary men and women, heroes and villains, leaders and common folk. They marshal facts to explain what happened and to provide accurate evidence.

This assessment tested basic knowledge of American history, and it asked for discrete information about events, people, and trends. We do not suggest that these facts (or any others) should be taught in isolation. That may be the very *worst* way to teach history.

Facts are very important, but they must be used judiciously, so that students are able to understand what happened in the past and why they should learn about it. The basic facts of history are meaningless unless they illuminate a significant story. History should be taught in context, and emphasis should be placed on the significance of major events, people, trends, and turning points in the past. Without such context, students cannot understand the relations among events or derive from their study of history any truly important conceptual understanding.

RECOMMENDATION: Devote more time to the teaching and learning of history. It should be studied from the earliest grades through high school. We cannot expect our students to learn the history of our country and the history of other countries unless there is enough time in the curriculum for these studies.

History cannot be well taught in a hurry. It needs to accumulate, slowly, carefully, steadily. One year out of twelve is not enough; neither are three years. When American history or world history is crammed into a single course, teachers are compelled to cover vast quantities of material without the time to examine anything in depth or in context. The study of history, like the study of any other subject, needs reinforcement from year to year, not by annually repeating the same survey course, but by engaging children with more challenging historical studies as they grow in maturity.

History should be taught almost continuously throughout the years of formal schooling, in forms that are well suited to children's ages and abilities. In the early grades, girls and boys should be reading and hearing and playacting historical tales of key events and great historical figures; they should learn about the nature of the past by constructing family histories and local histories. But instead of rich historical content, current social studies textbooks in the elementary years typically contain bland and banal materials about families-in-general and communities-in-general, offering little that is new or exciting to students. Social studies textbooks for the elementary years should include stories about major historical events and biographies of significant people in history.*

By the time they are old enough to take a "real" course in history, which usually occurs in the fifth or sixth grade, chil-

*Diane Ravitch, "Tot Sociology," *The American Scholar* (Summer 1987).

dren should already have internalized extensive knowledge of significant people and events in the past. The first formal history course in the upper elementary grades should be able to build on knowledge gained in the early grades, instead of introducing youngsters for the first time to the study of the past.

Historical studies should be part of every year of junior high school, and at least three of the four years in high school. Ten or eleven years of sequential study of the history of the United States and the rest of the world seems like a lot compared to the three or four years now available in most states and school districts; yet it is barely time enough to develop in-depth understanding of our own country and substantial portions of the rest of the world.

At present, the one or two years of historical study in high school are unduly burdened because of the paucity of background knowledge that students possess when they start their junior-year course in American history. Were history studied continually through the grades, high school juniors would *begin* their studies of American history already familiar with the basic knowledge that was covered in this assessment. By the time they are eleventh graders, they ought to be ready to dissect, explain, and rethink events whose specifics they already know quite well, to question conventional accounts, and to debate historical controversies.

RECOMMENDATION: All students should study at least two years of world history. This should include a close study of the evolution of the democratic political tradition. The historical interconnections among different nations and societies should be understood.

This assessment revealed the interesting fact that nearly half of the sample had studied world/Western history for one year. This is a salutary trend, but it must be recognized that fifty minutes a day for a single year is not enough time to learn the history of the world.

In recent years, there have been heated debates about whether high school students should study the history of

Western Europe or the history of the world. Those who argue for a course devoted to the history of Western civilization point out that our nation's laws, institutions, and political principles have been powerfully influenced by events in Western Europe and the Near East. They contend that if there is only one year of non–U.S. history it should be used to teach our students about the events, people, and ideas that shaped the democratic political tradition.

Others maintain that students must learn about the history of the major nations and cultures that lie beyond the boundaries of Europe in order to be well informed about the world they live in. Important though Western civilization is in our own history, they argue, it should not hold a monopoly on our students' knowledge.

There is something to be said for both arguments, but observe that the debate operates on the assumption that students will study world history for only one year. Frankly, we think that one year of international historical studies is inadequate under any circumstances. At minimum, students should study the history of Western Europe for a full year, and the history of other major nations and cultures for another full year. Even three years, with some of it in the junior high school grades, are hardly too much. In California, for example, the new state curriculum in history requires three years of world history: ancient history in sixth grade, the Middle Ages in seventh grade, and the modern world in tenth grade. Such an approach makes it possible to show the relationships among different nations and empires and to draw interesting historical comparisons. Other sequences are possible, but in every instance sufficient *time* must be provided for depth, context, and reflection.

RECOMMENDATION: Chronology must be recognized as a basic organizing concept in the study of history, in that it helps make sense of events in the past and the relationships among them.

Those who do not know the sequence of events cannot understand relationships among them, cannot imagine how one affected the other, nor speculate about causes and effects. Without knowledge of chronology, everything that happened in the past becomes truly puzzling, because there is no way of spotting patterns, sorting out sequences, or seeing connections. Without a secure sense of chronology, all that remains of history is a stew of facts and meaningless concepts.

During the 1960s and 1970s, there was a faction within the social studies field that derided the importance of chronology, treated it as a boring impediment, and preferred the study of topics and themes without regard to the chronological relationships among them. This point of view unfortunately took hold in many school districts. The results of this assessment suggest that it was a more potent movement than anyone imagined.

RECOMMENDATION: The study of history at every grade level should incorporate the study of geography. Geographic literacy enables students to understand how people and the places they inhabit influence each other.

While students' knowledge of geography is stronger than their knowledge of chronology, it is far from satisfactory. The geographic questions were not difficult. Most should have been answered correctly by 90 percent or more of the students, but were not. Students did best when all that was asked was a simple place identification—e.g., locating the Soviet Union on a map (92 percent did)—but worst when they were expected to integrate their knowledge of geography with their knowledge of history—e.g., identifying the area on the map of the United States that was purchased from France (only 57 percent knew).

Geographic knowledge of a basic sort is readily available to young people, in school and out. History textbooks have many maps, often colorful and richly detailed. So do newspapers and weekly news magazines. Nor is it uncommon to see maps on the nightly television newscasts, to enable viewers to understand a new development in Sri Lanka, San Salvador, or South Dakota.

To be sure, knowledge of geography is far more complex than merely knowing where to find different continents, nations, states, cities, mountains, and rivers on a map or globe. Geographic literacy begins with place awareness, and that includes not only where a specific location is in relation to other places but also the nature of its physical characteristics; the interaction of physical characteristics of the land with the human activities and settlement patterns found there; and the ways in which the interaction of people and physical environments change each other.

The assessment of geographic literacy was not a primary purpose of this project. NAEP plans a full assessment of geographic knowledge in 1988, to be carried out with the assistance of the National Geographic Society, which has been concerned about the teaching of geography in the schools. There is a widespread perception that geographic instruction has not kept pace with the need for geographic knowledge, and the 1988 assessment will establish whether this is the case.

For our purposes, we are concerned that students have not made the connection between history and geography. Geographic learning, including but not limited to place names, is an essential element of historical study. Past events occurred in particular places, and characteristics of the place often influenced human behavior. Students need to understand how the presence of isolating geographic factors, like a mountain range or a desert, affects cultural development, and how physical characteristics of the land affect migration patterns, trade routes, invasions, wars, and economic development. We were not able to investigate students' understanding of these more conceptual aspects of geography, and we hope that future assessments will not neglect the vital link between history and geography.

RECOMMENDATION: Enliven the study of history by the frequent use of narratives, journals, stories, biographies, and autobiographies. Students should understand that the past is not simply an unfolding of social, economic, and political trends, but is the story of men and women whose decisions, beliefs, actions, and struggles shaped the world as we know it.

Just as chronological history was in disfavor in the past generation, so too was narrative history. According to the students in the sample, the practice of reading stories and biographies is not common in American high school classrooms. Most class time is spent listening to the teacher explain the lesson, using the textbook, or taking a test. Only 36 percent of the students report that they read stories and biographies a few times a week; nearly half the students say that they do so less than once a week or never. We think this is unfortunate, because history as a tale well told is both an honorable tradition and a powerful teaching tool. Many of the great historians have achieved renown because of their power as storytellers, their ability to write absorbing accounts that are as exciting as fiction. Even young people who genuinely like the study of history have been wrongly persuaded that a thrilling story can't possibly be history.

Good history doesn't always have to be entertaining, but it never needs to be boring. Studies show, however, that many students designate history and social studies as their most boring subject. We wonder whether it is because of this ingrained notion that narrative history is somehow less accurate, less scientific, less scholarly than history as told by textbooks.

With rare exceptions, the textbooks follow the analytic mode of social science; curriculum writers do so as well. The trouble with this approach is that it tends to be so global, so alert to large social and economic trends, that the actions and fates of individuals tend to get lost or ignored. For students who comprehend abstractions, the social science approach is functional; many students, however, do not become engaged by this bloodless way of recounting the past. They become bored. We suspect that they would not be bored if they could learn about the past through exciting and true stories of men and women; through historically accurate and dramatic portrayals of human struggle, triumph, and tragedy. In other words, more stories, more biographies, and more autobiographies will help to infuse a sense of passion and excitement into the study of history.

RECOMMENDATION: Stress the human dimension—how individuals have shaped events—in order to engage the interest and fire the imaginations of boys and girls. Call attention to the struggles, accomplishments, and failures of men and women; the elements of character that made some men and women heroic and others villainous; the individual decisions that affected the lives of others and the course of history.

Girls did worse on the history assessment than boys, and somewhat better on the literature assessment. One explanation for the girls' superior performance on the literature assessment is that they read more in their free time than the boys do; they also do more homework than the boys. But why, we wondered, do they do worse in history?

We do not conclude that the test was biased against girls, or that history as a discipline is biased against girls. We looked at the items on which girls perform better to see if there were clues. Girls are more likely than boys to know who Susan B. Anthony and Jane Addams were and to know that women gained the right to vote in 1920. But boys are more likely to know that women worked in factories during World War II and that the Seneca Falls Declaration concerned women's rights. Girls outperform boys in identifying the meaning of *laissez faire, secession,* and *nullification.* More girls than boys know that President Washington warned against entangling alliances and that Woodrow Wilson tried to lead the nation into the League of Nations. They are also more likely to know that the great wave of immigration at the turn of the century came from southern and eastern Europe and that the "three-fifths compromise" in the Constitution concerned the counting of slaves for purposes of representation.

So far as we can tell, the questions on which girls outperform boys have no consistent thread or pattern. It is difficult, also, to get too excited about the girls' "superior" performance on these questions because even when they outscored the boys their scores were far from impressive. On none of the questions where the girls did better was their performance outstanding; and the same may be said for the boys.

Yet there is a consistent difference in performance on the history assessment, and it favors the boys. As we noted in Chapter 3, some observers think that the way to engage girls' interest in history is to include more material about women's role in history. We certainly agree that there should be more material about women's role in history, simply for the sake of historical accuracy and completeness. But it would be the rankest sort of sexism to propose that girls should concern themselves with women's history while boys attend to affairs of state and power.

The problem is not to find more topics or questions that girls will do well on, but to understand why girls, on the average, are not learning much history. Yet there is nothing in the assessment that explains why girls do not do as well in history as boys. Perhaps they have been socialized to believe that the usual subject matter of history—politics, war, and power—is reserved for men. Perhaps girls are interested in problems that involve people, human relationships, and emotions rather than abstract principles and war. We know that such issues are vigorously debated among social scientists, and we are not qualified to say whether either of these views is correct.

We do believe, however, that the results of the assessment suggest a resolution to this dilemma. The fact that girls tend to do better than boys on the literature assessment strikes us as significant. We believe that the girls do better because the materials in literature are typically presented in a lively, engaging, and dramatic fashion. By contrast, history textbooks tend to stress a dry, fact-by-fact recitation, strung together by social science concepts. This is unfortunate, because history contains as much drama, adventure, tragedy, and comedy as literature. But drama is not the form in which adolescents usually are introduced to history. In order to care about history, students have to understand that real people were involved, that they took risks, acted nobly or were cowardly or just survived; and that they never knew how things would turn out. Students must develop empathy and see the past as those living at the time saw it, in all its misguided certainties and obvious confusions.

As we observed in the previous recommendation, the best historians are great storytellers. Unhappily, this tradition of history seems to have disappeared from most textbooks. We believe that if this approach to history were emphasized in the schools, with equal stress on accuracy, controversy, and human drama, then girls and boys alike would find it a more exciting subject.

PROPOSALS FOR IMPROVING THE TEACHING AND LEARNING OF LITERATURE

Literature proved to be a difficult area to assess mainly because so little is known about what literary works have been read by today's eleventh graders. Yet much of value can be gained by improving the questions and regularly appraising the state of literature in the schools. One of the most informative questions on the assessment, we think, is the one that asked students which of ten novels they had read, and whether they read the book for school or on their own (see table, page 186). We hope that future assessments will expand this list substantially, adding well-known plays, short stories, and poems, so as to improve the state of knowledge of what is taught and what students read on their own. Here, too, would be an appropriate spot for an open-ended question for students: who is your favorite author? what is the best novel or poem or play or short story you ever read?

The most disturbing finding of the literature assessment was not the answer to any single item, but rather the cumulative impression that students do not know many of the common allusions, especially those drawn from the Bible and mythology, that regularly appear in serious literature. Classical mythology was once taught in all American schools to all children, not just to the gifted. This is how allusions to an "Achilles' heel" or a "Pandora's box" or a "Midas touch" became part of the everyday vocabulary of practically everyone. Virtually every schoolchild could explain what a Trojan horse was or whose face launched a thousand ships. The results of this assessment suggest that this kind of background information can no longer be taken for granted by writers and speakers, even by editorial cartoonists. Similarly, knowledge of key biblical references, once universal regardless of one's religion or lack of it, seems to be slipping away. If students had been asked to identify rock stars or sports celebrities, their scores would doubtless have been far higher. But by the time the results were published, the stars and celebrities of the day would already have changed. Besides, what sort of society has in common only its celebrities of the moment?

Children should become familiar with mythology and biblical stories not merely to increase their store of allusions and references, but because these are wonderful and often powerful stories with universal resonance. Stories from Greek and Roman mythology and from the Bible have survived for thousands of years because of their capacity to inspire, inform, entertain, and teach us. But they won't survive, except as part of elite culture, unless we teach them and ensure that all our children learn them. They should not be allowed to disappear from our cultural vocabulary, particularly when what is taking their place in some schools are stories of Wonder Woman,

Mr. T, the Incredible Hulk, and other figures from comic books and television. The adventures of comic-book heroes are neither better nor worse for children than other trivia that have been available at least since the invention of the penny press, but they are not appropriate as mainstays of the school reading program. In terms of their cultural value and their contribution to lifelong learning, they can't hold a candle to Odysseus, Medea, Achilles, Antigone, Oedipus, and Hector—or, for that matter, to any number of historical figures who lived heroic lives and provide models of character and valor for young people.

RECOMMENDATION: Devote more time and attention to teaching literature, beginning in the earliest grades and continuing in every year of elementary school, junior high school, and high school.

Classical mythology, fairy tales, legends, tall tales, and biographical stories of important historical figures ought to be part of the daily reading fare in every elementary school classroom, but they are not. Long before students reach high school, they should have read classic poems and short stories and other great works of literature for children. But the mass-market readers that are used in most school districts in the early grades are no help. With few exceptions, they manage to keep myths, folk tales, poetry, and short stories by classic writers like Nathaniel Hawthorne and Washington Irving to a bare minimum. Their pages are overloaded with nonliterary materials, like articles about topics in science and social studies, brief biographies of contemporary figures in sports and other realms of transitory achievement, and many pages of "skill-building" activities. The stories they contain are usually bland, mundane, undramatic, and forgettable. Seldom do they depict boys and girls who like to read, or adults whose education allowed them to make a great contribution to the good of society. Seldom do they contain memorable literature.

RECOMMENDATION: Publishers of readers for schools should include a generous proportion of important literary works among their selections. The space allotted to poetry should also be significantly increased and should include a balanced mix of classic and contemporary poems.

A half dozen reading series have the lion's share of the school "market." Research studies have shown that these readers are the primary tool for instruction in about 80 percent of elementary school classrooms. Their failure to include classic stories, poems, essays, and orations means that most children are unlikely ever to read the writings of significant authors who were well known to their parents' and grandparents' generations. Occasionally, conscientious teachers bring in literature that the approved textbooks do not contain, but it is hard to see why the presence of literature that is undeniably superior should be a serendipitous matter.

Poetry was once a major feature in school readers; children of an earlier time learned to recite poems by Longfellow, Whittier, Emerson, Poe, Rossetti, the Brownings, Stevenson, and other classic poets. Contemporary textbooks seldom contain more than one or two classic poems, and allot less than 3 percent of their pages to any poetry. We can't expect students in high school to be familiar with good poetry unless they have encountered it repeatedly, in every grade, beginning in kindergarten and continuing through high school.*

RECOMMENDATION: Textbook publishers should solicit the advice of English teachers and literature scholars in selecting the contents of the reading textbooks and anthologies that they prepare for the schools.

There are many reasons why today's mass-market readers are deficient, and their neglect of classic literature is only

*Diane Ravitch, "Where Have All the Classics Gone? You Won't Find Them in Primers," *The New York Times Book Review* (May 17, 1987): 46.

one of them. For the purposes of this assessment, however, it is critical. Perhaps they neglect classic literature because they try to be all things to all subjects, instead of literary readers. Or perhaps they are so grievously lacking in classic literature because their editors and boards of consultants rarely include anyone other than reading experts, curriculum specialists, and other educationists, rather than teachers and professors of literature. Of all the problems in the teaching and learning of literature, this one should be the most easily solved.

RECOMMENDATION: A hefty dose of good literature should be part of all students' English studies. Excellent fiction and nonfiction should not be reserved for the gifted, the college-bound, and the honors classes. Outstanding novels, plays, short stories, poems, and essays by great writers should be read by all students.

One of the most disturbing implications of these findings is that students from the most favorable circumstances, children of college graduates, in the academic track, and in nonpublic schools, spend significantly more time studying literature than students from less advantaged backgrounds. This practice reflects a widely held view that only the brightest students can read works by serious authors, even though many serious authors wrote literature for children or literature that is easily understood by anyone who can read.

Good literature should not be reserved for those who are already privileged. The average and slow students have as much right to be educated to enjoy and understand good literature as do the children who are bound for college. It is difficult to find the right novel, play, poem, or short story that will grip the imagination of slow readers, but the best English teachers have always known how. The effort must be made, for only by reading good literature with the assistance of a skilled teacher will children learn to appreciate the power of written language to make us laugh or cry or understand ourselves better; only by regular encounters with good writing will they develop the habit of reading good books. If average and slow students do not gain this appreciation and these habits in school, they are not likely ever to read the finest writers. They will remain forever ignorant of the writers present and past who have shaped our culture. Schools in a democratic society have an obligation, we think, to eliminate ignorance and not to distribute knowledge along social class lines.

Reading good literature carefully is an excellent way to develop critical thinking skills. Within the context of a gripping story, students can examine the way the writer uses language to affect their emotions, set a tone, build suspense, define character, and create a sense of reality or fantasy. Attention to meaning, to detail, to nuance, to differing interpretations and to a writer's language can be a wonderful exercise in developing what educators refer to as higher-order cognitive skills.

Reading good literature is also an excellent way to teach young people powerful lessons about values, character, and ethics. Great writers are seldom moralistic or didactic, but they do force their readers to think about what is important in life; they do place the values of their characters and of their society under a powerful microscope. And in so doing, they enable the reader to gain powerful insight into psychology, sociology, and moral reasoning. Both in fiction and in nonfiction, students encounter examples of men and women who had to make difficult choices; who made sacrifices for others; who pursued selfish goals and hurt others; who knew how to control and manipulate others; who changed the world through their vision or hard work. The lessons in character that great literature affords us are far superior to the soap operas and dramatic entertainments provided by the mass media. We may not always like the people we meet in great literature, but they compel us to think rather than merely amuse us.

RECOMMENDATION: Teachers, scholars, curriculum planners, and others concerned with the quality of literature in the schools should strive to define the essential ingredients of a coherent literature curriculum, from the earliest grades through high school graduation.

The results of the assessment raise formidable questions about the content of the English curriculum. We urge teachers, scholars, and others in the field to begin to work through the vexing, contentious, but supremely important issues of what does and does not belong in the curriculum, and at what grade levels. A strong core curriculum in literature should begin in the elementary grades and continue throughout every year of formal schooling. It should be built on a foundation of knowledge of mythology, folk tales, fairy tales, and biblical stories; it should be drawn from representative works by such major writers as Shakespeare, Dickens, Wordsworth, Keats, Twain, Whitman, Blake, Dickinson, Hawthorne, the Brontës, Chaucer, Dostoevsky, Emerson, Frost, Melville, Poe, Hemingway, Ibsen, Lincoln, Sophocles, Thoreau, Tolstoy, Baldwin, London, Donne, Fitzgerald, Kafka, Orwell, Plato, Stowe, Swift, Tennyson, Wright, Yeats, Austen, Byron, Coleridge, Eliot, Faulkner, Franklin, Shelley, Hardy, Carroll, Cather, Conrad, Crane, Defoe, Ellison, Scott, Stevenson, Woolf, Welty, Steinbeck, Bellow, Sandburg, Alcott, Hansberry, Doyle, Williams, Miller, Irving, Cooper, Solzhenitsyn, Cummings, O'Neill, Lawrence, de Tocqueville, King, Jefferson, Douglass, Machiavelli, Dubois, Mill, and Darwin, as well as such seminal documents as the Constitution and the Declaration of Independence. This is a massive menu of literary greats; it would not be difficult to add the names of other superb writers of fiction and prose from the United States and other countries. Of course, it is impossible to introduce students to all of them, but students should learn how to read and appreciate the best writers of our own and other cultures, both classical and contemporary.

The critical problems in shaping a coherent curriculum are

how to make selections; which works to offer at which grade
level; how to make connections between the mind of the student and the mind of the author; and how to use samplings of
larger works without losing a sense of the original. If such
issues are debated, there will doubtless be a faction that op-
poses any selection and that continues to advocate a policy of
no policy at all. We will cheer for the faction that lobbies for
a standard of the *best* literature for all youngsters: the best
novels, the best short stories, the best poems, the best plays,
the best essays. English teachers, like everyone else, will disagree on which are the best, but if they all try to find and teach
what they think is best, then there is bound to be considerable
improvement and greater consensus than now exists.

We think that efforts to teach the best literature appropriate
to the ages and abilities of the students will bring into the
mainstream curriculum some unjustly neglected writers such
as Zora Neale Hurston and will enlarge the attention paid to
superb authors such as Ralph Ellison and Richard Wright,
known now to so few students. It should cause a revival of
interest in writers long recognized as giants who have slipped
out of the regular curriculum and into the niche reserved for
classes for the "gifted and talented." Were there more time for
literature in the curriculum, there would be opportunity to
introduce the best writers from other countries as well.

RECOMMENDATION: Teachers of history and English should collaborate to select documents, orations, inaugural addresses, journals,
essays, and other nonfiction that have both literary merit and historical significance.

In the nineteenth century, literary readers for the schools
almost always included examples of important orations; dec-
lamation was then considered a valuable art and skill. Today
it is unusual to find an example of a major speech or historical
document in a literature textbook, even when it has great
literary and historical merit. The consequences show in the
results of this assessment. Lincoln was once regularly an-

thologized in literary readers, because he was a masterful and eloquent writer, as well as one who wrote and said important things. We are pleased that nearly three-quarters of the students recognized the stirring opening passage of the Gettysburg Address. We wish as many students were familiar with the somber and beautiful lines from Lincoln's Second Inaugural Address, "With malice toward none, with charity for all . . ." (only 45.7 percent were).

Just as students should read great novels, poems, short stories, and plays, they should also read outstanding essays, speeches, journals, and other nonfiction. An aptly chosen piece of nonfiction can illumine an issue, an era, a controversy, or the mind of an individual far better than any textbook summary. Lincoln's "House Divided" speech is a compelling description of the events that precipitated the Civil War; Fanny Kemble's depiction of life on a Southern plantation is dramatic and memorable; the Seneca Falls Declaration is a highly readable, pointed statement of the case for women's rights; Patrick Henry's speech to his colleagues in Virginia is forever stirring (and not just its last line); Frederick Douglass's speeches condemning slavery are as passionate today as when he lived. There is no substitute for reading and discussing the Declaration of Independence and the Constitution and Bill of Rights. The act of reading and dissecting such material can contribute substantially to students' ability to think critically about the connection between words and ideas, between ideas and action.

If English teachers do not include historical nonfiction in their classes because it is not quite literary enough, and if history teachers do not include such works because they slow down the onward march of events or the parade of concepts, then students will never have a firsthand encounter with some of the best thinking and most gracefully expressed ideas of our culture. No paraphrase can take the place of the real thing; unless the language of the original is too obscure for students, they should read it for themselves with the teacher's assistance.

Well-written, well-argued essays should also be read as models of expository writing. Not many students will be called upon in the near future to write a novel or a play, but most students are regularly faced with requirements to write an essay, presenting their views on some topic. What better preparation for their own efforts than to read first-rate examples of a brief, clear, persuasive argument? Editorials in the daily press are one source; but when students have the vocabulary to handle rich content, they should read the vigorous prose of writers like George Orwell, Virginia Woolf, and Ralph Waldo Emerson.

WHAT IS TO BE DONE? WHO IS RESPONSIBLE?

Education Policymakers and Administrators

We have discussed the importance of ensuring that all youngsters study more history and literature and ensuring that the history and literature they study are of worth and quality.

But wishing won't make it so and neither will admonishing. Decisions about what students encounter and accomplish in school are the stuff of education policy. For nine out of ten boys and girls in the United States, education policy is a branch of public policy, which is to say it is made by people who are directly or indirectly accountable to the electorate for the wisdom and utility of their decisions. But those attending private schools are also influenced by the public policies of many states as well as by the decisions of their schools' governing boards, religious denominations, parents' associations, and the like.

Much of the impetus to reform and improve American education is now coming from state capitols and governors' mansions; from business roundtables and lay boards; from civic leaders and economic developers. And these people—we have termed them policymakers, to contrast them with education professionals and parents—are given surprisingly often to nonincremental changes, to bold initiatives, to "thinking the unthinkable" once they are persuaded that it is apt to make a material difference in the performance and results of the education system.

Yet rarely do they seem even to think of history and literature, let alone take forceful action to strengthen the teaching and learning of these fields. Every month reports pour forth, urging various education reforms at the national, state, and local levels. They are full of dolorous conclusions and fervent recommendations about basic skills, higher-order skills, math and science, technology and computer literacy, teacher preparation and certification, and on and on, but we could count on our fingers those we have seen that seriously engage the subjects of history and literature. Similarly, the legislative enactments and policy decisions of state and local officials practically never treat these subjects directly, though it is not unusual for bits and pieces of them to get attention under the weary (and in our view inappropriate) headings of social studies and language arts.

This neglect ought not to persist. Policymakers disposed to strengthen the teaching and learning of history and literature possess a number of functional tools and powerful levers that they can operate. Perhaps the most direct approach is for policymakers to make proper use of their control over both the amount of exposure to these subjects that students have en route through school, and the "outcome standards" that youngsters must meet at various stages in the educational process before moving on to work or to further education.

RECOMMENDATION: Require all schools to teach a solid core curriculum of history and literature to all students at every grade level, and require individual students at appropriate points in their school careers to demonstrate satisfactory attainment of substantial amounts of historical and literary knowledge, concepts, and skills before moving on.

The two suggestions need to be linked, of course. An "outcome standard" is either unfair or meaningless if students lack the means of attaining it; but a "process standard"—take history for three or four or eleven years instead of one, two, or four—without accompanying expectations of attainment can quickly decay into busywork or a new label on the same old bottle.

It is within the power of policymakers to direct a wholesale revamping of the humanities curriculum to accent history and literature for most of the twelve years of primary and secondary schooling. What is needed in both subject areas for all students is a *core curriculum,* a commitment by the schools to teach history and literature to all students, as appropriate to their age and ability. Furthermore, we suggest that a genuine core curriculum is inconsistent with tracking as it is now practiced in American schools. One of the clearest findings of this assessment is that tracking serves to limit the exposure of certain groups of students to the study of history and literature; those who are in the college-bound track study more of both than those who are in either the vocational or general track. In effect, those with the most advantages get the best education.

It also lies within the authority of policymakers to stipulate the "exit standards" in these subjects, much as has been done in many jurisdictions with basic skills. Except for elementary facts about history, however, we would caution against the widespread adoption of multiple-choice or fill-in-the-blanks tests as major means of enforcing standards and appraising individual performance. Let the students instead be asked to write a competent book review, to analyze a good poem, to produce a brief essay setting forth the moral lessons of a short story, to write a history term paper, or in other ways demonstrate their ability to handle information, concepts, analysis, and expression at the same time.

RECOMMENDATION: Adjust the school schedule, calendar, and homework policies as needed to expand the time devoted to history and literature without taking time away from other core subjects.

We are not proposing that history and literature take the place of math, science, foreign languages, or the arts. There is room for all the major academic subjects, provided ephemera, busywork, and distractions are purged from the school day; provided the school day and year are long enough; and provided that enough homework is assigned (and done by students and reviewed by teachers).

It is not, of course, sufficient to say that students shall learn more without regard to the resources that will be needed. This is especially important when we are proposing universal inclusion of students in history and literature, instead of the restriction of these key subjects to gifted youngsters, elite schools, or advanced placement courses.

The principal resources that policymakers must concern themselves with are time, teachers, and instructional materials. We have already indicated how we'd find the time: shift the emphasis in existing courses at every grade level from social studies to history, and from language arts to literature; lengthen the total time commitment of students, both in school and out; give priority to history and literature over less important subjects and activities that compete for time under the rubric of social studies and language arts. In addition to increasing the time available for the study of history and literature within the curriculum, teachers should expect students to spend more time outside school reading and writing about these subjects.

RECOMMENDATION: Purchase first-rate history books and supplementary materials and a diverse array of good literature, so that teachers at all grade levels have suitable instructional materials readily at hand. Empanel textbook selection committees that include historians and literature scholars as well as classroom teachers. Improve school libraries.

As with time, a shift and sharpening of priorities can increase the availability of better materials: schools can purchase first-rate textbooks, readers, and supplementary materials instead of mediocre ones, and stop squandering resources on worksheets, workbooks, and costly doodads. One way to find the first-rate textbooks is to cease using irrelevant standards for textbook selection, like the number of illustrations or the mentions of superficial facts or the quantity of consultants and advisers on the masthead. Textbooks should be judged solely by the quality of their content. History textbooks should be selected for the vigor and accuracy of their presentations, and should be supplemented in the classroom with biographies, stories, documents, and so forth. Reading textbooks should be judged by the quality and quantity of the literature they contain. First-rate teachers manage to find the panoply of good materials that are needed; there could be no greater incentive to the production of more such materials than a clear signal that the demand for them exceeds the supply.

RECOMMENDATION: As additional history and literature teachers are needed, open up the ranks of prospective teachers to include all adults with degrees in these fields who are willing to teach what they know to children. Simplify entry into the classroom for such individuals and make provision for on-the-job and in-service training programs, supervised entry years, and other such arrangements by which they can improve their instructional skills without a protracted period of preservice professional study.

We are not entirely sanguine about the availability of enough additional excellent history and literature teachers to transmit a markedly larger amount of first-rate history and literature to a much larger population of students. But the main problem here is not with the potential supply; it is with the sharp constraints that most states slap onto the certification of teachers. The United States contains a very large number of people who majored in English literature or history in good colleges over the past few decades but who are not teaching school. In many cases they are not teaching their subjects in school because they have not attended an approved program of teacher education, and therefore cannot be certified. Much of this problem could be solved by the stroke of a policymaker's pen: redefine the population of prospective literature and history teachers to consist of all adults who are well educated in either of those subjects. And then, through alternative certification, internships, apprenticeships, summer institutes, and short, intensive programs of supervised practice teaching, enable them to acquire in a reasonable period of time whatever additional training they may need in order to transmit their knowledge effectively to students.

Those who love their subject matter and are genuinely interested in young people must take the time to learn the art and craft of teaching, to observe mentor teachers, to familiarize themselves with the strengths and weaknesses of instructional materials, and to learn how to manage a classroom of active youngsters. It is no less important to have well-educated principals and supervisors in these fields, who can assist new teachers, maintain the integrity and continuity of the program in history and literature, monitor the quality of teaching and materials, and protect their staff and programs against unwarranted interference by politicians or pressure groups.

RECOMMENDATION: Only those who are well educated in history or literature should teach those subjects in the schools.

If the ranks of truly outstanding teachers are to increase, then in addition to opening entry to those who did not graduate from colleges of education there should be barriers to those who lack proper training in the disciplines they propose to teach. Anyone who teaches history or literature courses should have at least a bachelor's degree in the subject, and postgraduate study is highly desirable, too. Teachers of the primary grades should have a well-balanced liberal education that includes a substantial quantity of both history and literature. States should require prospective history teachers to have their degree in *history*, not one of the social sciences. Local school boards should cease and desist from using coaches to fill in as history teachers, a practice that is as contemptible as it is common.

The Role of Teachers

Among the ranks of the nation's teachers are many dedicated men and women who love history and literature and who have taught these subjects, year in and year out, despite the failure of the school, the education profession, and the larger society to recognize their value.

RECOMMENDATION: Teachers of history and literature should not only participate in the selection of textbooks and other teaching materials; they should also work collegially to establish curricula for their subjects from kindergarten through twelfth grade, so that children will have a carefully sequenced and developmentally sound preparation in history and literature. Wherever possible, history teachers should enrich their courses with literature, and literature teachers should enrich their courses with history.

Too often these heroic teachers find themselves forced to use textbooks that they do not respect; judged by measures that do not assess their knowledge and skill; saddled with a curriculum that stresses basic skills and competencies but not knowledge of subject matter; burdened by students who were inadequately prepared in the earlier grades; and abandoned by professional associations that have failed to defend the integrity of their disciplines. Despite the disincentives, these teachers bravely persevere. Most improvise: they invent classroom activities; they bring in books, biographies, stories, and documents in order to build a classroom library of worthwhile materials; and, more often than not, they must pay for their ingenuity out of their own pockets.

These teachers need the professional support of their colleagues in higher education; they deserve public recognition for the valiant work they do on behalf of the rest of society. They need a curriculum in which history and literature are accorded an honored place in every grade. They need the freedom and the resources to use "real" books and stories to supplement or even supplant the state-selected textbooks. And they need professional associations that fight for them and the interests of the disciplines.

RECOMMENDATION: Outstanding teachers should be enlisted as expert advisers by the media, libraries, museums, civic organizations, public agencies, and parent groups that want to create programs, materials, and activities to increase the community's knowledge of history and literature.

Teachers are community assets far beyond the walls of their classrooms, but too seldom are they invited to participate in the myriad nonschool affairs in which their knowledge would be valuable and from which they might derive some of the additional status, income, community appreciation, and personal gratification that are scarce commodities in the lives of many teachers.

RECOMMENDATION: Provide all history and literature teachers with ample opportunities to keep up with their subjects, perhaps through summer institutes and workshops conducted by scholars in the field; with ready access to appropriate journals and professional meetings; and with sabbaticals and other recurrent opportunities to read, reflect, and do research in their professional disciplines.

Teachers need to get their batteries recharged from time to time; they need professional renewal and collegial relationships; and they need to keep intellectually keen. As with any professionals, much of this is their own responsibility and that of their peers and professional associations. But those in charge of schools and education policy must also be mindful of these needs and make proper efforts to accommodate them.

RECOMMENDATION: Authors, historians, editors, and other active professionals should be invited into classrooms so that children can meet people who are daily engaged in these fields. They should be encouraged not only to talk about their own work, but to join with teachers and students in discussing historical events or literary works.

Every community has writers, and most have a number of historians, editors, and others who are professionally engaged in these fields. Here and there a local or state humanities council has underwritten a small program to place a "humanist in the school" or a "scholar in residence." For most writers, the opportunity to talk to young people about their art and craft is not only stimulating but a welcome change from their usual isolation. The presence of these professionals provides an object lesson about how writers and editors work, how historians judge evidence and decide what to include, and how poets choose their words and images. Meeting a person who has done these things will help students realize that the authors they read in class were not born as giants but had to learn a craft and find ways to express their ideas, not unlike the students themselves.

Bringing professionals into schools on a regular basis will help to break down the distance between the school and the world of work and ideas; provide a valuable professional interchange for teachers; introduce practitioners in these fields to the way their field is taught in the classroom; and enrich the students' understanding of history and literature as challenging activities that are part of real life, rather than static textbook exercises.

The Role of Higher Education

Other than the schools themselves, no institutions bear greater responsibility for the condition of history and literature than colleges and universities. Not only do they train teachers, but they also set standards of admission for entering students that signal to students, teachers, and school authorities whether the study of history and literature is necessary to enter or succeed in higher education. Their direct responsibility goes still farther, for these institutions maintain departments of history and literature where the humanistic disciplines are studied, criticized, preserved, and redefined. The professors of literature and history in these institutions belong to professional organizations like the Modern Language Association, the American Historical Association, and the Organization of American Historians, which exist to promote the interests of their disciplines.

The results of this assessment lead us to conclude that higher education in all of its different roles has failed to support and defend history and literature in the schools. In every area where the academy's responsibility is clear, its silence, absence, or abdication has been equally clear.

RECOMMENDATION: The quality of teacher-preparation programs should be dramatically improved by strengthening ties between education faculty and faculty in the history and literature departments. Those who expect to teach future teachers need themselves to be first-rate authorities on these subjects as well as superlative practitioners of the craft of teaching.

Nearly all of America's teachers are educated and professionally trained in our colleges and universities. Yet teacher training has been allowed to become the pariah of higher education. Teacher-education programs have low standards of admission, low standards of graduation, and low status on campus. Seldom are their students required to study history and literature; seldom do departments of history and literature become actively engaged in preparing those who will teach their subjects in the schools. In particular, those who will teach elementary school are not expected to know much of either subject, even though they deal with critical years of children's intellectual and emotional development. One year of children's literature is not enough, nor is a single year's course in teaching social studies. Even prospective elementary school teachers—*especially* prospective elementary school teachers—need strong preparation in the subject matter of history and literature. The more solid their preparation, the better equipped they will be to incorporate good literature and to find engaging ways to make the past come to life.

RECOMMENDATION: Higher education should upgrade the quality and quantity of history and literature that are taught in the schools by requiring that students demonstrate a high degree of knowledge and proficiency in these subjects before entering college.

With only a few exceptions, America's colleges and universities lowered their requirements for admission and graduation in the late 1960s. In doing so, they withdrew from their responsibility to inform students about the kind of preparation that is necessary in order to pursue higher education. Furthermore, when state universities and prestigious private colleges no longer required the study of history and literature for admission, the schools ceased requiring them as graduation requirements. This pattern resembles that of the foreign languages, which suffered a deep decline in enrollments when colleges lowered or abolished their entrance requirements. Only the state legislatures, which had less knowledge of curricula than either universities or schools, continued to impose mandates, which were more likely to respond to special-interest campaigns than to reinforce such core subjects as history and literature.

Colleges and universities can turn this situation around by revising their entrance requirements. More than half (52.3 percent) of these eleventh graders plan to attend a four-year college, and an additional 20.6 percent intend to enroll in a two-year college. This means that the vast majority of them will respond readily to the conditions laid down and the signals sent by colleges and universities. So will their high schools.

RECOMMENDATION: Colleges and universities should expand contacts with schools, in order to develop collaborative projects of many kinds, including research seminars, summer institutes, textbook review projects, and curriculum-development activities.

As leaders of their fields, professors have neglected the needs of their colleagues in the schools. The university community accords little professional reward or status to faculty members who take responsibility for teacher preparation, lead research seminars for teachers, or work in curriculum-development projects for the schools. Yet without this involvement by professors, teachers are cut off from the sources of professional stimulation that nourish their intellectual development and their continued vitality in the classroom.

Many professors enjoy deriding their students' abysmal ignorance of history and literature, but few of them have been willing to work collaboratively with schoolteachers in their fields or even to interest themselves in the challenges of teaching their subject to young children and adolescents. It is not coincidental that general knowledge of history and literature in the schools appears to be imperiled at the same moment that specialists in the universities devote themselves to arcane debates among deconstructionists, structuralists, neo-Marxists, and other specialized schools and esoteric interpretations. We do not question the value of healthy theoretical debate within the academy, but we hope that professors of history and literature will stop turning their backs on the needs of the schools, where the foundations for general literacy must be built. Ignoring John Donne's famous admonition, professors of history and literature have acted as if higher education were an island, detached from the problems of the schools. The cultural ignorance of which professors endlessly complain may in part be attributed to negligence on campuses where teachers failed to receive a solid liberal education.

The Role of the Family

Children arrive in school from vastly different home backgrounds. Some come from households where parents read to them, talk to them, take them to museums and plays, and engage in other activities to enlarge their knowledge of the world and their capacity to think about what is going on around them. Others lack these advantages. Yet the schools must educate all children, regardless of their social and cultural origins. We believe that it is an integral part of the responsibility of the schools to try to bridge the gaps created by these initial disparities of circumstance. One way that schools can do this is by giving all children keys to the well-stocked storehouse of history and literature. Failure to make this cultural knowledge part of every child's inheritance serves to reinforce invidious social class distinctions.

As the background data for this assessment show, the family is the child's first educator. In countless ways, families powerfully influence children's attitudes toward learning. There is a vast research literature on the role of parents in promoting children's cognitive development during infancy, by means such as supplying manipulative toys, visual stimulation, emotional rewards, and a supportive environment. Parents also choose whether to send their children to a nursery school or prekindergarten, where children are apt to gain social skills and to engage in learning activities.

Children who live in a literate environment are more likely to do well on an assessment of history and literature than those who do not, and it is families that create such an environment. Parents supply the home with dictionaries, encyclopedias, newspapers, magazines, and books, and their use of these tools of literacy sets a model for their children. Families also provide a television set (though they seldom regulate its use) and, less frequently, a home computer.

The interactions in the home between adults and children are no less important, and possibly even more important, than the presence or absence of printed materials and electronic devices. Children often value what their parents value. Children's interest in the past can be developed by mealtime discussions, by tales of "when-I-was-your-age," by conversations with grandparents, by excursions to historical sites and exhibitions, by attention to the historical content in movies, documentaries, and the daily news, and by reading biographies and histories written for children. In similar fashion, love of literature may be encouraged by parents who read to their children, who share favorite childhood books and poems, who take their children to the local public library and to plays, who read their children's homework with interest, who encourage their children to read and write, who give them books for special occasions, and who find diverse ways to show that they value good literature.

We suspect that one of the reasons the quantity of parent education figures so strongly in student performance is that educated parents are likelier to have the knowledge, motivation, and resources to do these things with their children. But as we also know from the data, there are significant numbers of high-scoring children whose parents do not have a college education. Perhaps their parents gave them as much stimulation as college-educated parents would. Or perhaps these students had other sources of motivation and interest in these subjects, such as a teacher who sparked their curiosity and need to know. There is a voluminous body of research on the role of parents, but there is no equivalent fund of knowledge about inspiring teachers; yet we know from memoirs that they touch the lives of many students who are not expected to succeed.

One of the most important contributions that parents can make toward their children's growth in knowledge of history and literature is to encourage them to read more, beginning at an early age. According to the 1985 Report of the Commission on Reading, "the amount of reading students do out of school is consistently related to gains in reading achievement." The report cites a study of fifth graders which shows that most devoted five minutes or less per day of their free time to reading from books, compared to 130 minutes per day watching television.* Parents who read to their children at bedtime, set aside a special quiet time for reading, read with their children, or make regular trips to the public library can help their children read better and acquire more knowledge. There is a substantial body of research demonstrating that parents can help their children become better readers by reading to them and talking to them about what they read.†

Aside from helping their own children learn, parents can become a potent force in the local community to improve their schools. By joining parent groups, they can become informed about what happens in their children's schools and can advocate stronger programs in history and literature. Parent groups can make their voices heard by policymakers and school officials by insisting on a solid curriculum in these fields, a well-supplied library, homework assignments, and well-educated teachers. When teachers are doing a fine job, or when school officials put more emphasis on history and literature in the curriculum, parent groups can help by expressing support and appreciation.

The Role of the Media

The mass media and especially television powerfully influence children. There may be households where television has even more influence than either the school or the family, because of the preponderant number of hours that the child's attention is focused on the set. As we saw in the background data, a reasonable amount of television-watching is not harmful, and may even be beneficial, presumably because it ex-

---

*The Commission on Reading, *Becoming a Nation of Readers* (Washington, D.C.: U.S. Department of Education, 1984), 77.

†*What Works: Research About Teaching and Learning* (Washington, D.C.: U.S. Department of Education, 1986), 9.

poses some youngsters to a broader range of experiences and information about the world than they would have if there were no television in their home. However, we found that students who watch more than three hours per day of television tended to have lower scores on the assessment than those who watched less. According to the students, few of them have family rules about how much television they are permitted to watch. Parents should consider restricting television-watching and establishing a daily time for reading and study.

Many teachers are convinced that excessive television watching subverts students' motivation to learn. According to Patrick Welsh, an outstanding high school English teacher and author who served on the learning area committee for the literature assessment:*

> When I asked some of these kids what they'd do if they were assigned three hours of homework a night, many replied that they'd refuse to do it. "If you mess with people's TV, they'd quit school. I can't read your books because I've got my programs to watch," says one delightful girl who's yet to finish more than 20 pages of any novel I've assigned this year. These same kids can rattle off every character and detail in the soap operas and sitcoms but have little knowledge of our common cultural heritage. Recently when a class was studying "Hamlet," many of the students thought that Shakespeare was born before Jesus; not one member of the same class knew who Cain and Abel were.

We do not suggest that television is an unmitigated evil, but it is hard to dispute Welsh's conclusion that "excessive TV has been one of the major factors in making many kids intellectually lazy." And as with any sustained self-indulgence, it can also lead to dependency, poor self-discipline,

*Patrick Welsh, "Our Teens Are Becoming Lookworms—Instead of Bookworms," *TV Guide* (May 23, 1987): 3.

an inability to defer instant gratification, and other bad habits that undermine one's character. "To many kids," Welsh writes, "TV seems like drugs or alcohol. They speak of themselves as addicts and are embarrassed by the time they spend in front of the tube. 'I've been hooked since I was 9. It started with the soaps. I always say that I'm going to stop, but I never do. It's gotten so bad that I take my portable TV along in my car so that I won't miss anything,' says an 18-year-old senior girl."

Of course, the medium of television also has genuine potential for good, and leaders of the broadcasting industry should conscientiously reflect on how they can use their vast power to promote interest in history and literature. Series like *Roots* and *Holocaust*, though they have been criticized for fictionalizing historical events, were enormously successful in bringing the past to life for many millions of viewers. There must have been many among their audiences who learned for the first time about the brutality of black slavery and the Nazi campaign to annihilate the Jews of Europe. Even among those who already knew, these programs had an immediacy that was deeply affecting. The dramatic presentation of these events was a powerful history lesson, and it may well have inspired many viewers, young and old alike, to search out books on these subjects.

Television productions of great dramas have had a similar effect. When a commercial network broadcasts a play by Shakespeare or Beckett, millions of people see it, more than would ever see it if it ran for years on Broadway. When *Nicholas Nickleby* was televised, all eight hours of it, a new demand was created for the book. And *Silas Marner*, which had been dropped from the high school curriculum because of its lack of relevance, may at last have been redeemed by Ben Kingsley's television portrayal of the old bachelor. For many communities distant from major cities or university towns, the television screen may offer their only connection to dramatizations of history and literature.

In recent years, the film industry has largely neglected history and classic literature as a source for scripts. During the 1930s, '40s, and '50s, however, the film industry regularly turned to great books as sources for mass-market movies. The film version must surely have inspired many viewers to read the original, the "real thing." Many Americans read *Moby-Dick* only after seeing Gregory Peck as Captain Ahab. Others bought their own copies of books by Dickens or the Brontës after seeing the movies on late-night television. The power of movies to stimulate the wish to *read* the story is proved by the curious trend in recent years to write a book based on a movie—a process now known as "novelization"—in order to capitalize on the success of the latter.

The mass media can help children and their teachers by dramatizing significant events in history and great works of literature. We have seen from our background data that movies and videotapes are used in classrooms to catalyze students' interest in the subject matter. The television industry already understands that an important program with educational value should be accompanied by teachers' materials and background information and should be publicized through the schools.

Unfortunately, television has virtually abandoned a variety of formats in which knowledge of history was explicitly enhanced. For example, in the early days of television, there were regular discussion programs where historians and knowledgeable participants talked about critical issues, relating past to present. And there were regular documentary programs like *See It Now* and *You Are There* which brought history to life with the vigor and immediacy that television specializes in. Even game shows once rewarded people with superior knowledge of history and literature; today, game shows place no premium on knowledge of anything but popular culture or television lore.

We don't expect that commercial television will invest in unprofitable ventures, but we can at least hope that the major networks will find ways to popularize history and make it come alive, as they have done in the past.

The evolution of new video technology is creating additional possibilities for information distribution in homes and classrooms. We hope that interactive software, videodisks, videocassette recorders, and whatever other gadgets and gimmicks the future holds will not be limited only to the amusing, the useful and the mundane, but will also serve to record the best writing and thinking of the ages; it seems just that the inventions of the future should be employed to preserve the momentous events of the past. Hints of the future are already at hand, in the form of computer software that analyzes historic decisions and of commercially produced film encyclopedias for classroom use containing footage of historic figures and events.

It should go without saying—but we will say it anyway—that the new technology ought not to become a substitute for print. Some forms of literature, like a play or sometimes a poetry reading, can be presented better on film than in a book. But a movie of a novel is not a substitute for reading the novel; the film should motivate the reader to turn to the original, not to ignore it. The movie of *Great Expectations* should be used as an appetizer for the authentic novel, which contains delights that cannot be translated into film.

This generation, as well as their younger siblings, has been weaned on television and movies. It takes more than a textbook and a lecture to awaken their interest and grab their attention. Inspired teachers can get their attention by the sheer energy and zeal that they bring to their classes. But even they will welcome the support of those in the media and the assistance of flexible new technologies in the ongoing battle to bring students into ever closer encounters with the best of history and literature.

The Role of Other Agencies

RECOMMENDATION: Public and private agencies, like libraries, museums, historical societies, universities, and others with education programs, should recognize their responsibility to increase the public's knowledge of history and literature and should design their exhibitions, with the assistance of teachers and scholars, not merely as displays but as educational experiences.

Schools are not the only institutions responsible for educating the young, nor should they be the only agencies responsible for fostering young people's interest in history and literature. Other agencies have useful roles to play, too. Public libraries and museums, for example, should no longer think of themselves as institutions where books are stored or where art is exhibited. They, and institutions like universities and historical societies, should make the general education of the public a high priority. In planning exhibitions, they should bear in mind that a significant part of their potential audience knows nothing about the subject of the exhibition.

Public libraries must acknowledge an obligation to *foster* literacy and knowledge. Acting as a repository of information is no longer sufficient to define their mission, if ever it was. They must join hands with the schools and agencies of adult education to attract new audiences and to develop new programs that educate the public. Good libraries have long offered story hours for young children, great-books discussion clubs for adults, and exhibitions on special literary or historical themes. These services may now need to be expanded to include basic reading programs, book clubs for teenagers, and book-and-author programs for students.

Public libraries should also take a different approach to their exhibitions. In the past, it may have been sufficient to mount a display of Shelley's letters, a rare illuminated Bible, or a first edition of Herman Melville, with each item accom-

panied by a two-or-three-line description. The assumption behind such a display is that viewers know a great deal about the
subject and want only to see the actual objects with their own
eyes. Such an assumption is no longer valid. The public today
needs to be educated by such exhibitions; it needs written
material to accompany the objects in which the historical
setting and context are fully explained. The letters of a poet
must be accompanied by his or her poems and critical comments on the poet's style, life, and milieu. The significance of
each displayed item must also be explained. Those who create
these exhibits must see them as exercises in public education,
not confined to the cognoscenti, but intended for a sizable
portion of the public that is interested but uninformed. Such
strategies are not merely a matter of public responsibility for
libraries but a recipe for survival.

When public libraries and museums celebrate Black History Month, for example, exhibitions should be designed not
merely to commemorate some aspect of black history, but as
an education for visitors who know little or nothing about the
past. Libraries, museums, and schools should work together
to develop curriculum materials, so that the general public as
well as schoolchildren will have the chance to read the background material that explains photographs, films, and objects.
Exhibitions of this kind provide an excellent opportunity for
collaboration among high school history teachers and professional historians to create background material for use both
at the exhibition itself and in schools. Bibliographies should
be made available, referring interested persons to books that
are easily obtainable in the library or bookstores.

Other public agencies can measurably increase their contributions to public literacy. The National Endowment for the
Humanities, for example, has sponsored scores of excellent
television programs about history and literature. These programs, produced at great public expense and greeted with
critical acclaim, are typically shown on public television once
or twice and then disappear. It would be of enormous value

to schools and to the public if these programs were transferred to videotape and made available to public libraries and schools all over the nation.

The same principle holds for public television, which has also sponsored excellent programs—plays, operas, ballet, documentaries, discussions, historical essays—which are seen once or twice and then consigned to oblivion or permanent storage. Perhaps the advance of technology will make it possible one day to dial up these superb visual presentations for individual viewing, but until that day arrives, there ought to be a well-organized, well-publicized way to rent or borrow or at least rerun these outstanding programs that had their season and then vanished.

HOW CAN FUTURE ASSESSMENTS BE IMPROVED?

RECOMMENDATION: Knowledge of both history and literature should regularly be assessed, just as other core subjects are, among students at various grade levels with questions appropriate for their ages. The emphasis should be on important knowledge rather than content-free skills.

One self-evident but fundamental need is to keep gathering the information by which it will be possible to know whether the situation is improving or worsening. The present effort establishes a baseline for subsequent appraisals of students' knowledge of American history and literature. Future analysts will be able to judge whether students are progressing or not, because they will have comparative data. Although there has never before been a national test of this kind in the subject of history, NAEP appears determined to assess it regularly in the future. This we applaud. Any future national tests or assessments of literature will similarly benefit from the mistakes of this venture as well as from whatever has been learned that proves valuable.

We do not doubt that knowledge of history, especially

American history, can be assessed successfully, because the body of knowledge to which children are exposed is identifiable, finite, and coherent. Literature presents a different and less tractable problem, because of the inherent diversity of the curriculum. The effort to appraise students' knowledge of literature still needs refinement. We are not satisfied with questions that ask for simple associations of titles with their authors or with questions such as the one that asks whether students know that Byron, Keats, and Wordsworth were poets. We wish that the test might have been more subtle, more demanding, more complex. But we also wish that more students could correctly answer some of the extraordinarily simple questions that *were* on this assessment. A better test, in our view, would not simply retreat behind the neutral façade of content-free skills, of questions that ask students to analyze a passage they have never seen before or to fill in a missing word. Literature is one of the chief wellsprings of the background knowledge that literate people require to communicate effectively in modern society. We continue to hope that future literature assessments will gauge whether our youngsters are assimilating the background knowledge that can be gained *only* from literature.

For the future, we hope that those individuals and professional associations like the National Council of Teachers of English and the Modern Language Association that are committed to the survival of good literature will collaborate to develop a better literature assessment. Mindful that test results help to shape the national agenda, those concerned about the quality of literature in the schools should not shun a national assessment of it. In the absence of such studies, those activities that are regularly tested and quantified, like decoding, basic skills, elementary competencies, and other content-free literacy activities, will continue to hold the attention of policymakers and the public.

RECOMMENDATION: Future assessments of history and literature should include a variety of ways to answer questions, not just multiple-choice options. Whenever multiple-choice questions are used on an assessment of knowledge, students should be allowed to select "I don't know" as an answer.

We hope that future assessments will also find ways to improve the manner in which questions are posed. While there are some situations in which a multiple-choice question is efficient and appropriate—for example, chronological questions that allow students to select a period among segments of twenty or fifty years—it ought to be possible in other situations to ask other kinds of questions in which students can answer briefly in their own words. The results demonstrate, we think, the limitations of the multiple-choice format. We understand that this method is cheaper and simpler and less controversial to score, since it can be done quickly by computers. But the drawbacks are substantial, particularly where the purpose is to test knowledge rather than some abstract skill.

Whether questions are posed as multiple-choice or in essay formats, we strongly urge the use of a "don't know" option. When students do not have any idea what the answer is, they should be allowed to admit it, especially when they know that their confession of ignorance will not be held against them. We see no virtue in encouraging random guessing. We admire the student who honestly says "I don't know" instead of wildly stabbing at an answer that looks plausible but is totally wrong. There is nothing shameful about admitting that you don't know something.

Allowing students to check off "I don't know" also has the salutary effect of reducing or nearly eliminating totally random guessing. This in turn would make the assessment results more meaningful. Knowing that random guessing would produce a 25 percent response for any of four possible answers, we could not feel sure about the significance of the results. If 40 percent answered a question correctly, did that mean that 15 percent *really* knew it, and the others guessed randomly? Or that a full 40 percent truly knew the correct answer? We learned in the preliminary field test of this assessment that students are quite willing to mark "I don't know"; test-makers should allow them to do so.

What we saw repeatedly in examining wrong answers was evidence that many boys and girls have become "testwise." They have learned, sometimes from experience, sometimes from direct instruction, that there is a technique to answering multiple-choice questions. The canny test-taker eliminates the clearly wrong answers, then makes a calculated guess between the remaining reasonable possibilities. Smart kids can "psych out" the test-makers by using good test-taking strategies. The difficulty is that the test then rewards students not on the basis of what is ostensibly tested, but on their mastery of test-taking skills.

That path, if followed long enough, will produce a nation of guessers. Perhaps it already has. Intelligent estimating is a skill worth honing, but it seems to have been developed to excess by our dependence on multiple-choice tests. Time and again, we found examples of answers that drew a high response because they were logical, though completely wrong. Other times we realized that word clues within the questions pointed to one or another answer. This kind of gamesmanship distorts the purpose of the assessment and confuses the meaning of the results.

Thus we urge those who design future assessments in history and literature not to rely exclusively on multiple-choice questions, but to devise testing instruments that contain a variety of formats. Where appropriate, multiple-choice questions should be used; where it is not, test-makers ought to permit essay answers. The short-run cost of scoring these answers seems to us to be less than the long-term, invisible cost imposed by a method that encourages superficiality and rewards guessing.

SOME REMAINING QUESTIONS

Is Print Literacy in Peril?

Many people believe that this generation of young people will never be readers because of their immersion in television and various other electronic devices; trying to curb their addiction to blinking screens, it is said, is like trying to squeeze toothpaste back into the tube. Based on what students said in the background questionnaire on this assessment, we disagree. Most of them like television and watch quite a lot of it, but the overwhelming majority also say that they read on their own time. About four out of every five students say that they read at least occasionally for their own enjoyment. This is true for whites, blacks, and Hispanics. It is true whether students went to public school or private school. It is true regardless of the region of the country or the type of community that youngsters live in. Even among students who are "selected" for their lack of academic ability, those in the general and vocational tracks, three out of four say that they read for their own enjoyment.

Unless the students are vastly exaggerating their reading habits, then we have to believe that they have learned that books and magazines provide something that they cannot get from television, rock music, or the movies. Whatever taste they have for literature—and many report that they like to read novels, short stories, and poems—we must credit at least in part to the steadfast efforts of their English teachers. However disheartening the results of the assessment, it is good news that this generation knows that reading confers special rewards.

How Important Is Relevance?

In both portions of the assessment, black youngsters perform better than average on some of the questions that deal with events or authors of special pertinence to the black experience in America. What conclusions should be drawn from these findings? Some may conclude that blacks will perform better overall if they are taught more black history. There is a case to be made for this claim, but we think it is essentially misdirected and altogether too modest a goal. Just as girls need to have sound knowledge about the Constitution and affairs of state, so too do black students need a solid grounding in American history, and not just in that portion that pertains directly to the black experience. (We refer here by implication to other minority groups as well.)

Our own sense is that white students should be as knowledgeable about black history as black students are, because the events and issues that directly affect blacks are important events in *American* history. It should not be the case that blacks know more than whites about Jim Crow laws, the Ku Klux Klan, the "three-fifths compromise" in the 1787 Constitution, and the *Plessy* and *Brown* decisions. All of these are signal developments in the evolution of our national story, some exemplifying milestones of oppression, others signifying the advance of our national commitment to justice and equal rights. This is not a black story, but an American story. This history should be known by all students, not just those whose ancestors suffered. Without the whole story, which depicts the evolution of our contemporary understanding of civil rights, American history is distorted and diminished.

Conversely, we believe that black students should be as knowledgeable about American history in general as white students are. As Americans, they have the same need to understand the past as their classmates, the same need to comprehend the institutions and laws of the society in which they are citizens. No less than whites, they should be knowledgeable about chronology and geography, about the Constitution and the Bill of Rights, about the forces and trends that have shaped the nation they live in. They too need to know who Churchill, Hitler, and Stalin were; they too should know about Watergate, Sputnik, and the Great Depression. They too will be voters and will need the knowledge about the rest of the world that enables them to understand public issues, to become active participants in the democratic process, and to comment critically on the actions of their elected representatives.

We do not dismiss the issue of "relevance." We recognize its value in some of the results of this assessment. But we urge educators to construe it broadly, not narrowly along racial or sexual lines. The challenge is to enable students of all backgrounds to understand the relevance of history and literature to the world today and to their own lives; to help them recognize universal themes and dilemmas in literary works written in other ages and other societies; to encourage them to see the significance of historical decisions that were made a hundred or a thousand years ago. You don't have to be Jewish to weep for the men, women, and children who were shepherded into gas chambers during the Holocaust; you don't have to be black to share the despair of the men, women, and children who were crammed into slave ships, bound for a lifetime of slavery in an unknown land. Not only history, but great literature has the capacity to carry us beyond our own ancestry, our immediate sphere, to mourn with the family of Hector, to cry with Janie (in *Their Eyes Were Watching God*), to feel devastated by the death of Mrs. Ramsay (in *To the Lighthouse*), to experience the terror in novels like *Darkness at Noon, 1984,* and *The Painted Bird.*

The best literature is always relevant in the sense that it makes us aware of our common humanity. Even when it deals with people who are from a distinctive race, religion, or culture, it has the power to touch the lives of whoever reads it, to make them understand themselves better because of what they have read, to make them sensitive to the joys and sufferings of others, to awaken them to knowledge and emotions that are both particular and universal.

Why Study History and Literature?

We urge the study of history and literature because we believe they are important. It is not simply because they are repositories for our cultural heritage; nor is it merely that they help us understand the past. Those who study these subjects become more knowledgeable, more perceptive, and more thoughtful by doing so. They learn about the forces, individuals, trends, and events that shaped the present; they discover from their own experience the power of novels, poems, plays, and stories to move, delight, entertain, inform, shock, and reveal us to ourselves. History and literature are the essential studies of the humanities because they interpret for us the human experience. To the extent that we are knowledgeable about these subjects, we are better able to communicate with one another. And the more knowledgeable we are, the more complicated are the discussions that we can have together. Paradoxically, the broader our shared background knowledge, the better able we are to argue, debate, and disagree with one another.

But will we all possess a sufficiency of that shared knowledge, or will it become the near-exclusive property of the more fortunate among us? Remember that not all members of the 17-year-old generation are equally at risk. Some possess a decent reservoir of knowledge of history and literature, and these tend (with significant exceptions, as described in Chapter 3) to be the children of the well educated, the well employed, the well motivated, and the well off.

It is a pattern as old as civilization: a society's elite nearly always strives to ensure that its sons and daughters acquire enough of the knowledge, the cultural lore, and the intellectual traits associated with success in that society. And while success in American society—be it gauged in terms of wealth, prestige, public office, business acumen, social status, or whatever—does not automatically follow from being well versed in such subjects as history and literature, one's prospects are certainly enhanced by being "culturally literate." Hence we can take for granted that the elite will continue to do its best to equip its own children with this knowledge and to send them to schools that furnish substantial quantities of it. But neither our culture, our politics, our civic life, nor our principles of equal opportunity can be satisfactorily maintained if large numbers of youngsters enter adulthood with little knowledge of this kind.

It is on that conviction that we base our reply to all who will inspect the evidence in this book and conclude that the students did better than might have been expected, that they did reasonably well, that they did well enough, that the proverbial glass is a bit more than half full. It is not just that the complacency of this attitude irks us; it is also that the elitism lurking within it must not be condoned by the citizens of a democracy. We cannot settle for an education system that imparts "passable" amounts of important knowledge to its more fortunate students while the majority learn less than the minimum required for successful participation in the society they are about to enter. To rest content with a "half-full glass" is to condone mediocrity as well as inequality.

Nor need we be fatalistic about this distribution of knowledge. It is not adventitious. It is within the capacity of adults—educators, parents, librarians, television producers, and all the rest—to take the steps by which all our youngsters learn enough to participate in selecting our leaders, in shaping our culture, in renewing our civic life, and in discussing and resolving the important issues before us. One premise of our democratic society, as Jefferson recognized two centuries ago, is that for it truly to succeed, all its members must have an education that will "enable every man to judge for himself what will secure or endanger his freedom." We believe that this remains a valid premise now and for the future.

We hope it is clear in these pages that we do not make a case for a monolithic, immutable body of knowledge that is to be transmitted from one generation to the next like an uncut diamond. Both history and literature are shaped and transformed by the social context in which they are studied. As a nation and a people, we continually add to, reconsider and redefine the history that we study because we tell a story to ourselves about who we are and how we got that way. Others who disagree with the consensus version write conflicting interpretations, and these are often so persuasive that in time they change the way we see the past. In this way, history changes, as it is revised by new discoveries, fresh interpretations, and altered understandings of what American society is, has been, and should be.

Literature changes, too, as new writers add their contributions and emerge as important voices in the American dialogue. Our conceptions of literature also are changed by the discovery of writers whose works were ignored when they wrote but whose voices now seem prophetic, speaking to our own time with an urgency that was neglected during their lifetimes.

No one can know everything. It is possible to spend a lifetime studying history or literature without reading every important book or learning about every significant event. The most we can hope for in the years of formal schooling is that students learn to tell the important from the unimportant; that they know enough about literature to distinguish for themselves what is fine and what is dross; that they know enough about history to inform themselves about the vital connections between the present and the past; that they cultivate a desire to learn more; and that they acquire a foundation of knowledge on which to build for the rest of their lives.

This is a tall order. But we do not think it is an impossible order. Nor do we think it is beyond the capacity of our educating institutions. Certainly it is not beyond the capacities of our 17-year-olds.

Afterword and Acknowledgments

The Foundations of Literacy project evolved over several years and benefited from the support and participation of a great many individuals and organizations. It was sponsored and underwritten from the outset by the National Endowment for the Humanities, a small but very important federal agency. We are deeply grateful to the Endowment and to its chairman, Lynne V. Cheney. We also thank William J. Bennett, who initiated the Endowment's constructive engagement with elementary and secondary education when he served as its chairman and who launched this NEH project in 1984.

The project has been overseen throughout by Jeffrey Thomas, a capable and imaginative NEH program analyst who is notable for preferring to solve problems rather than aggravate them. It has benefited as well from the counsel of Deputy Chairman John T. Agresto and the assistance of Celeste Colgan, special assistant to the chairman. However, nothing in this book necessarily represents the views of the National Endowment for the Humanities or its staff members and employees, past or present.

The Educational Excellence Network was the organizational aegis for this project. Founded by the co-authors in

1981, the Network is a loose confederation of individuals (now numbering about 800) who share an interest in the reform and improvement of education, principally in the United States and primarily at the elementary/secondary level.

We are grateful to fellow Network members for their colleagueship, assistance and enthusiasm. More than a few of them are daily engaged in the issues this book addresses and many have made signal contributions to the quest for better education. We pay special tribute to Network member E. D. Hirsch, Jr., whose early articles on "cultural literacy" brought him to our attention, who has participated in other Network projects, and who is the author of the superb recent book *Cultural Literacy*. Hirsch was a member of the learning area committee that developed the literature portion of this assessment. We are deeply appreciative, too, for the hard work of Stephen Clements, Janice Riddell, and Gilbert Sewall, who served *seriatim* as the Network's administrative officer during the span of this project. But no Network member, donor, or employee is responsible for the views of the co-authors.

Finn and Ravitch also wish to express their deep gratitude to the members of the history and literature learning area committees who designed the objectives of this assessment and reviewed the test items. Their names are listed in Chapter 1. Everyone involved gave of his or her time with the expectation that this assessment would ultimately contribute to the improvement of knowledge about these subjects and to the betterment of teaching in these subjects. We hope that their participation is rewarded with success.

When the project began, the Educational Excellence Network was housed within Vanderbilt University's Institute for Public Policy Studies. At that time, the project director was co-author Finn, professor of education and public policy at Vanderbilt, a position from which he is presently on leave while serving in the federal government. The co-authors are grateful to the staff of the Vanderbilt Institute for Public Policy Studies, especially professors Erwin Hargrove, Frank

Sloan, John Folger, and Lottie Strupp; to Vanderbilt chancellor Joe B. Wyatt and provost Charles M. Kiesler; to Dean Willis C. Hawley of Vanderbilt's George Peabody College for Teachers; and to Steven Smartt of the university's Office of Sponsored Research. Again it should be noted, though, that Vanderbilt University, its officers, and its employees are in no way responsible for the contents of this book.

When Finn went on leave from Vanderbilt to join the Education Department in the summer of 1985, the entire project moved to Teachers College, Columbia University, where Ravitch is professor of history. The Educational Excellence Network moved its headquarters as well. NEH entered into a new contract with Teachers College, and Ravitch became project director. At that point, Finn withdrew entirely from the management and direction of the project but continued with his commitment to co-writing its final report—this book—in a private, unpaid capacity. Thus the views of his employer, the U.S. Department of Education, are not necessarily reflected in the pages of this volume.

As principal investigator and project director, Ravitch has benefited from the wise counsel and constant support of Michael Timpane, president of Teachers College; Judith Brandenburg, dean of the college; Barbara Russell, grants officer at the college; and Victor Mainente, controller of the college. She owes a special debt of thanks to Eileen Sclan, her energetic and tireless research assistant. She continues to be indebted to Lawrence A. Cremin for his understanding of educating institutions. Neither Teachers College nor any of these individuals is responsible for the views, findings, and opinions expressed in this book.

In the assessment-planning, test-development, and data-gathering phases of the project, before this book was written, the vast majority of the work was performed by the Educational Testing Service (ETS). In conducting the history and literature assessment, ETS followed the procedures and protocols it customarily uses in carrying out the National Assessment of Educational Progress (NAEP), which is funded primarily by the U.S. Department of Education.

That assessment was conducted in hundreds of schools across the United States. We and the readers of this book owe perhaps the heartiest thanks to almost eight thousand young Americans enrolled in the eleventh grade during the 1985–86 school year, who sat for the history and literature portions of this assessment. Though we're not generally contented with what they know, we're grateful indeed for their willingness to reveal it! The validity of the entire enterprise hinges on the truthfulness and reliability of these boys and girls, as well as on the accuracy of the statistical sample of all eleventh graders that ETS's experts say they are and, of course, on the integrity of ETS's administration of the assessment itself.

As is their customary practice, ETS staff assigned to NAEP compiled and analyzed the data and made the results available for use by the NAEP project, the co-authors, and the general public. The data have been accessible to all since the spring of 1987, when a public-use data tape was produced by ETS.

Throughout the entire process, the ETS staff has been gracious and helpful. Particular thanks are due to Archie Lapointe, director of NAEP, and to Ina V. S. Mullis, deputy director. Words are really insufficient to repay Ina, who among many acts of selflessness spent Mother's Day reading a draft of this manuscript. They not only saw to the fulfilment of ETS's contractual responsibilities to this project; they also went the extra mile to give the co-authors sage advice and help guard against errors of fact and analysis. We are also grateful to ETS for encouraging this project at the outset; we especially thank its president, Gregory R. Anrig. None of these individuals or organizations is in any way responsible for anything that appears in this book, neither its authors' conclusions and recommendations nor any factual errors that may have crept in.

Other ETS employees assigned to NAEP who have been

helpful during the course of this project include Laurie Barnett, Fran Blumberg, Anne Campbell, Nancy Mead, Norma Norris, and Rebecca Zwick. We thank them, too.

In addition to the analyses produced by ETS, the project obtained analytic help from Dr. Fred W. Quelle, Jr., an independent number cruncher and computer wizard whose inspired handling of this very large data set yielded some of the most interesting findings and provocative relationships set forth in this volume. He, too, bears no responsibility for the conclusions we have drawn, but we are grateful indeed for his assistance.

Ravitch wishes to thank Martin Kessler of Basic Books; Ed Burlingame of Harper & Row; and Carol Cohen of Harper & Row, the superb editor of this book.

As is ordinarily the case with a major project of this kind, we have incurred countless personal debts of gratitude to friends, relatives, colleagues, and associates. They offered, at various times and in various styles, advice, solace, encouragement, insight, imagination, tolerance, tips, cautions, and chicken soup. Diane Ravitch thanks Mary F. Butz, a heroic teacher and friend, for all of the above, plus heroism and friendship; her sons, Joseph and Michael, who know far more about history and literature than she; Kirk Winters and Patricia Hobbs, for their kindness, thoughtfulness, and all-around brilliance; Irene Labourdette, for being there; and Ruby Ratliff and Ruth Reeves, her favorite high school English teachers. She also thanks Checker, who is not only a reliable source of wisdom, courage, friendship, and ineffable wit, but also was willing to learn to use her software.

Chester Finn extends thanks and much love to Renu, Arti, and Aloke for enduring a husband and father whose long days at the office were for many weeks rivaled by evenings and weekends in thrall to his word processor. He also thanks Diane, his most cherished professional colleague, who supplied not only the aforementioned software but also most of the energy, intellect, and determination that pushed this ambitious venture to completion.

A portion of the proceeds of this book is dedicated to the New York Public Library, one of the nation's finest institutions of literacy and learning.

Appendix

Name of cluster	Number of questions	Percent correct	"Grade"
Chronology	26	51.1	F
Maps and geography	12	71.3	C—
Important people	25	61.6	D—
The Constitution	19	54.4	F
Women in history	8	52.6	F
Civil rights	21	58.2	F
Demography and migration	8	51.0	F
Science and technology	10	71.3	C—
Labor and industry	14	61.1	D—
International affairs	38	58.3	F
Pre-National and colonial	13	49.0	F
Revolution–War of 1812	24	58.9	F
Territorial expansion–Civil War	19	54.4	F
Reconstruction–WWI	24	49.5	F
WWI–WWII	33	60.2	D—
Post-WWII–present	20	54.7	F

AVERAGE SCORES ON LITERATURE CLUSTERS

Name of cluster	Number of questions	Percent correct	"Grade"
Title-author relationships	29	39.5	F
Author information	10	51.0	F
Literature of the Bible	15	66.8	D
Classical mythology and literature	15	56.4	F
Epics, myths, and legends	16	60.7	D−
Shakespeare	7	68.4	D+
Passages and quotations	18	60.5	D−
Short stories	11	46.2	F
Novels and novelists	35	44.9	F
Poetry and poets	17	48.6	F
Plays and playwrights	8	43.6	F
Nonfiction	12	54.9	F
Literature of women and blacks	13	48.6	F

ITEMS TESTED ON THE U.S. HISTORY ASSESSMENT

Weighted Percent Correct in Descending Order by National Performance

Description	Total	White	Black	Hispanic	Male	Female
Thomas Edison invented the light bulb	95.2	97.0	90.6	89.0	95.4	94.9
Find Soviet Union on map of Europe	92.1	94.5	78.8	87.9	93.2	90.0
Alexander Graham Bell invented the telephone	91.1	92.4	90.5	80.8	88.7	93.5
George Washington was president between 1780–1800	87.9	90.1	79.5	77.2	89.3	86.5
Find Italy on map of Europe	87.7	90.9	69.6	83.4	89.3	86.9
The Underground Railroad was secret network to help slaves escape	87.5	89.1	90.7	69.7	88.4	88.4
Adolf Hitler was leader of Germany during World War II	87.4	89.4	83.1	73.1	86.6	86.1
Thomas Jefferson was main author of Declaration of Independence	87.4	90.6	75.9	75.3	86.7	88.3
The assembly line was introduced by US auto industry	87.2	90.0	79.4	74.4	87.5	86.7
Find area of 13 original states on map of US	84.8	87.7	73.6	71.2	88.4	80.6
Ku Klux Klan used violence to oppose minorities	83.9	85.4	82.1	71.2	84.2	83.5
Harriet Tubman was leader in helping slaves escape	83.8	84.2	92.4	66.7	82.8	84.9
Find Rocky Mountains on map of US	81.3	82.5	76.5	75.0	83.3	79.3
Guarantee of free speech and religion found in Bill of Rights	81.3	82.4	76.2	74.2	80.1	82.7
Japanese attack on Pearl Harbor led US into World War II	80.0	81.7	75.0	68.7	84.9	74.9
US dropped first atomic bomb on Japan in World War II	79.9	84.4	59.0	67.4	85.7	73.0
Washington was commander of American army in Revolution	79.2	83.7	60.0	66.1	83.1	75.4
Churchill was prime minister of Great Britain in World War II	78.1	81.0	62.2	66.4	80.8	75.2
TV became new feature in American homes after 1950	78.1	81.5	66.9	62.7	80.4	75.4
Watergate led to resignation of Richard Nixon	77.4	79.4	73.2	59.7	81.1	73.7
Women worked in factories during World War II	77.3	81.2	65.1	54.9	80.3	74.2

263

ITEMS TESTED ON THE U.S. HISTORY ASSESSMENT *(Continued)*

Description	Total	White	Black	Hispanic	Male	Female
Jamestown was first permanent English colony	76.1	78.2	69.9	60.8	75.9	76.4
Find West Germany on map of Europe	76.1	81.0	52.0	64.4	82.3	69.7
Lindbergh made first solo flight across Atlantic	76.1	80.2	62.3	56.5	81.1	70.2
Nazi decimation of Jewish people in Europe called the Holocaust	75.8	80.1	57.5	61.2	75.4	76.2
The Great Depression was a period of mass unemployment	75.1	77.4	64.9	70.8	79.2	73.5
"Prohibition" refers to ban on sale and consumption of liquor	74.6	79.1	56.0	56.6	76.1	73.1
The Great Depression occurred between 1900–1950	72.2	77.4	50.6	54.6	79.2	65.4
Vietnam War had strongest citizen protest movements	72.1	74.0	61.3	67.2	77.7	65.6
Civil rights movement of 1960s focused on equality for minorities	71.7	73.1	71.8	59.9	71.6	71.8
Discovery of gold in California was a cause of westward movement	71.3	74.5	57.0	61.8	76.3	66.4
Find area on US map that fought for independence from Mexico	71.0	73.6	53.7	73.9	75.0	66.9
Invention of cotton gin stimulated plantation economy in South	70.7	73.1	65.7	55.5	72.7	68.7
Germany and Japan were main US enemies in World War II	70.7	75.0	50.8	59.5	80.6	60.9
World War II ended between 1943–1947	70.7	72.3	61.6	71.6	77.7	63.7
Indians were put on reservations after Civil War	70.5	73.3	60.4	58.8	71.7	69.3
Find Mississippi River on map of US	70.3	74.4	51.0	60.1	76.6	64.1
Find Great Britain on map of Europe	70.2	75.7	44.2	54.2	76.6	63.8
Most people in English colonies of North America worked as farmers	69.7	70.0	70.1	64.8	73.8	65.6
"Secession" refers to withdrawal of Southern states from Union	69.7	74.4	49.2	49.0	67.4	72.2

Susan B. Anthony was a leader of women's suffrage movement	68.9	70.0	63.6	61.4	66.3	71.9
Columbus discovered the New World before 1750	68.1	72.6	47.1	54.6	71.6	64.1
Abraham Lincoln wrote the Emancipation Proclamation	68.0	69.3	67.8	50.5	69.0	66.9
The Declaration of Independence was signed between 1750–1800	67.8	70.1	57.3	57.1	72.6	63.1
The Declaration of Independence marks colonies' break with England	67.6	71.6	49.4	53.1	71.3	63.9
Stamp Act of 1765 was attempt by English to tax colonies	67.3	71.1	55.1	44.5	65.2	69.3
US policy after World War II was to provide aid to Europe	67.2	68.8	63.3	58.0	69.9	64.4
Find France on map of Europe	65.8	69.1	46.4	61.3	70.0	61.4
US provoked to enter World War I by German submarine attacks	64.6	66.7	63.3	48.9	69.4	60.0
Watergate occurred after 1950	64.5	69.1	46.7	47.3	71.1	57.0
Brown decision of 1954 ruled school segregation unconstitutional	63.7	66.4	55.5	47.5	60.8	67.1
Alexander Hamilton known for urging strong national government	63.5	65.1	50.4	61.3	63.6	63.3
Find area of the Confederacy on map of US	63.4	67.6	47.6	46.7	71.5	55.2
Sputnik was the first man-made satellite	62.7	67.6	46.3	47.2	69.1	56.4
Plessy vs. Ferguson decision approved racial segregation	61.4	64.9	53.6	40.4	60.4	62.3
The southwestern US was explored and settled by Spain	61.0	63.5	48.1	52.1	62.9	58.7
United States Constitution was written between 1750–1800	60.9	63.8	49.0	44.1	65.4	55.7
East Coast of US explored and settled mainly by England	60.6	64.3	49.2	44.8	64.2	57.0
Woodrow Wilson appealed for American entry into League of Nations	60.2	62.0	52.4	52.2	58.2	62.3
Japan bombed Pearl Harbor between 1939–1943	60.0	62.1	50.4	56.1	65.9	53.9
"Checks and balances" divides power among branches of federal government	59.9	63.1	50.2	44.1	62.2	57.6

ITEMS TESTED ON THE U.S. HISTORY ASSESSMENT *(Continued)*

Description	Total	White	Black	Hispanic	Male	Female
Heavy immigration in 1970s–80s came from SE Asia and Latin America	59.5	61.0	46.6	61.2	62.0	57.0
Articles of Confederation were first Constitution during Revolution	59.4	61.2	54.0	47.5	60.2	58.4
Representative government existed in Colonies	58.0	63.0	38.7	39.3	57.5	58.5
John D. Rockefeller formed Standard Oil	57.8	58.9	51.3	52.0	62.9	52.7
US foreign policy after World War II was containment of Communism	57.7	61.9	44.2	43.8	61.8	53.6
World War II was between 1900–1950	57.3	62.3	32.9	46.3	67.8	45.1
Booker T. Washington was major black leader before World War I	57.1	57.9	55.2	52.2	58.5	55.5
Find area of map of US purchased from France	57.1	61.4	40.8	40.5	61.5	52.7
"Prohibition" occurred between 1900–1950	56.4	61.2	40.0	36.2	62.5	49.3
Before 1800 most immigrants came from northern and western Europe	56.3	59.1	43.2	49.5	62.0	55.7
Eisenhower was president between 1946–1963	55.6	58.2	46.2	49.0	59.2	52.0
Israel has never been invaded by Soviet Union	55.4	57.5	40.3	55.8	62.2	48.9
Japanese-Americans were forced into camps during World War II	55.2	57.4	40.8	54.1	63.4	47.1
Nixon established relations with the People's Republic of China	55.1	57.0	45.0	49.3	55.8	54.4
A cause of population movement in 1800s was reasonable land prices	54.7	59.5	35.8	34.3	60.5	48.0
Social Security system was introduced during the New Deal	54.7	56.6	46.3	52.8	57.1	52.3
US gave military support to South Korea with United Nations	53.9	56.7	40.5	43.8	61.9	45.9
Dust Bowl of 1930s fostered movement to California	53.8	56.9	41.7	44.6	55.4	52.2
Amendment of 1920 granted women right to vote	53.7	54.8	50.2	47.3	49.7	57.7
Stalin was leader of Soviet Union during World War II	53.6	51.7	39.7			

Populist Party advocated government support for farmers	52.8	53.2	54.2	44.9	49.1	56.5
New Deal identified with changes in social, economic policies	52.3	53.9	44.6	44.8	49.5	55.4
Franklin Roosevelt was president between 1929–1946	52.0	56.1	36.2	42.3	57.1	46.9
Before Civil War, nation debated spread of slavery	51.6	53.2	43.7	42.1	54.7	48.5
"Give me liberty or give me death"—Patrick Henry	51.1	53.6	46.0	33.3	50.4	51.7
"Laissez-faire" means minimal government regulation of economy	51.0	53.6	38.9	38.4	49.3	52.9
Monroe Doctrine said Europe should not gain land in western hemisphere	50.9	53.8	35.7	45.1	53.3	48.4
Washington's Farewell Address warned against foreign alliances	50.3	51.7	46.4	43.7	47.0	53.7
Canada and Mississippi valley first explored by France	50.3	54.0	32.6	41.4	52.5	48.1
Samuel Gompers was first president of AFL	49.8	50.3	48.9	48.9	52.3	47.4
Martin Luther King, Jr., rose to prominence in Montgomery bus boycott	48.9	45.6	71.9	38.8	50.6	47.2
US dropped first atomic bomb between 1943–1947	48.6	51.7	34.0	36.8	57.7	39.4
Valley Forge was lowest point in Revolutionary War	47.9	50.6	37.6	35.3	49.5	46.1
Women's right to vote was not guaranteed after Civil War	47.3	50.1	37.8	38.7	53.5	41.0
An issue in War of 1812 was Great Britain's interference with shipping	47.0	47.4	48.0	46.6	51.8	42.3
Andrew Carnegie was associated with development of steel industry	46.9	48.4	41.7	38.0	48.5	45.4
Thomas Jefferson was president between 1800–1820	45.6	46.8	40.8	39.5	46.6	44.5
The Constitution divides powers between states and federal government	43.8	45.2	39.1	34.7	48.4	39.3
Missouri Compromise admitted Maine as free, Missouri as slave state	43.0	43.6	40.7	36.3	43.4	42.5
Woodrow Wilson was president between 1912–1929	42.9	45.2	31.9	37.9	48.6	37.2
Senator Joseph McCarthy involved in controversy about Communism	42.6	43.9	33.9	38.9	43.0	42.1

ITEMS TESTED ON THE U.S. HISTORY ASSESSMENT (Continued)

Description	Total	White	Black	Hispanic	Male	Female
"Nullification" related to states' rights	42.4	44.0	40.1	32.9	39.1	45.7
Hoover, Franklin Roosevelt were presidents during Depression	41.1	44.5	30.1	26.8	46.7	35.6
Jane Addams founded settlement houses to help the poor	41.0	41.1	41.1	34.9	37.1	44.8
"Reconstruction" occurred between 1850–1900	40.2	42.3	27.8	35.2	40.7	39.6
The Federalist advocated adoption of Constitution	40.1	40.5	40.2	35.5	39.5	40.7
Dred Scott decision: slave who moved to free state was not free	39.5	41.0	36.6	28.1	40.1	38.8
D-Day occurred between 1943–1947	39.5	41.5	31.2	33.7	44.4	34.4
Renaissance was characterized by cultural, technological advances	39.3	41.4	31.0	26.9	38.7	40.1
Paine's Common Sense argues for colonial independence	38.3	42.4	24.9	19.1	39.3	37.3
Emancipation Proclamation freed slaves in Confederacy	38.2	36.3	43.6	40.2	40.4	36.0
Union membership grew in the 1930s because of new laws	38.2	40.3	22.1	36.0	39.6	36.6
Jamestown founded before 1750	38.0	42.4	21.7	18.1	43.7	31.4
Restrictions on immigration were not part of New Deal	37.8	39.1	30.1	37.0	39.4	36.2
"Three-fifths compromise" in Constitution defined status of slaves	37.7	40.1	27.3	24.0	35.4	40.0
Immigration from southern and eastern Europe grew, 1890–1910	37.6	36.2	42.5	43.3	36.0	39.2
Immigration restriction in 1921, 1924 aimed at SE Europeans	37.3	39.2	31.0	26.2	38.0	36.5
Scopes trial was about teaching evolution	37.2	39.2	24.3	30.9	40.8	33.6
Upton Sinclair, Lincoln Steffens, Ida Tarbell known as muckrakers	37.1	38.3	32.4	30.8	39.0	35.3
Theodore Roosevelt was president between 1895–1912	36.9	38.0	32.2	34.0	40.9	32.9
Articles of Confederation failed to provide adequate taxing power	36.8	38.1	33.9	26.8	38.9	34 7

Find region on US map acquired from Mexico in war	36.2	35.2	33.3	46.3	39.3	33.1
Religious toleration in colonies due to common interest of many groups	36.0	36.2	29.4	42.7	35.5	36.4
Jonas Salk invented polio vaccine	34.3	37.3	23.6	22.7	30.5	38.0
Spanish-American War made US an international power	33.0	35.1	27.3	22.2	35.5	30.6
American foreign policy after World War I known as isolationist	32.3	34.8	18.0	23.5	32.2	32.5
The Civil War occurred between 1850–1900	32.2	33.9	25.8	22.6	38.5	26.0
US foreign policy in early 1900s: "Speak softly, carry a big stick"	31.6	32.9	28.9	27.8	36.2	27.0
Purpose of Jim Crow laws was to enforce racial segregation	30.7	30.6	31.8	20.8	34.2	26.5
Magna Carta is foundation of British parliamentary system	30.6	31.2	26.0	33.8	31.9	29.3
Andrew Jackson was president between 1820–1840	29.9	31.1	22.1	26.1	32.0	27.8
Reformation led to establishment of Protestant sects	29.8	29.8	28.8	27.6	30.5	29.0
The United Nations was founded between 1943–1947	25.9	28.6	16.4	19.3	34.4	17.3
The Seneca Falls Declaration concerned women's rights	25.8	25.9	25.9	22.5	27.2	24.4
Abraham Lincoln was president between 1860–1880	24.7	26.0	17.5	21.2	31.3	18.0
Lyndon Johnson's term included Medicare and Voting Rights Act	23.9	24.7	20.0	19.5	26.3	21.4
Betty Friedan and Gloria Steinem led women's movement in 1970s	22.8	24.3	14.1	23.1	23.5	22.2
"Progressive movement" refers to reforms before World War I	22.6	23.7	16.7	18.8	25.5	19.6
"Reconstruction" refers to readmission of Confederate states	21.4	21.9	16.9	20.9	24.7	18.1
John Winthrop and the Puritans founded a colony in Boston	19.5	18.4	21.6	26.1	19.4	19.5

Note: The descriptions above are paraphrases of the information tested. The answers are not identical to the material on the test. In some instances, for reasons of space, the information is incomplete as presented here. Wherever a bloc of time is in the answer, students were presented with several choices on a timeline; some timelines were divided into half-centuries, some into twenty-year periods, and some into even shorter spans.

ITEMS TESTED ON THE LITERATURE ASSESSMENT
Weighted Percent Correct in Descending Order by National Performance

Description	Total	White	Black	Hispanic	Male	Female
In Bible, Noah gathered pairs of creatures into ark	94.0	95.7	88.4	84.7	91.4	96.4
In Bible, Moses got 10 commandments, led his people from Egypt	92.3	93.2	89.0	90.0	92.6	92.1
Romeo and Juliet hindered by feuding families	89.7	91.1	83.9	86.5	86.7	93.1
Martin Luther King, Jr.: "I have a dream . . ."	88.1	87.7	92.7	86.0	86.9	89.4
Hamlet: "To be or not to be . . ." (5 lines)	87.8	89.5	84.1	81.0	86.6	89.0
Ebenezer Scrooge was stingy character in "A Christmas Carol"	87.2	89.9	79.7	71.2	83.5	90.9
In Greek mythology, ruler of gods is Zeus	86.7	88.5	81.7	77.5	86.2	87.2
White Rabbit, March Hare, etc., are in *Alice's Adventures in Wonderland*	86.1	87.3	78.7	84.8	80.9	91.2
Robin Hood is known for stealing from rich to give to poor	85.7	89.1	75.4	71.3	88.9	82.0
Cinderella's rags turned into gown and she met prince	85.1	86.9	80.5	78.2	78.9	91.4
Robinson Crusoe was shipwrecked on an island and survived	83.6	88.5	63.7	69.1	84.1	83.2
"The Lord is my shepherd . . ." (3 lines) is from Psalm 23	82.4	82.8	86.1	70.7	79.7	85.0
The magician who advised King Arthur was Merlin	80.5	83.2	68.3	68.2	82.4	78.6
Adventures of Huckleberry Finn is about orphan boy and runaway slave	80.5	83.5	70.1	65.9	77.7	83.8
In Bible, Book of Genesis includes account of creation	79.5	80.9	76.2	71.9	76.0	82.9
Plato and Aristotle are best known as philosophers	79.0	82.0	68.9	62.6	78.3	79.7
Victory of unknown team parallels Bible story of David and Goliath	78.0	81.5	61.6	68.9	82.4	73.6
"Rip van Winkle" is about man who slept for 20 years and awoke	76.3	79.9	68.1	54.7	73.5	79.1
E. A. Poe wrote "Pit and Pendulum," "Fall of House of Usher," etc.	75.2	78.2	67.5			

"Friends, Romans, countrymen . . ." is from *Julius Caesar*	74.9	77.0	64.1	69.4	74.7	75.1
Juliet said, "What's in a name? That which we call a rose . . ."	74.2	76.1	62.6	70.1	71.4	76.9
Gettysburg Address: "Four score and seven years ago our fathers . . .," etc.	73.9	77.7	65.6	54.2	73.0	74.9
Mary Shelley's novel *Frankenstein* is about scientist who created creature he could not control	73.8	75.2	67.7	66.3	73.4	74.1
Novel that helped the antislavery movement was *Uncle Tom's Cabin*	73.4	75.8	69.3	57.5	71.2	75.5
Epic about a Greek war leader's voyage home is the *Odyssey*	73.0	75.7	60.6	60.9	69.5	77.1
Oliver, Micawber, Pip, and Gradgrind appear in novels of Dickens	72.7	76.3	62.2	49.7	69.4	76.5
Lucifer is another name for Satan	72.3	74.1	61.0	75.3	71.8	72.8
Legendary King Arthur presided over knights of Round Table	72.0	74.4	62.1	65.9	70.5	73.5
In Bible, Samson is known for great strength	71.8	72.0	71.5	70.5	74.0	69.3
Jesus was betrayed for 30 pieces of silver by Judas	69.5	70.7	68.4	65.0	69.2	69.9
Emily Dickinson was American poet who lived in solitude, wrote often about death (lines from 2 poems)	69.3	70.2	67.1	61.3	67.5	71.3
Moral of tortoise and hare: slow and steady wins the race	67.7	70.8	54.6	52.8	65.1	70.6
In Cain and Abel story, jealous young man kills brother	67.3	68.0	64.3	62.8	62.4	72.1
Sherlock Holmes is main character in *Hound of the Baskervilles*, etc.	67.2	68.7	62.4	63.8	68.7	65.8
Edgar Allan Poe wrote poems "Annabel Lee" and "Raven"	67.0	71.1	54.0	45.8	64.5	69.5
In Roman mythology, Venus is goddess of love	66.5	68.1	57.2	58.6	66.0	67.0
"We hold these truths to be self-evident, that all men are created equal . . .," etc., is in the Declaration of Independence	65.7	67.5	60.4	52.2	64.4	67.2

ITEMS TESTED ON THE LITERATURE ASSESSMENT *(Continued)*

Description	Total	White	Black	Hispanic	Male	Female
"We, the people of the United States, in order to form a more perfect union," is from the Preamble to the Constitution	65.7	67.7	64.6	49.1	64.0	67.6
Play by Thornton Wilder about typical New England village is *Our Town*	65.6	69.2	51.0	51.7	66.2	65.0
Aesop is best known for writing fables	65.3	68.3	53.9	51.5	62.8	67.8
In Greek mythology, multitude of evils escaped from Pandora's box	64.0	64.2	61.7	66.4	62.9	65.2
Hemingway wrote *For Whom the Bell Tolls, The Sun Also Rises*	63.2	65.9	53.8	52.1	61.0	65.8
Jack London wrote *Call of the Wild* about dog in Yukon	62.5	66.7	44.7	47.0	64.7	60.4
Robert Frost wrote poems ("But I have promises to keep . . .", "Two roads diverged in a wood . . .")	62.5	65.2	52.2	53.1	60.4	64.6
In Melville's *Moby-Dick*, Captain Ahab's obsession is revenge	61.8	64.6	52.2	52.8	68.5	55.0
Lilliput, country of little people, is part of *Gulliver's Travels*	61.7	62.5	53.3	61.3	63.8	59.6
The Red Badge of Courage is about young soldier's struggle to overcome his fear in Civil War	61.6	62.5	63.0	53.8	58.3	64.9
In Greek mythology, Atlas has to support heavens on his shoulders	61.1	62.7	50.7	59.6	66.3	55.9
In Bible, King Solomon is famous for his wisdom	61.0	60.8	64.6	55.1	57.9	64.6
The *Iliad* is an epic poem by Homer	60.6	64.0	49.0	43.0	58.9	62.4
In biblical story, Jonah is swallowed by big fish	60.2	62.9	50.0	43.6	62.7	57.7
In Mark Twain novel, Tom Sawyer is known for clever ways of avoiding work, trouble	59.8	62.6	45.4	55.6	61.6	57.9
Midas was mythical king whose touch turned objects to gold	59.5	62.4	52.3	42.0	56.7	62.8
The Scarlet Letter is novel about woman who was unfaithful	59.4	61.1	53.5	49.3	56.0	62.7

Item						
To Kill a Mockingbird is novel about 2 children affected by community conflict when father defends black man	59.1	63.3	41.6	49.3	55.7	62.3
Dickens's novel Tale of Two Cities occurs during French Revolution	59.0	59.9	58.2	50.2	57.4	60.5
Longfellow wrote poem about Paul Revere that includes "One if by land, / Two if by sea"	58.8	61.7	52.2	44.7	56.2	61.3
Franklin Roosevelt said, "The only thing we have to fear is fear itself" and "Yesterday, December 7, 1941,—a date which will live in infamy . . ."	57.2 / 57.0	58.0 / 60.2	51.8 / 44.5	54.4 / 47.1	57.0 / 53.5	57.5 / 60.6
In addition to plays, Shakespeare also wrote sonnets						
Young man who wastes fortune, comes to his senses is like prodigal son	56.5 / 56.2	57.8 / 60.2	53.8 / 38.8	46.5 / 41.0	55.5 / 58.1	58.1 / 54.2
In Roman mythology, Mars is god of war						
Winston Churchill said, "I have nothing to offer, but blood, toil, tears, and sweat" and "From Stettin in the Baltic to Trieste in the Adriatic, an Iron Curtain has descended across the continent"	55.7	59.3	46.6	35.4	54.6	56.9
Arthur Miller wrote The Crucible and Death of a Salesman	53.7 / 53.2	55.6 / 51.9	47.3 / 63.8	43.4 / 51.8	53.0 / 50.6	54.3 / 55.8
A Raisin in the Sun is about experiences of black family	52.7	54.2	47.2	45.5	57.1	48.3
John F. Kennedy: "And so, my fellow Americans, ask not what your country can do for you; ask what you can do for your country"	52.5	53.4	48.8	49.3	55.5	49.2
In Greek mythology, Jason traveled in quest of the Golden Fleece	51.7	55.7	35.3	38.0	47.1	56.4
The Great Gatsby is novel by F. Scott Fitzgerald about pursuit of wealth and status in 1920s	51.7	53.6	41.0	46.7	48.9	54.5
Character in ancient Greek play who unknowingly killed father and married his mother is Oedipus	51.5	52.7	48.7	40.9	51.8	51.1
"Achilles' heel" means weak point in strong person						
In Greek mythology, Daedalus and Icarus make wax wings, fly too close to sun, fall into sea	50.2	51.5	42.8	52.6	53.7	46.1

ITEMS TESTED ON THE LITERATURE ASSESSMENT (Continued)

Description	Total	White	Black	Hispanic	Male	Female
Odysseus is mythical Greek hero who journeys home after Trojan War	49.8	50.9	48.8	42.0	48.4	51.2
Byron, Keats, and Wordsworth are chiefly known as poets	48.1	49.9	40.6	42.6	47.2	49.1
Shakespeare's play *Julius Caesar* is about the fate of his assassins	48.0	49.9	37.2	44.1	48.5	47.5
Don Quixote was Spanish knight who attacked windmills, thinking they were giants	47.9	49.9	34.0	49.2	48.3	47.5
Macbeth is play about man whose ambition to be king led him to murder	47.3	49.1	40.8	40.1	44.9	49.5
"To every thing there is a season, and a time to every purpose under the heaven: a time to be born, and a time to die": the Bible	46.7	45.6	54.0	48.5	42.8	51.2
In *Beowulf*, the hero battles with the monster Grendel	45.8	48.1	38.8	37.4	49.0	42.0
Abraham Lincoln: "With malice toward none, with charity for all . . ."	45.7	47.3	41.7	41.0	43.9	47.5
T. S. Eliot wrote *The Waste Land,* "The Love Song of J. Alfred Prufrock," and "The Hollow Men"	45.4	48.3	31.7	39.3	44.7	46.2
In Greek mythology, Trojan War starts because Paris kidnapped Helen	45.4	46.8	32.8	40.8	46.6	44.3
"A penny saved is a penny earned" and "A small leak will sink a great ship" are maxims from Franklin's *Poor Richard's Almanack*	43.6	45.6	35.9	29.4	44.6	42.6
"The Minister's Black Veil," "Young Goodman Brown," "Rappaccini's Daughter" were written by Nathaniel Hawthorne	43.3	44.9	37.2	38.5	40.2	46.4
The Old Man and the Sea is novel about man who battles great fish	43.0	46.3	31.6	26.1	45.5	40.3
Walden by Henry David Thoreau is about simplifying						

John Milton's *Paradise Lost* is about rebellion of Satan, fall of Adam and Eve	41.2	42.3	34.9	38.5	37.5	45.0
Walt Whitman wrote *Leaves of Grass*, which includes line, "I celebrate myself, and sing myself"	40.2	41.2	40.0	30.6	42.6	37.7
Steinbeck's *The Grapes of Wrath* is about family that migrates from Dust Bowl to California	39.7	41.3	29.8	32.9	42.6	36.8
Antigone is Greek play about woman who defies king to honor her dead brother	39.1	40.2	35.8	38.6	40.1	38.3
"Things fall apart; / The center cannot hold . . .", etc., is from "The Second Coming" by William Butler Yeats	38.9	39.6	34.4	38.3	41.2	36.6
In Greek mythology, Prometheus is chained to a rock for stealing fire	38.5	41.2	24.9	30.7	39.9	37.2
In Jane Austen's *Pride and Prejudice*, the Bennet daughters find husbands	38.0	39.5	30.5	31.0	33.2	42.9
Wuthering Heights is about Heathcliff's obsessive love of Catherine	37.9	41.4	22.2	23.7	31.0	45.0
George Bernard Shaw wrote *Pygmalion, Arms and the Man*, and *Saint Joan*	37.5	39.0	34.5	26.3	35.2	39.8
In the Bible, Job is known for his patience during suffering	37.2	37.9	40.2	30.1	33.4	41.0
Walter Mitty had dull existence but exciting fantasy life	36.6	38.1	33.3	26.7	38.5	34.7
Langston Hughes was poet of Harlem Renaissance who wrote "Hold fast to dreams," etc.	36.2	34.4	52.8	27.1	35.7	36.8
Geoffrey Chaucer wrote *The Canterbury Tales*	36.1	38.6	26.6	21.9	32.7	39.7
Herman Melville wrote *Billy Budd*, "Benito Cereno," and "Bartleby the Scrivener"	35.9	36.4	29.9	32.6	36.5	35.2
1984 is novel about dictatorship that watches everyone to stamp out individuality	35.5	36.9	28.3	28.5	38.9	31.6
Lord of the Flies is novel about children stranded on island who try and fail to lead civilized life	35.3	37.6	20.2	27.9	35.6	35.0
Herman Melville and Joseph Conrad are authors of novels about the sea	34.7	37.1	23.9	22.4	35.1	34.2

ITEMS TESTED ON THE LITERATURE ASSESSMENT (Continued)

Description	Total	White	Black	Hispanic	Male	Female
In the Bible, the cities of Sodom and Gomorrah are destroyed because of wicked inhabitants	33.4	33.9	30.7	31.1	34.2	32.6
The South was setting for many of William Faulkner's novels	33.3	33.5	32.4	30.7	35.2	31.1
Dante's *Divine Comedy* is about journey through Hell, Purgatory, Heaven	32.8	35.0	19.5	32.6	31.5	34.2
Richard Wright wrote *Native Son* (about black life in Chicago) and *Black Boy*	32.3	29.1	50.2	35.0	30.5	34.2
D. H. Lawrence is English author who wrote "The Rocking Horse Winner" and *Sons and Lovers*	28.7	26.4	37.7	37.1	28.3	29.2
Willa Cather wrote about settling of West in *My Ántonia, O Pioneers!*, and *Death Comes for the Archbishop*	28.2	29.8	23.4	18.7	22.5	33.8
Tennessee Williams wrote *A Streetcar Named Desire* and *The Glass Menagerie*	27.6	29.3	18.8	20.8	27.3	27.8
Ernest Hemingway wrote "In Another Country," "The Short Happy Life of Francis Macomber," and "The Killers"	27.3	27.4	25.7	28.3	24.2	30.5
Thomas Hardy wrote *The Return of the Native, Tess of the D'Urbervilles, The Mayor of Casterbridge*	24.4	22.7	30.7	30.2	25.5	23.3
Catcher in the Rye is novel about 16-year-old boy who is expelled from school, goes to NYC for weekend	22.5	24.4	14.8	19.2	21.8	23.2
Henry James wrote about American/European life in *Daisy Miller* and *Portrait of a Lady*	21.9	21.2	22.7	32.9	24.3	19.4
Henrik Ibsen wrote *Hedda Gabler, A Doll's House, An Enemy of the People*	20.3	19.9	20.7	18.8	19.5	21.4
Joseph Conrad wrote *The Heart of Darkness, Lord Jim*, and *The Secret Sharer*	19.3	19.1	16.4	21.0	16.8	21.8
Ralph Ellison's *Invisible Man* is about young man who grows up in South, moves to Harlem	18.3	17.2	23.9	24.5	19.5	17.2

Item						
Dostoevsky wrote *Crime and Punishment* and *The Brothers Karamazov*	17.1	18.1	13.5	11.7	17.6	16.6
James Joyce is Irish author who wrote *Ulysses*, *A Portrait of the Artist As a Young Man*, "Araby" and "Eveline"	15.6	15.9	12.4	16.4	17.8	13.4
De Tocqueville was European who traveled in US and wrote *Democracy in America*	15.5	16.5	12.2	9.6	14.6	16.5
Eudora Welty and Flannery O'Connor are known for stories set in South	14.4	13.5	19.0	15.1	14.0	14.8
William Blake refers to a tiger in poem, "——! ——! burning bright / In the forests of the night, / What immortal hand or eye / Could frame thy fearful symmetry?"	13.6	15.4	6.1	9.1	13.6	13.5
John Bunyan's novel *Pilgrim's Progress* is about the temptations that Christians face in life	13.4	14.3	11.4	9.6	13.2	13.6

Note: These descriptions are paraphrases of the information tested. In most instances, for reasons of space, the information is an abbreviated and sometimes incomplete version of the item on the assessment.

Index

279

About the Authors

Diane Ravitch is Adjunct Professor of History and Education at Teachers College, Columbia University. She is author of *The Troubled Crusade: American Education, 1945–1980; The Schools We Deserve;* and *The Great School Wars.*

Chester E. Finn, Jr., is Professor of Education and Public Policy at Vanderbilt University and is currently serving as Assistant Secretary of the U.S. Department of Education, the policies of which are not necessarily reflected in these pages. He has written or edited five books, including *Against Mediocrity* and *Challenges to the Humanities.* Ravitch and Finn are co-founders of the Educational Excellence Network.